ABOUT THE AUTHOR

John Oliver OBE, BSc, MSc, Director of Optima Personnel Services, is the former Chief Executive of Leyland Trucks, the largest UK truck manufacturer. He was a prominent member of the buy-out team that rescued Leyland from receivership in June 1993. John now devotes himself full-time to the teaching and development of new concepts in employee involvement and empowerment. He is much in demand as an entertaining speaker on the subject of "Profiting Through People".

In 1989, John devised the now widely known Team Enterprise concept, transforming Leyland Trucks from an unprofitable, declining truck-maker into the most cost-efficient operation of its kind in Europe. Leyland's success and indeed profitability over the period 1993–1998 led to its acquisition by US giant, PACCAR Inc. In 2000, Leyland Trucks was deemed to be the "Best Engineering Factory in the UK" by the prestigious *Management Today*/Cranfield judging team.

John has helped a leading further education college, Runshaw College, similarly transform itself from virtual insolvency to sector exemplar in his capacity as Chairman of Governors. John is also Chairman of North and West Lancashire Business Link and Chair of the North Western Business Support Council. John was presented with the OBE by Prince Charles in recognition of his work in education. He recently was appointed by Government Office North West to the Lancashire Learning and Skills Council and now acts as Chair of that high-profile group.

The Team Enterprise Solution

*A Step-by-Step Guide
to Business Transformation*

John Oliver OBE

Oak Tree Press
19 Rutland Street,
Cork, Ireland.
www.oaktreepress.com

A catalogue record of this book is
available from the British Library.

ISBN 1-86076-225-5

*All author's royalties from the sales of this book will
be donated to BEN, the motor industry's benevolent
fund (Registered Charity no. 297877).*

Printed in Ireland by Colourbooks Ltd.

CONTENTS

ACKNOWLEDGEMENTS

A book of this nature is by definition a team effort. The derivation and the confirmation of the principles involved probably touch a few score managers and key influencers. Some will be mentioned later in the book, but most will not. We have merely used names to illustrate points and not to ascribe contribution. My apologies to those wonderful people at Leyland who contributed so much over this period, and are not specifically named later.

My thanks also to my successor, Stuart Heys, for proving that I wasn't indispensable. I'll forgive him one day. And my appreciation goes to all those Optima clients for the great joy of watching them struggle and then improve so dramatically. Stewart Pierce and Clive Memmott did sterling work in helping me cut the original tome down to size; and Sue Kirk, God bless her, kept me on schedule and in shape in my first, and probably last, attempt to write a book.

But above all, my appreciation goes out to two figures who have been totally inspirational. The late Les Southworth, former Works Director of Leyland Motors when it really was a company, had the characteristics of every guru's ideal of a modern manager, way ahead of his time. He influenced a whole generation of management across the Leyland empire and beyond. Secondly, the wonderful Bernard O'Connell, Principal of Runshaw College, who epitomises what this book is about.

Thank you.

John J. Oliver OBE
September 2001

Dedication

To Deirdre

FOREWORD

The operating environment faced by the motor industry is one of intensified and growing competition, largely as a result of the removal of trade barriers and the resultant opening of markets. The improved quality of product, in becoming widespread and assumed, has also contributed to this environment, in which the vehicle manufacturer must achieve the best possible efficiency and cost levels in order to give it a fighting chance of survival, whatever the market throws at it. In a nutshell, there is nowhere for the inefficient to hide.

This is no more apparent than in the commercial vehicle sector. The commercial vehicle is an intermediate product needed purely for business reasons. There are few, if any, of the psychological factors that come into play for purchasers of motor cars. To compete in such a world, the commercial vehicle maker, like any other company, must make products people want in the most cost-effective way. *The Team Enterprise Solution* describes how Leyland Trucks achieved this and thus provides "a step-by-step guide to business transformation" that has general applicability in all areas of manufacturing and, dare one say, in many areas of service provision as well.

The story of Leyland is in many ways a tragic one, but one which had a positive conclusion as the operation entered a new era under the control of a well-funded and visionary American truck-maker. The decline of the British-owned truck industry was an industrial disaster of monumental proportions. However, when all seemed lost, with the total disappearance of heavy truck-making in the UK being a real possibility, the 1990s saw a revival, of which Leyland has been a major contributor.

The business philosophy that is Team Enterprise revived the fortunes of what seemed a terminally wounded company. As such, it should encourage others to embrace it to their own benefit. The operation of Team Enterprise from 1989 to 1998 began with Leyland as part of DAF; with the collapse of the latter in 1993, Leyland operated as a standalone UK enterprise; but the need for larger scale meant that, in 1999, it was sold to the US company PACCAR, which already controlled DAF and Foden. Team Enterprise made Leyland an attractive purchase, but it also facilitated successful assimilation.

Team Enterprise is no more than empowered people working towards mutually beneficial objectives. It sounds simple, but great ideas always do when they are explained. The difficulties arise in deciding on the correct course of action and implementing it. The rewards of doing so are huge. In the case of Leyland Trucks, the operating costs and breakeven point were reduced greatly, quality improved, and production efficiency and employee morale were transformed.

If Leyland Trucks in its perilous condition could do this, then so can any other enterprise with a real desire to learn and improve. *The Team Enterprise Solution* is a manual for those wishing to attain the level of performance that gives them a real chance of surviving the rising tide of competition. Its authority comes from the fact that it describes a success story and how Team Enterprise was a major ingredient in that success. It demonstrates that manufacturing in the UK really can be world class.

Professor Garel Rhys OBE
SMMT Professor of Motor Industry Economics and
Director of the Centre for Automotive Industry Research
Cardiff Business School

CHAPTER 1

INTRODUCTION

This is a book about a philosophy, a philosophy so powerful that it reversed a seemingly inescapable decline in the fortunes of a medium-sized commercial vehicle manufacturer called Leyland Trucks. Since then, the key concepts and elements of this philosophy have been transferred to a host of differing institutions, often engendering step-changes in performance. The philosophy, called Team Enterprise, has been constantly refined and developed over a decade by Optima, Leyland Trucks' personnel services consultancy, of which more later. It has traditionally been taught on a face-to-face basis by skilled practitioners, but increasingly the customer base has demanded a book, a manual or a comprehensive guide, something for the Optima practitioners to leave behind when the client is left to fend for themselves. They wanted something to remind them of the basic principles and tenets involved, alongside those nuances and subtleties that are often forgotten due to a lack of immediate relevance.

This book is intended broadly as a manual, to be dipped in and out of as the need arises. If, for example, you feel that your company communication systems are somewhat underperforming, then dip into Chapter 7 and extract what you think fit. If you want to review your team's management behaviour, then go to Chapter 9 and do likewise. Digesting the contents at one continuous sitting is recommended only for the three-Shredded-Wheat brigade. In general, we've attempted to structure the book around the more obvious concepts of Team Enterprise. We might have missed the odd pointer but, then again, we don't want to render the Optima consultants totally redundant!

Understandably, much of this book revolves around Leyland Trucks. The trials and tribulations of the once-proud British Leyland empire have filled countless newspaper columns and editorials over the past four decades. Whilst manufacturing may be slipping fast in the fashion stakes as new and more exciting career paths emerge, the appetite of the public for tales of gloom and doom in the automotive sector seem insatiable. From the politics of the sixties through the Ryder report, strikes and associated militancy, and on to struggles with macro-economic disruption and global competition, the story of Leyland has been headline news for far too long now — and for all the wrong reasons. Leyland is seen by many as a microcosm of that traditional brownfield practice in which we Brits excel only in our mediocrity. The decline of mining, shipbuilding, steelmaking and their ilk is seen as part of a natural continuum with Leyland, in its various forms and gestations, leading the way — downwards.

The public mind has often found it difficult to distinguish Leyland Trucks from Leyland Cars. In truth the relationship between truck-making and the car industry within Leyland was more academic than real. Forced together by political rather than economic motives in the late sixties, these widely different sectors had little in common within the company, aside from answerability to corporate control. However, it is of little surprise that the public fails to distinguish between the two parts. Both share a cycle of decline over the past three decades which is as alarming as it is saddening. The reversal of fortunes in British truck-making is just as dramatic as that of its counterparts in passenger cars. In 1969, over 201,000 trucks were produced by factories in England and Scotland, including

Leyland's. Compare that to 1999, when only a pitiful 13,300 emerged from the nation's domestic manufacturers.

The story of how Team Enterprise has been able to reverse the fortunes of one so battered should be of great encouragement to others seeking to go down the same path. It is possible, I suppose, but I doubt whether many reading this book can consider themselves to be in such parlous difficulties as our subject. However, we should strongly emphasis from the outset that this isn't just about truckmaking or even heavy engineering. The principles of Team Enterprise are universal. As you will see, if your company employees *people* and has *competition*, then at some point in the near future you're going to have to think very carefully about moving into the exciting and highly profitable world of involvement and participation.

Over the past eight years, Optima has been working in companies a world away from Leyland Trucks. And the spectacular successes seen at Leyland have been repeated in the field of chemicals, paint manufacture, glass, education and local government, to name but a few. At first sight, one can't imagine sectors of greater differentiation. But the commonalities come thick and fast, the parallels seen over and over again. Management nowadays, thanks to the emergence of new technology and changes in society, is increasingly focused on the maximisation of individual contribution. It is no longer totally technically oriented, focusing on the best use of assets. Management has ceased to be purely about managing things but instead emphasises managing the *people* who manage the *things*. So the commonalities between apparently totally different concerns are less surprising.

Having mentioned Optima twice already, we should explain its origins. On 14 October 1993, Optima Personnel Services came into existence. Leyland Trucks had just emerged from a bruising and near-fatal receivership. Its reputation, never that good at the best of times, had taken a battering. Every public pundit forecast an early bath for this fledgling truck-maker. Competitors speculated gleefully on the prospects of the "phoenix being strangled at birth and remaining in the ashes", a quote frequently fed back to us. Suppliers reacted cautiously to requests for a restoration of normal credit terms. All in all, not a pretty picture.

To be successful, the marketing gurus tell you that you have to have a USP, a Unique Selling Proposition. Unfortunately, one was hard to find. Leyland was a British manufacturer selling in a British market, so the opportunity for a sentimental or emotional spin was perhaps a possibility. However, unlike the light commercial market where such factors were relevant, the bigger truck buyers rarely exhibited any such loyalty. They would buy from Germany, Italy or Timbuktu if the package was right. So that wouldn't wash. The more we analysed, the more we realised that our key strength, our own differentiating factor, was the highly individual sense of teamwork we had created in 1989.

Due to the baggage of a highly chequered history, Leyland had been forced to approach business improvement through a wholesale change in culture, first and foremost. The traditional mechanistic techniques allegedly successful elsewhere had been tried at Leyland without really energising performance. TQM, MRPII, SPC and a host of structural initiatives had their moments but never created the quantum improvements essential to business survival. But the philosophy, initially termed Lean Enterprise and then hastily renamed Team Enterprise when we discovered what the former was really about, had generated quite startling results in a relatively short period of time. Whilst the rest of the world may have still regarded Leyland Trucks as a true descendant of the British Leyland Empire, with all its inefficiencies and inadequacies, we knew that the first 30 months of Team Enterprise had literally transformed the company to a standard to compare with the best in European class. Unfortunately, we never bothered telling anybody outside the plant about this change in fortunes. We were manufacturers, not marketers.

We'd like to claim that the Optima idea was all our own, a flash of internal inspiration, but that's not true. It took the promptings of the local Training and Enterprise Council, LAWTEC, to bring the proposal to the forefront. Encouraged by a national competition entitled "The TEC Challenge" and funded by Gillian Shepherd's DfEE (Department of Employment and Education), LAWTEC asked Leyland for its ideas on increasing employment in the manufacturing sector. At the time, we explained, we had few suggestions on actually *increasing* employment; our sole objective was to maintain it. Survival was quite definitely our number one priority, particularly as the company had leapt from the jaws of receivership literally weeks earlier.

The TEC persisted, however, and in truth probably knew us better than we knew ourselves. They argued that local dissemination of the practices and principles embodied in Team Enterprise would benefit North and West Lancastrian manufacturers and hence provide a solid foundation for future growth. Their persuasive skills, and the not insignificant attraction of the substantial cash grant, won the day. We agreed!

Our initial contract was to run a one-day seminar for local managing directors or senior decision-makers. From this group, we would find a number of companies who would be trained via a series of three-day programmes. This would be augmented by an ill-defined "buddying" exercise where we would send line executives from Leyland to visit these companies to give them practical advice on their first tentative steps towards a genuine Team Enterprise.

Despite all our fears and concerns, the one-day programme was a huge success. The response of the attendees was unexpectedly enthusiastic and encouraging. What became apparent was the sheer frustration many in medium-sized businesses feel about the plethora of business opportunities surrounding them. Bombarded daily by mailshots encouraging the adoption of more and more exotic improvement initiatives, and similarly chastised by a host of well-intentioned business support agencies, few know where to turn. Most felt they had neither the time nor the resources to undertake any of these conventional programmes. Life in business is never easy at the best of times and 1993 was certainly not the best of times! The Leyland Trucks' approach, however, struck a chord in its relative simplicity and its grounding in apparent common sense. Nobody could dispute the theory that all companies had an untapped reservoir of hidden talents and expertise within their employees. Few could argue that the devices proposed by Leyland were either controversial or difficult. The whole approach of Team Enterprise, alongside clear evidence of a transformation of an archetypal brownfield organisation, seemed to awaken an empathy in the audience.

Word of mouth quickly spread and before long sufficient demand arose to run another "Chief Executive Day", as the session was grandly titled, even though chief executives were relatively scarce. The second course was even more successful. Some of the presenters were invited to make speeches elsewhere and demand grew further. The Chief Executive Day soon became a regular event, once every two months initially before stabilising at one per month. Despite its longevity, the day continues to be successful with appreciation levels consistently above 90 per cent and frequently over 95 per cent. However, before long, simply preaching was deemed insufficient. Clients wanted more active support within their factories or offices for training or perception gap analysis (see Change Initiation, Chapter 6). Optima's part-time staff (they all still had full-time line responsibilities) became more and more engaged outside the company. From those modest beginnings, Optima has grown to a medium-sized company in its own right. Hence the need for a book to satisfy the increasing demands of the hundreds of visitors to the Leyland plant.

The book is intended to broadly mirror the recommended sequence of activities needed to optimise Team Enterprise. Whilst not an iron rule, we suggest that the steps in Figure 1 are followed. These will be explained in more detail in Chapter 15.

The path towards Team Enterprise is, as you will find, a far-from-easy one. It will tax even the most talented and committed organisational leaders. However, the benefits are ultimately enormous, both in quantitative and qualitative terms. Once well on the road, you will find it difficult to perceive of any other way. All the hard work, the hours and the frustrations of seemingly repeatedly revisiting your steps will be worth it. I guarantee it.

Figure 1: Getting Started — The Preferred Path

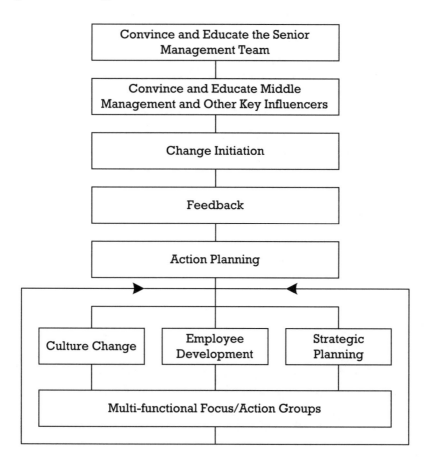

CHAPTER 2

TEAM ENTERPRISE — WHAT'S IT ALL ABOUT?

A Philosophy Defined

Back in 1989, we felt there was a need to define succinctly our new ethos and the task was given to me. My excuse for the cumbersome nature of the outcome is that at the time we were full of "management-speak". Plain English was deemed inadequate to convey the rich, intellectual depths of our intentions, and instead we resorted to a classic piece of cliché-ridden jargon. My only defence is that we knew what we meant and it didn't do us any harm. Team Enterprise was defined as:

> **Empowered People working towards**
> **Mutually Beneficial Objectives**

and remains so within Leyland to this day. The rather outlandish contention behind this whole book is that if your organisation can achieve the state of grace envisaged by this clumsy mangling of the Queen's English, then you will have in turn transformed every single operating parameter in your business. Now the extravagance of that statement depends very much on where you start from, but you are hardly likely to be reading this book or attending one of our courses if your company is in A1 condition. For the mere mortals amongst us, the potential is enormous. The point we should emphasise here is that we are talking about *every* single operating parameter. We are talking cash, we are talking profitability. We are talking efficiency and we are talking quality. This is not some well-intentioned piece of social engineering conjured up by the Human Resources Department. There are numerous and very welcome social spin-offs, but these are tangential. The whole justification for Team Enterprise is that it's the safest, quickest and most cost-effective means of improving your bottom line, long-term and permanently. And don't get hung up on the "long-term". Done correctly, Team Enterprise will start to pay back in months, not years.

If that's the case, then what exactly do we mean by our definition? The first word, "empowered", is a much-debated concept, particularly by the more mechanistic breed of management. Where does it start? Where does it end? How do we define it, measure it and monitor it? I have spent many fruitless hours exploring these and the many other questions that naturally follow, with zero benefit. Perhaps it's a useful debate for the academics but it is hardly likely to add any value to the process of making money. A colleague once richly described this as a classic piece of intellectual masturbation, or words to that effect. He was right, if a little intemperate in his choice of vocabulary.

All we would implore you to do here is simply to give your employees a discernible increase in their range of accountabilities, responsibilities and decision-making. The extent of those accountabilities, responsibilities and decision-making is largely down to you. The bigger the step you make, the bigger ultimately is the payback. But the bigger the step you make, the bigger the risk is that things may go somewhat awry. So most prefer to move a little at a time, with one important precondition. People must know about it! They have to be aware not just of the changes themselves but also the thinking behind them and the expected consequences. Ideally, they should be consulted, not simply informed, and given some time to reflect on the questions, "What does this mean for me?" and "What's in it for me?"

For those in a hurry — and we see this all the time in Optima — this may seem to be an unnecessary process, a definite case of not adding value. However, skip this stage at your peril. The most significant lesson learnt by Leyland Trucks over the past ten years is that:

> **Empowerment cannot be given;**
> **empowerment has to be taken**

Management can provide the framework, the infrastructure for empowerment, but it cannot force acceptance on people. Instead, all it will achieve is merely enlarging job descriptions without the benefits of a more committed, involved and eventually proactive workforce. Empowerment only exists when the employee enters into the new arrangement with a view that this new way of working could be worthwhile, for them as well as for the company.

In most traditional or "brownfield" establishments, carrying all the baggage of history and less-than-ideal experiences, one shouldn't expect an immediate conversion. If you're lucky, you might get a general response characterised by a quizzical curiosity or perhaps even a guarded willingness to Give It A Go. But inevitably there will be the cynics, the "seen-it-all-before" brigade and those who are downright hostile. Don't worry too much about this. If you've done your best to communicate in a participative fashion, flagging up a future of greater harmony, experience tells us that the workforce will eventually see the wisdom and the benefit of a better way of working. They'll cautiously dip their toes into the waters. And that's all you can expect at this stage.

Psychological Gainsharing

All the foregoing sounds very mid-seventies-ish, when participation was all the rage. And those experiments are littered in retrospect with phrases like "abdication not delegation", a "recipe for anarchy" and *"laissez-faire* management". There are obvious dangers that must be avoided and will be if we manage to achieve the second element of the definition — "working toward mutually beneficial objectives". This is very much the difficult bit. Somehow we must ensure that our employees perceive that they will use these newfound accountabilities, responsibilities and decision-making to work towards objectives which not only satisfy the objectives of the corporation or company but also meet the requirements of the individual involved. We are looking for win-win; we are looking for that area of common interest which creates a "psychological gainsharing" opportunity. The selection of the mutually beneficial objective is therefore all-important.

I use the expression *psychological gainsharing* to emphasise that, in my view, conventional financial gainsharing rarely works here. I am aware that this is not a widely held view and hence I've said "rarely works", when I really mean "never works"! I am convinced that we are looking here for a purer form of motivation than simply earning more money. For Leyland in 1989, the obvious banner to fly was job security. In the early 1970s, between 12,000 and 14,000 people had been employed in the manufacture of trucks and buses in the small towns of Leyland and Chorley. By 1989, it had fallen to a little over 4,000. So those who had survived the succession of radical plans, restructurings and redundancies had seen scores of friends, acquaintances and close family members lose their jobs. It was little wonder that the prevailing emotions in the plant were insecurity, fatalism and not a little guilt at being one of the lucky ones.

By focusing on this latent desire for survival, we were able to develop a common focus for employees and companies alike. Our mutual interest was therefore described as maximising the number of long-term jobs within the company by utilising all of our collective resources. There were no guarantees, just an awareness that whatever we had all been doing for the past 20 years wasn't working. Surely, went the argument, there must be a better way of working together to ensure that those factors which we could control should be handled to the best of our collective ability. There was enough to worry about with issues completely beyond our influence — market changes, exchange rates and relative inflation rates, to name but a few — without too frequently shooting ourselves in the metaphorical foot. The enemy lived outside the factory gates, not inside them.

We were therefore able to articulate a common purpose, our mutually beneficial objective. Convincing the workforce was a completely different proposition. The inherent and powerful distrust of management and a suspicion of our motives proved a huge barrier. Breaking down this barrier was never going to be easy or immediate. After all, the Leyland workforce had for years been familiar with a succession of well-intentioned senior managers, each in turn dedicated to reversing the seemingly irresistible decline in the company's fortunes.

There was no easy answer to this dilemma. It was not and still isn't an unusual situation. Lots of directors and senior managers find themselves in similar circumstances. Fortunately, the whole management team appreciated that these attitudes were not going to be overturned quickly. We had generations of perceived misjustice and mismanagement to overcome. We had to accept that, even with the grandest scheme we could conjure, transformation of mistrust and suspicion was likely to take years rather than months. But we consoled ourselves that even a few steps along the journey would be beneficial. The techniques we used will be described later in the book, so I will not bother the reader with great detail here. All required enormous management commitment, lots of time and constant repetition.

For Leyland, therefore, in 1989 the "mutually beneficial objective" was long-term job security. I suspect that's equally valid for most companies, as competition in most sectors nowadays falls in the "ferocious" category. Some companies worry about the potential downside on morale if this common purpose is defined in such a negative way. This is a valid concern. There is little prospect of gaining the desired unity of purpose if the prevailing atmosphere in the company is one of fear. Fear will kill creativity, imagination and the ability to innovate. It will arrest the necessary process of continuing change as people naturally see the preservation of the status quo as a key element in job protection. The message must be conveyed realistically. I have no truck with those organisations that only communicate good news, but it must also emphasise the very real benefits of a collective and positive response. Remember: we are seeking to motivate, to inspire and to instil a major leap in "average employee mindset". Negative messages will strangle this at birth.

Many organisations, however, cannot use long-term job security as the key motivator. It just doesn't apply to their operation. They have difficulty in identifying this common theme, this unity of purpose. In these cases, I'm 100 per cent with Tom Peters, who argues that people respond best to a perceived crisis: "If you haven't got a crisis, invent one!" The crisis may be competitive pressure, the threat of legislation or major market changes. It could be the need to grow the business or to diversify or to focus. Either way, a great deal of thought needs to go into the derivation of a mutually beneficial objective. In monopolistic or semi-monopolistic situations, such articulation may be difficult. But it's not impossible, as demonstrated by successful moves in this direction in educational establishments. Here, for example, *the pursuit of excellence* has proved to be very powerful in a workforce with a strong sense of vocation. Whatever you do, don't start this initiative until you are confident that you can develop a theme or purpose which fulfils the requirement of being **mutually beneficial**.

Our ambition within Team Enterprise is to replicate the motivating forces often seen in owner-management across the whole organisation. We want every employee to feel a strong sense of identification with the business. We want them to feel that their role is naturally proactive, seeking to constantly challenge the status quo in pursuit of continuous improvement. We want them all to feel valued, to have personal pride and a strong sense of self-esteem in the way they go about the world of work. In our very early days, we mused about "winning the hearts and minds of the workforce" but decided that, as a statement of intent, it would be seen as too pat or patronising. The old saw about "grabbing them by the balls and the hearts and minds will follow" was too near former management styles for comfort! But winning hearts and minds is exactly what Team Enterprise is all about. The true dynamic behind the phenomenal success of the initiative is this strong empathy between employee and company goals, where the difference between management and the managed is increasingly blurred.

Empowerment and Process Control

One of the key concerns of those naturally resistant to participative systems is the fear of losing control. Applied incorrectly, this is a very real possibility. My memories of the 1970s experiments in this arena are littered with examples of this happening. Moving, for example, from an outdated and adversarial piecework system to a far more socially acceptable measured day work scheme allegedly cost Leyland Motors 20 per cent in productivity within a year. I once heard Peter Wickens from Nissan describe one of the prerequisites of increasing empowerment as being an attendant increase in process control. Note that we are talking here of *process* control, not *management* control. Figure 2 shows the profile we are seeking. As we release empowerment into the organisation, or more accurately as empowerment is taken up by the workforce, we put in place measures to ensure that process controls are increased. This is achieved by delegating properly, of which more later. Quadrant D in Figure 2 represents the Team Enterprise zone, high empowerment associated with 6σ (Six Sigma)-like control. Quadrant A, displaying low control and low empowerment, is *anarchy*. Quadrant B is *autocracy* characterised by high control but little empowerment, the traditional hierarchical approach.

Quadrant C is where those cautious or cynical about Team Enterprise fear their organisation will finish up — *abdication*.

Figure 2: Delegating with Confidence

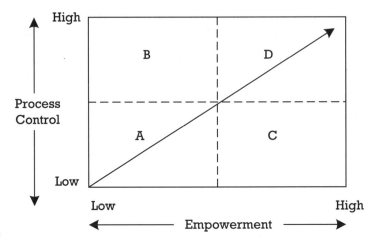

If all the guidelines in this book are followed closely, there is little chance of a quadrant C outcome. But the concerns do highlight the need for a step-change in process conformance in tandem with the cultural changes advocated through Team Enterprise. A significant reduction in process variability would also be welcome. Whether you decide to pursue your business improvement strategy through either Lean or Team philosophies (see below), the point is equally valid. Inadequate process controls are known to create organisation waste, but they also contribute to frustration, demotivation and interfunctional strife. Improving process conformance is a necessity, a prerequisite in achieving the harmonious organisation envisaged throughout this book. The difference between the two approaches is that, in Lean, process controls are effected from above. In Team, we delegate that responsibility to the organisation but with a clear expectation of a successful outcome. Before too long we find a natural momentum towards greater predictability.

Lean Enterprise and Team Enterprise

One of the great confusions in the minds of those approaching participation for the first time is the difference between Lean Enterprise and Team Enterprise.

Strangely, for two entirely different philosophies, the end products, measured as deliverable outputs, are theoretically almost identical. Lean Enterprise attempts to achieve world class levels of efficiency, quality and productivity through the maximisation of added value and the elimination of waste. The approach is very much management-inspired and executed using a highly structured methodology. Process flows and attendant procedures are optimised in this search for a truly streamlined operation. Teams and teamworking are often found but usually only because they represent the most efficient and effective means of achieving corporate goals.

A true Team Enterprise aspires structurally to have the same end product. However, the key difference is in the surrounding culture. Team Enterprise should exhibit the "loose" characteristics such as empowerment, recognition, participation, etc., as well as the "tight" ones found in high levels of process conformance. Some people argue that the two philosophies are incompatible; that Lean systems will always offer a greater potential for savings than a participative approach. They might well be right, in the extreme. But most entrants into this arena will be more than satisfied with the potential that the allegedly "softer" option offers.

Benefits to the Organisation

The reader might by now be feeling a little daunted by the difficulties in implementing a Team Enterprise culture. We have stated earlier that Team Enterprise is the safest, quickest and cheapest means of improving operational performance but we didn't say that it was the easiest. Any successful implementation will be the result of a lot of hard work, planning and monitoring. The levels of complexity involved demand at least the same attention as if you were implementing a sophisticated piece of software. In many ways it could be more difficult since we are dealing with far more intangibles. Team Enterprise may be viewed as a "soft" approach but it certainly is no soft option. Whilst we can guarantee that the rewards will flow in copious volume if you get it right, we can't ignore the hard work, commitment and open-mindedness which are all essential ingredients of a successful execution.

So before the aspirant Team Entrepreneur gets totally deterred by the degree of difficulty in implementing a successful Team Enterprise, let us spend a few pages examining some of the benefits. Leyland Trucks is a prime example of what can be achieved when the whole manufacturing organisation initiates and drives change through this process. Note that we refer only to the manufacturing operation. For reasons covered in Chapter 4, we at Leyland in 1989 were unable to simultaneously bring on board sales, marketing and engineering. Theoretically, therefore, the benefits could have been much higher but, as you will see, are quite impressive on their own.

The total cash-out for Leyland over its first two years spent on Team Enterprise amounted to just £30,000. This compared to a local turnover of over £200 million per annum. In absolute terms, this expenditure was therefore insignificant and in fact hidden under existing budgets to avoid declaration to the "Centre". We feared that corporate involvement would inevitably result in unnecessary bureaucracy, fears that turned out to be well-founded. The attractions of going it alone and developing a model designed to be compatible with local culture were irresistible. It should be strongly emphasised that cash was not the only resource input. As a matter of policy, we elected to do all training in-house with line management teaching and instructing. If you can afford the time and have the luxury of making more than the odd mistake, this approach is well worth considering.

Figure 3 shows some of the benefits gained over these first two stumbling, fumbling years. Chapter 4 will describe in greater detail how these were achieved. For the moment we should concentrate on the scale of the benefits that Team Enterprise can deliver. In pure financial terms, a return of £10 million per annum for a cash-out of £30,000 beats the hell out of every other management initiative we've every tried at Leyland and, believe me, we've tried most of them. The consequent halving of breakeven point was a vital step in the survival of the company. We weren't to know it at the time, but the year of initiation, 1989, was the last year in the UK for mega-volume truck sales, over 69,000 in total. The following year the market collapsed to 32,000 and has never fully recovered due to improvements in logistics, technology and truck longevity. A breakeven point of 11,500 trucks per annum became totally unsustainable for a company heavily dependent on a UK market dominated by foreign competition. Team Enterprise's role in reducing the break-even to 5,500 was, in retrospect, really a matter of life and death.

Figure 3: The Benefits of Team Enterprise at Leyland Trucks, September 1989 to December 1991

- ♦ Within two years, a reduction of 24 per cent in operating costs generating a saving of £10,000,000 per annum.

- ♦ Within 30 months, a halving of breakeven point.

- ♦ Within 30 months, a 35 per cent reduction in warranty costs and an equivalent improvement in build quality.

- ♦ A more responsive and flexible organisation.

- ♦ A step-change improvement in employee attitudes and satisfaction levels.

The financial benefits of Team Enterprise are therefore mighty impressive. Similar results have been achieved in many other businesses that have trodden a similar path. This emphasises the point that Team Enterprise is a *business philosophy* not, as often perceived, a human resources initiative designed to improve the sociability of the world of work. There will also be many benefits in the latter's direction, as we will discuss shortly. But the overriding result from all the cases noted in this book is a substantial and ongoing improvement in bottom line performance.

There are many other equally impressive consequences of moving in this direction. Product quality improved markedly over the first 30 months of Team Enterprise, yielding a 35 per cent reduction in warranty costs and an equivalent improvement in build quality. This was vitally important to the company's image. Whilst I have always been profoundly impressed by the financial opportunities offered by Team Enterprise, it is the last two items on Figure 3 which personally generate the greatest enthusiasm.

The benefits of a much more responsive and flexible organisation are difficult to quantify but represent the most surprising and delightful outcome for those who work within a successful Team Enterprise implementation. I have often heard the near elimination of interdepartmental strife being described as an unexpected benefit of the change, but perhaps it shouldn't surprise. With a new emphasis on multi-functionalism and on dynamic teams based on process flows rather than departmental sub-objectives, it is clear that the silo mentality characteristic of far too many organisations is likely to erode.

The consequences for delivery times, project implementation, responsiveness to market changes and so on are therefore extremely powerful. In 1994, just five years after commencement of the process at Leyland and just one year after the integration of the Product Development department into Team Enterprise, Leyland initiated a complex new product introduction with a target capital cost of 60 per cent of previous estimates and just 40 per cent of the normal cycle time. It wasn't the most comfortable project any of us have been associated with, but it certainly rewrote the rulebook for future schemes.

For many people, managers and the managed alike, the world of work is like a battleground. Hostility, mistrust and suspicion can create stresses and strains that make the daily grind unpleasant and uncomfortable. Simply generating the will to get up in the morning and face yet another day of quarrelling, backbiting and general negativity can be a major effort. And yet in this increasingly competitive world, with the emergence of the so-called "knowledge worker", getting the best of employees is absolutely paramount. Team Enterprise has the benefit of attacking some of the key causal factors that create this negative atmosphere. As you will find later, improved communication systems, recognition systems, organisational structures and management behaviour all help to reduce most of the root causes of frustration and dissatisfaction.

The Leyland Trucks journey towards Team Enterprise had lots of unexpected gains in this area, even in its very early days. Whilst never quite aspiring to the utopian situation often described elsewhere, a quite discernible step-change in attitudes and morale was very much in evidence nevertheless. Through the Change Initiation Surveys (see Chapter 6) we were able to measure the transformation in some detail, although the improvement was self-evident in both formal and informal contact with the workforce. People, we found, were willing to accept the trials and tribulations imposed by external factors but are far less tolerant of those hardships which are seen to be caused by management inefficiency or laxity. The transparency created by Team Enterprise alongside a more collective focus on problem-solving erodes the traditional "us and them" attitudes which pervade so much of the world of work. This in turn opens the door to greater acceptance of more sophisticated work systems such as autonomous work groups, multi-functional project teams and greater levels of empowerment.

The benefits of Team Enterprise are therefore huge and cannot be ignored by any manager wishing to improve their business performance. It is, of course, not the only route forward. I'm sure that there are many examples of mechanistic and autocratic organisations which can claim significant successes over an extended period. However, I would venture that such situations are highly dependent on the energy, personality and cha-risma of a small number of key individuals. Whether this is sustainable in the long term as these *wunderkinder* grow old or depart is questionable. For those of us who might not possess these rare characteristics, Team Enterprise promises to be the safest, quickest and cheapest means of creating a world class workforce.

CHAPTER 3

SIX PITFALLS OF TEAM ENTERPRISE

A friend of mine, Tony, tells the following story. Apparently Tony, who's a bit of an action man, went off skiing with a colleague of his, Peter, who shared the same love of risk. Not for them the orthodoxy of the normal ski runs — they preferred instead to risk the dangers of the unknown, venturing far off-piste and challenging each other to greater and greater deeds of derring-do. After a thoroughly exhilarating and entertaining morning wandering who knows where, they eventually stumbled on a particularly nasty piece of descent. At this point Tony began to come to his senses and suggested that they turn back but Peter would have none of it. Tony initially resisted the pleadings and cajolings until his friend offered him a challenge. If Peter could manoeuvre his way down to the bottom, would Tony follow? Tony knew the sensible and safe answer was no but found it hard to say so and caved in.

Peter boldly set off at pace but after only a few yards lost control. He plummeted head-over-heels down the icy slopes. Tony watched in horror as his mate tumbled at increasing speed, losing a ski, falling further, losing another ski, and then his head came off. Or so it seemed until close examination revealed this to be only his rucksack, much to Tony's (and no doubt Peter's) huge relief. After several hundred metres of this terrifying spectacle, this now distant figure lay still in the snow, his debris scattered behind him on the mountainside. Tony peered anxiously into the gloom and was just about to turn away and seek help when he suddenly detected movement. To his surprise, Peter slowly and agonisingly hauled himself to his feet, gingerly dusted off the snow and ice and painfully cupped both hands to the face. And then called out, "Come on down, it's a piece of piss!"

Throughout this book I have often felt like Peter. For me and my colleagues, the first faltering steps along the road to Team Enterprise are but a distant memory. Our journey, it has to be said, has been an extremely fortunate one. Difficulties have been encountered and occasionally tracks have had to be re-traced, but rarely has the overall momentum been arrested. For Leyland Trucks, Team Enterprise has been an exercise in in-creasing optimism and enthusiasm from day one.

But we know now that we were one of the lucky ones. Many companies have big problems at some stage in the process and, as a consequence, give up. It has been estimated that as many as four experiments in five relating to teams and teamworking fail. Worryingly, your involvement with Team Enterprise could follow a very similar profile unless some key pitfalls are avoided.

Fortunately, we think that we can identify most of these pit-falls. The other good news is that they're not difficult to under-stand. But doing something about them might be a little more troublesome! The following issues appear time and again when my colleagues and I visit companies in trouble. I am sure that this is far from a complete list but these six little lessons proba-bly account for about 80–85 per cent of failures, if Optima's ex-perience can be seen as representative.

PITFALL NO 1: TEAM ENTERPRISE IS A SERIOUS BUSINESS

In the late 1990s, most organisations realised to their horror that they had a nasty problem called the Millennium Bug coming their way. Despite forecasts of widespread disaster and disruption, in the end very few concerns encountered any real difficulty. The reason for this was that, almost without exception, the problem was addressed from the standpoint of a major complex endeavour. Ramifications were quantified, options scrutinised, project architectures constructed and detail review and monitoring processes investigated. This may have been extended into Conference Room Pilots, User Sign-offs, etc., etc. In summary, what we saw was the construction of professional and coherent project plans to maximise chances of success. All this is eminently sensible. With a complex piece of new software, we wouldn't dream of doing anything else. We know the consequences of getting it wrong and therefore we fully appreciate the value of detailed planning and preparation. Sensible? Clearly. Optional? Hardly.

Few would disagree with any of the foregoing. And yet, why do organisations rarely take the same trouble with a sophisticated and complex programme like teamworking or Team Enterprise?

My colleagues and I are often staggered by the apparent naivety displayed when it comes to introducing culture change programmes in all sorts of organisations. We have seen implementations where the sole forethought seems to have been, "Let's get rid of supervision and see how it goes." This approach seems to stem from the conviction that a harmonious organisation will ultimately be self-determining once the necessary structural alterations have been put in place. Similar thinking is commonplace when it comes to teamworking. Again, a simplistic view prevails that all management has to do is to think up a structure and the system will sort itself out.

Why do such organisations fall into this very obvious trap? Well, there appear to be three key reasons. Firstly, management doesn't understand the existing culture, let alone the new one. Secondly, they're simply afraid of it; and thirdly, they place little importance on such initiatives. Many prefer the intellectual and mechanistic basis of orthodox programmes such as TQM, MRPII and BPR to what they perceive as touchy-feely personnel-speak.

It is this last one which I find so frustrating. Surely by now there is sufficient evidence to convince anybody that the quickest, safest and cheapest way to improve profitability is through the better use of people in employment? This can no longer be regarded as some politically correct piece of social engineering — nice to have but not really anything to do with proper management. F.W. Taylor seems to be the one true hero in many eyes, even today.

Figure 4 shows some of the factors that need to be thought about before teamworking is introduced. It's not a comprehensive list, merely a few pointers. These are some of the parameters that will dictate whether your brave new world is going to be successful. If you don't at least think about them, then who will?

Figure 4: Thinking About Teams . . .

◆ Team structures, dynamics and leaders

◆ Range of responsibilities, accountabilities and authorities

◆ Measurement criteria and reporting mechanisms

◆ Communication and recognition

◆ Discipline and "consequences"

◆ Support from ancillary areas and infrastructure

◆ Pay and pay differentials.

The preferred approach is to address Team Enterprise in the same way that senior management would tackle a major capital investment programme. The key deliverables need to be determined and the key variables understood. But once described, the rest of the project organisation is left to get on with it and concentrate on doing what they do best.

PITFALL NO. 2: WITH TEAM ENTERPRISE, YOU MUST THINK 70 PER CENT CULTURE, 30 PER CENT STRUCTURE

This is by far the most common weakness seen in participative systems. When it comes to developing any "people-based" initiative, you must focus approximately 70 per cent of your development time on understanding and implementing changes to the culture of the organisation and not more than 30 per cent on systems or structure. A simple statement but one that most managers meet with sheer incredulity. As well they might. In these more enlightened times, management has ceased to be an art acquired through breeding or years of practical experience. It is now an accepted subject for detailed academic treatment. Managers at all levels nowadays are trained either before they take up the reins or during their very early days in the job.

However, due no doubt to the prestige associated with formal qualifications, many managers fall into the trap of assuming that they now have the full toolkit! They sincerely believe that working life can be distilled neatly into the academic and formulaic structures so ardently taught in the management and business schools. Many aspects of working life can be treated so but, unfortunately, others cannot. I have often wondered whether this is the reason why so many well-educated and highly intelligent young people fail abysmally when thrust into management. Years ago I came to the conclusion that the most important characteristic one sought when interviewing potential management candidates was a certain *nous* or streetwisdom.

To illustrate this theme, let us examine the process of a fairly routine management activity — problem-solving. Most of us find the challenge of sitting down armed with only pen and paper or in front of a PC, attempting to resolve a particularly thorny problem, very pleasing indeed. The intellectual satis-

faction of working through several variables of previously uncertain dimensions and arriving at a practical resolution can be
one of the more pleasant excursions of workaday life, particularly if we think the outcome to be elegant or surprisingly
imaginative.

However, finding a potential solution by scouring our knowledge of organisational structures and systems is, unfortunately,
not the same as solving the problem. Implementation, the hard
bit, necessitates involving other people and that is where the
uncertainty begins. Other people may not react as positively or
enthusiastically as we would like. The overall responsiveness of
our colleagues is said to be a function of the "culture" of the organisation. Accordingly, it seems sensible to take the view that
systems, structure and culture should be in some form of "balance" if we are to be consistently able to identify and implement change. Figure 5 illustrates this process.

Figure 5: Balanced Problem Solving in the World of Work

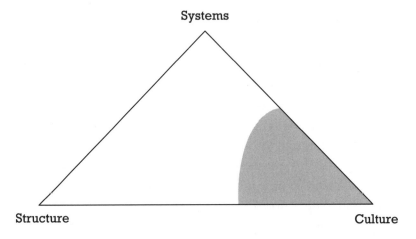

Unfortunately, few of us attain this balance. We generally prefer
working on the system–structure axis. Life here is predictable,
controllable and understandable. It is a comfortable world
where uncertainty rarely appears since few problems in management require the application of rocket science. But the
shaded zone is a different proposition altogether. Here, we're

exposed to the irrationality, variability and often emotional responsiveness of people in the world of work. This area, the culture zone, doesn't seem to conform to any mathematical norms. Nor is it consistent or stable. For apparently little reason, cultures can shift dramatically at a stroke, dependent on whims or fancies. For an overworked, constantly harassed manager, this can be totally perplexing or downright frustrating. They can't understand it, can't rationalise it and simply can't accept it. So the perceived irrationality is ignored, often making the problem worse.

For most of us in management, the shaded zone is too difficult. We retreat to the comfort of the systems–structure axis, where our left-brain logic works so well. We spend our time with our peers, focusing our attention on meetings, reports, agendas and conferences where life returns to a uniform conformity. The shaded area becomes a no-go zone, often viewed fearfully because of its painful unpredictability. We convince ourselves that effective management can be executed from the comfortable left-hand axis, working life being reconstructed as "painting by numbers".

It is little wonder that Change Initiation engenders a far from flattering picture of most managers. Not only are they perceived as remote, they are often seen as out of touch and lacking an understanding of the reality of the workplace. This is extremely worrying if the central premise of the book is to be believed: that in today's world, getting more out of your employees' talents and expertise is essential. If so, then the way most of us manage is the first major bottleneck! We have to be prepared to move into the shaded zone and accept all the uncertainty and unpredictability that goes with it. We have to understand the real culture of our particular place of work and that means communicating, listening and observing what really goes on. We need to find ways of discovering for ourselves what turns our people on, what turns them off, what they find troublesome and what they find acceptable. And given the unavoidable conclusion that most managers have been neglectful of this area for decades, we need urgently to redress the balance. Hence our contention that, as a rough guide, 70 per cent of "development" time should be spent getting to grips with creating the preferred new culture and only 30 per cent on building new systems and structures to accommodate it.

This is not to say that Team Enterprise is anti-structure. Far from it: throughout this book, you will find numerous suggestions for helpful structural change. But the emphasis must be on culture, as Team Enterprise is primarily a motivational tool. And only rarely do people get excited about new systems!

PITFALL NO. 3: PERCEPTION IS REALITY

Our objective with Team Enterprise is to win the hearts and minds of the workforce so that we can all work together to our utmost to achieve our mutually agreed unity of purpose. Our task as managers is therefore to inspire and to motivate those who work for us to this end. As we said earlier, however, empowerment cannot be given — empowerment has to be taken. People have to empower themselves and they will only do so if they *perceive* that the whole endeavour is worthwhile. And it is this "perception" wherein lies the key. We must clearly understand that **the perceptions of the workforce are their reality**. You as a manager might feel that their perception is wrong or misguided, but it's still their reality. And if this erroneous perception is preventing progress, then it's down to you and only you to change that perception so that their new one matches reality. The example we quote on our seminars often seems harsh as well as crude: "You might think you're the best manager in the world, but if the people who work for you think you're a tosser . . . well, guess what, you are a tosser and you will remain a tosser until you change that perception!"

Some managers find this very unfair. They will agree with the perception but say things like "But that's what they think of *all* the managers in our place." That doesn't matter. You are paid to do the job and the responsibility lies with you. Your task is to "manage the *people* who manage the process". And you're obviously not doing it!

Nobody said the world of work had to be fair and reasonable. If people perceive the situation as unhelpful or unsupportive, then we need to find ways of changing this perception to support a more positive outcome.

In many respects, the difficulty starts here. Because knowing what our subordinates, peers and colleagues actually think is a skill denied to most of us. And yet it is this knowledge which is so essential in the world of motivation. If we don't know what turns our people on or what turns them off, how can we possibly achieve the synergy so necessary in a successful Team Enterprise? Figure 6 shows our dilemma:

Figure 6: The Perception Dilemma

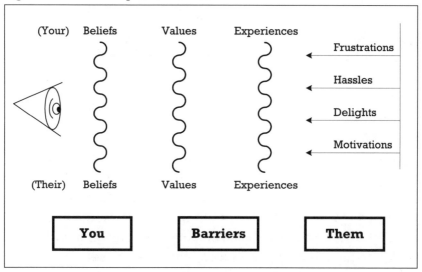

You as a manager are challenged to bring out the best in your people. You need to know what they are thinking, what frustrates them and what gives them hassle. And more positively, what delights them and what motivates them to giving more in the cause of mutually beneficial objectives. But it isn't easy. There are unseen barriers between them and us, which cloud our judgement. Our own belief systems, our values and our experiences may clash with theirs.

We cannot ignore these barriers. They exist but they must be overcome. We need devices to get through them and find what the perceptions of the situation really are. Fortunately, there are many tools to do this. We can communicate more effectively, perhaps through perfecting our listening skills, we can utilise the perception gap analysis known as Change Initiation (covered in Chapter 6). But don't fall into the trap of thinking that *you're* not the problem here. Enough research has been done to indicate that management's view of the needs of their workforce is almost invariably at odds to the workforce's view of their own needs. The consequences of getting it wrong are horrendous and yet we do it all the time. Just think of the hours and costs wasted in developing new payment and performance approval schemes only to find them ineffective and unpopular at the death. I had years at Leyland where my time in manufacturing management was totally dominated by site-based productivity schemes designed originally to motivate people to higher efficiencies but which had no such effect. All that was created was a legacy of mistrust, suspicion and misunderstanding that took a long time to wane.

To illustrate this point, let me relate one of my own experiences. For years, I had developed the habit of "Managing by Walking About" (MBWA). Each day I would wander around the factory confident that I was spending my time gainfully by providing the shopfloor with access to senior management as well as identifying the hot spots in daily affairs for myself.

However, one day I started my daily tour in the usual place and was just about to stride forth when a colleague from the assembly lines approached me. The face was familiar but I hadn't really talked to him before, since he seemed a quiet, conscientious sort who normally appeared too busy to interrupt. On this occasion, however, he approached me and said, "Can I ask you a question?" This simple and polite request took me a little by surprise, but I answered in the affirmative: of course he could.

"You won't be offended then?" he added mysteriously. "Of course not," replied I, the self-acclaimed Prince of Democracy; "Fire away." He took a deep breath, this being obviously difficult for him, and said, "OK, why do you have to be a *pillock* to be noticed in this place?" The tone and nature of the question took me by surprise, so I asked him to repeat it to make sure I'd heard it correctly. When he did, I gently said that I did not know what he meant and would he care to elaborate. There was no stopping him now: "Take you, for example; nearly every day you come down to the shopfloor. Just *exactly* what are you trying to do?"

Remaining calm and ignoring the latent aggression in his voice, I simply explained the need to make myself generally available so that I understood the real issues of the workplace and that people could feel comfortable about accessing one of the key decision-makers in the company.

He fixed me carefully with his gaze and said, cynically, "And *who* do you speak to when you walk around the plant?" I should have realised that this was the trick part of the question, but I waxed on regardless about varying my route to ensure I talked to a representative cross-section of the workforce. His demeanour darkened and he interrupted, "That's *bollocks!* You don't do that." Now I pride myself as being a caring, sharing, democratic manager but in situations like this, my old autocracy creeps out and unfortunately a bad-tempered exchange took place. The blame for which, I stress ashamedly, was entirely with me. The upshot was that I ended up challenging him to tell me that, if I was so wrong, exactly with whom did he suppose I spent my time. He answered curtly, and with some venom, "Don't ask me, ask anyone around here. The only people you speak to are the *dickheads*, the *barrack-room lawyers* and the *loony tunes*." Now I confess he had me at a disadvantage here. I had no idea what a "loony tune" was, but I got the drift. But I ploughed on regardless and we parted, to my dying shame, in rancour and disagreement.

I was now in a temper. My blood pressure was no doubt up and I strode off, muttering darkly, in the direction of solace — my somewhat-to-the-right-of-Attila-the-Hun manufacturing manager. "John," says I, "have you heard what this nutcase over there said?" and I continued to tell the story. John became increasingly pensive as the tale unfolded and commented at the end, "You don't think he could be right, do you?"

Despite my rigorous denials to the contrary, John persisted. He suggested that we both took a few minutes to write down the names of those people we had spent time with over the past few days. So we did. I petulantly sat in a corner and obliged. The list was passed over to John to spend a minute or so consolidating our contributions. He then read out the conclusions. All I heard was . . . "barrack-room lawyer, dickhead, loony tune, barrack-room lawyer, dickhead, loony tune" . . . and on, and on.

To our mutual horror, the chap had been right. We had been wrong! Frighteningly, it took all of five minutes to work out why. There are two forces at work here. Firstly, MBWA isn't easy. Few of us are extroverts. Most of us find walking up to relative strangers, who invariably are busy or otherwise preoccupied, quite a daunting proposition. This can be doubly difficult if the recipient of your attentions is less than garrulous or is somewhat in awe of authority. The net result can be an uncomfortable, halting progression from person to person. Unless, of course, we find people who want to speak to us; who want to engage in conversation; who have issues to talk about. This is much easier and therefore very welcome. But, unfortunately, there exists in this category a high proportion of the negative minority, those "moany-faced sods", to quote Jack Black, who thrive on those situations. They use the opportunity to offload all their negative baggage, whinging and whining. And we rise to the bait every time.

The other force in evidence here concerns the tedium of workaday life. A full shift on an assembly line can be a boring business, so most look to do something to brighten up their day. Some work exceptionally hard, seeking variety and challenge to add a little interest. Others may engage in extra-curricular activities, playing chess, joining a racing pool and so on. But for some, a little mischief is a far more attractive proposition. And what could be better than having a go at the boss. You may lose the argument, but you've had a bit of fun and your status amongst your peers will rise as they admire your gumption for taking on the establishment. It is therefore little wonder that most managers — for this is not an isolated tale — spend so much time with the bottom 20 per cent (attitudinally) of the work population. And as we continually fall into this trap, it is no surprise that the remaining 80 per cent simply cannot comprehend why we would place so much value on the negative minority by spending a disproportionate amount of our scarce time with them.

This was a learning point and a half. Had I, in my early days, bothered to seek opinion on my daily promenade, then no doubt someone would have given me a clue. Instead, I spent the best part of two decades doing something so routinely and so wrongly without having the sense or humility to check it. Their perception, that my own version of MBWA was a total waste of time, was indeed their reality and the only reality that mattered.

The key lesson from all this goes back to the fundamental definition of a manager's role. If our task is nowadays "to manage the *people* who manage the assets" rather than simply "to manage the assets", then understanding perceptions is all-important. If you don't know what people think is wrong, how can you possibly fix it?

PITFALL NO. 4: KEEP THE ATMOSPHERE POSITIVE!

Our challenge as managers is to harness the creativity, imagination and innovativeness of our charges. The more we do that, the more successful we are likely to be. A few minutes walking around any organisation and talking to a random cross-section of employees can frequently be enough to assess the likely success or otherwise of local management. Psychologists might view this as anecdotal or experiential, but it seems to work! The more positive the atmosphere, the greater the chances of achieving a truly effective Team Enterprise. Encountering the reverse usually means the company is either failing altogether or is about to fail.

If we accept the statement on the first line of the above paragraph, then the need for a positive climate is self-evident. People are not going to feel inclined to give their best intellectually and enthusiastically if the prevailing atmosphere is dominated by fear, apathy or complacency. Every world-class or aspirant world-class organisation I have encountered seems to possess a pervasive ethos of positivity, whether expressed as cheerful optimism or as a collective "can-do" spirit. Disasters and tribulations are looked upon as challenges with little tendency to being either overawed or depressed. This is not just a consequence of ongoing success or the luxury of trading in a stable and unthreatening environment. The former helps but the latter is beyond most of us in this increasingly competitive and hostile age. Within the same market sectors under the same circumstances, some companies seem able to engender a positive spirit, others quite the reverse.

Looking at Leyland Trucks in 1989, for example, the prevailing atmosphere, for reasons detailed elsewhere, was highly negative. A sense of fatalism abounded. The workforce had seen their numbers shrink and hence the view "it's just a matter of time" followed. Couple this with a profound mistrust of management, a distinct coolness between functions and a discernible impression of guilt at personally having survived successive redundancies, then you have the recipe for a heady cocktail of negativity. Whilst history could be largely blamed for this state of affairs, the communication channels hardly helped. Too much information was delivered second-hand via trade union representatives who had neither the inclination nor the obligation to ensure that the necessary nuances were effected. Top-level communications were delivered via sophisticated pseudo-newspapers, videos or mass briefings. This form of delivery tends naturally to depersonalise the message but the problem was compounded by our parent company's view that only good news should be cascaded. The logic of our Dutch masters seemed to be that if you talked enough about bad news you created the danger of a self-fulfilling prophecy. Unfortunately, the only emotion generated by what was seen as the company propaganda machine was complacency, followed inevitably by the emergence of disasters as the consequences of the unspoken bad news finally came home. With the latter came shock and disbelief, as nothing had been done to prepare the workforce for these downsides.

Positivity is definitely not peddling good news for the sake of it. It is all about generating a collective "will to win", where bad news can be handled maturely and seen as a challenge rather than the presager of disaster. My personal view is that you should always strive to communicate the simple facts in a balanced fashion without over- or under-emphasising the message. This must be coupled with a sense of determination to meet any new challenges constructively and aggressively.

The story of how Leyland accelerated a positive climate is told in much more detail in Chapter 14 where the subject of Team Enterprise and Mindstore is debated. Most companies will find the logistics, cost and seemingly outrageous approach difficult to swallow. But nevertheless I do commend that you read it carefully. In the end, the use of Jack Black and his box of tricks had a profound and lasting impact on the entire company. Through him we created a more positive language. It made us all profoundly aware of the damaging consequences of negative behaviour. And it enabled us to tackle the change process with a sense of fun, excitement and togetherness. Whilst there might be some cynicism about the technique, particularly from those used to the rigour of academia, there is no escaping the fact that it worked. Or to quote Jack, it only works!

If I was asked to use one word to describe the change in climate pre-Team Enterprise to post-Team Enterprise, then I

would chose *positivity*. When the prevailing ethos is so optimistic, a general enthusiasm to tackle anything abounds. It makes
life more enjoyable for everybody, management and the managed alike.

To conclude, therefore, you will improve your chances of
success with any participative system if you can do likewise and
generate this feeling of optimism. Creating a positive ethos
takes years and just one mistake is capable of setting you back
dramatically. However the ultimate benefits more than justify
the effort.

PITFALL NO. 5: MANAGERS MUST MANAGE

I have been participating in courses run by Optima for many
years now. More often than not, it is a rewarding experience
with curious visitors coming in droves every month and, for the
most part, leaving as converts to the "Profiting Through
People" cause. In our early days we limited attendance to chief
executives or their direct reports, for reasons which will hopefully become obvious after the next chapter. Change as radical
as this will only happen with this group's enthusiastic sponsor-
ship and commitment. However, in discussions during these
sessions, or frequently in follow-up visits, we detected a general if somewhat unhealthy trait. We found that all chief executives energetically demanded change from their organisations
in order to meet what they perceived to be a major change in
the competitive climate. We talked at length about potential
bottlenecks. A common theme developed. Most of this group
believed that the key constraints to an effective participative
system within their companies lay in the attitudes and behaviour of middle management, with occasional reference to front-
line supervision as well. However, in parallel discussions with
the aforementioned middle management strata, we heard them
state that the biggest obstacle involved, in their view, was senior management attitude and behaviour! Obviously they can't
both be right. Although they could both be wrong!

All this may have been left as merely interesting if somewhat amusing but we discovered a further tendency in a large percentage of chief executive types. This group believed emphatically that radical behavioural change had to take place in order for their companies to be more successful, but that change had to take place beneath them. They were neither willing nor convinced of the need to change themselves. On more than one occasion, I've had senior executives dismiss out of hand any suggestion that they should adopt a prime role in Change Initiation, purportedly on the grounds that they are already performing more than acceptably! The true reason behind this stance may be sheer arrogance, or it may be simple fear, particularly the fear of having to answer criticisms of personal behaviour from more junior staff.

Why is this important? Because what we attempt to do through a Team Enterprise initiative is to change both the individual and collective mindset. Changing any habit or custom is usually fraught with difficulty, hence the fortunes made in smoking remedies and diet plans. Changing familiar habits and practices in the world of work may not be on the same scale as the latter but is nevertheless still something of a challenge. But there will come a point when each individual, having hopefully answered the "what's in it for me?" question positively, will be tempted to get on board. At this juncture, the tendency is to look around and seek inspiration to justify this significant alteration of personal behaviour. Peers and colleagues may be influential, as may be immediate superiors. But the key exemplars are those at the top of the tree, the people who make the decisions and who hold the strings. If the individual sees that the change is actively supported by the *behaviour* of these key influencers, then they may be minded to move. However, if the prevailing view is that senior management behaviour is the same today as it was yesterday, and we know full well that it'll be the same tomorrow, then why bother? If it's not good enough for them upstairs, then it certainly can't be that important or relevant. So the revolution is killed off before it starts!

Senior management must recognise that they have an active and ongoing part to play in this process. All the truly remarkable cases of radical and rewarding transformations through participation have evidence of strong and committed leadership. In an organisation of any size, at least one key figure needs to become identified with the process, seen to be evangelically enthusiastic about the rightness of the path. This works best when the key figure is also perceived as the organisational decision-maker. So for a company this would be the managing director or CEO, for a plant it might be the general manager or manufacturing director or for a function it may be the departmental head. Even if these people aren't the leading light in the process, they need to be seen as 100 per cent behind it. Otherwise, the initiative will lack credibility from the outset.

One person isn't enough. Several players in the senior management team need to be perceived by the organisation to be actively involved in the process. Any doubters at this level must be converted or silenced, otherwise uncertainty will spread, starting from the doubter's function.

In summary, managers must manage and be seen to be managing. Team Enterprise, as we said before, is a top-down initiative, first and foremost. Without the top-down commitment, we will not achieve bottom-up participation.

PITFALL NO 6: ONCE YOU'VE STARTED, YOU CAN'T GET OFF!

Team Enterprise is a philosophy, not a programme. It therefore doesn't have an expiry date. Once people get a taste of the benefits that Team Enterprise bestows, they are extremely unwilling to let go.

I remember talking to a middle manager in a large city council in the northwest of England who told of his delight at being part of a bold experiment in participation. Being part of a high performing team had engendered such enthusiasm that it had changed his whole attitude to the world of work. His three or four years working for his visionary manager had been the most enjoyable of his career. But then the speaker was promoted, across functions. Despite the higher pay and status, he found the re-immersion into the world of autocracy, bureaucracy and functionalism incredibly depressing. His attitude to work suffered along with his health. He couldn't wait to transfer to a unit similar in philosophy to the one he had left behind.

The consequences for a division, factory or company to go through a similar trial are enormous. It may take a little time, depending on the robustness of the momentum of the Team Enterprise culture but eventually it will erode rapidly and, in certain circumstances, almost irreversibly. I have seen factories that had once been alive and exciting return to traditional mundanity in no time at all. The participative culture is hugely rewarding but it is also a fragile animal. It needs constant nurturing to keep it healthy. Senior executives must keep its development continually at the head of the management agenda. Turn your attention away from it, even accidentally, and the organisation will immediately begin to believe that it's no longer a priority. Changing managers can have the same effect.

Team Enterprise is the most powerful initiative available to management. To pinch a cliché from elsewhere, you either use it or lose it!

Chapter 4

The Leyland Story

Back in the Fold . . .

My first stint with Leyland Trucks lasted from 1972 to 1986. Over that period I was fortunate to have a number of senior manufacturing jobs in a variety of businesses. I ran engine plants, a foundry, a large fabrication shop, a large machine shop and a military engine business, amongst many other fascinating positions. The jobs were great, the people wonderful, but the business . . . well, the business was only going in one direction — down. Coupled with a growing frustration at having to look increasingly inwards as we seemed hell-bent on fighting with each other instead of our competitors, in 1986 I decided that enough was enough and departed to pastures new.

Fast forward three years later: I was approached by a former colleague, Stewart Pierce, who asked me if I'd like to return. In the intervening years, Leyland had been "acquired" by DAF Trucks of the Netherlands and life, allegedly, had changed. No longer part of a nationalised lame duck, the company was now a key player in an international concern and had the prospect of exploiting the many opportunities coming its way. It sounded good and, alongside an invitation to run the truck assembly plant, which had always been my longstanding ambition, the offer proved irresistible. On 28 May 1989, I arrived back in the little Lancastrian town of Leyland, eager and enthusiastic to accept the challenge.

Despite my earlier years at Leyland, my contact with the assembly plant had been somewhat peripheral. I'd heard stories of the peculiar culture that prevailed in the operation but had always taken them with the proverbial pinch of salt. Earlier, for example, people had talked in the same way about the fabrication division as being some horrible bastion of militancy and Ludditism, yet I had actually enjoyed the experience. I had therefore little in the way of apprehension about my new home.

The Size of the Problem becomes Apparent

It was a rude awakening. I immediately had two shocks, one pleasant and one far from it. On the positive side, I was highly delighted and impressed with the quality of local management, both at senior level and below. The plant had obviously benefited from being the centre of Leyland's little universe and the talent had followed. We were well supported in all areas, ranging from the best manufacturing engineer I have ever encountered right through to an enthusiastic and evangelical quality manager. And in between lay a rich array of similarly highly talented individuals. Unfortunately, that was the end of the good news!

The bad news came with general attitudes and morale. As I walked around the plant trying to gauge strengths and weaknesses on the "people" front, my apprehension about the size of the challenge facing the management team increased rapidly. The stance of the majority of employees could best be described as passive neutrality or perhaps even grudging acquiescence. There seemed to be little natural affinity between their personal goals and ambitions and those of the company. Perhaps it was due to a latent fatalism. After all, most employees had been at Leyland a long time (average service levels being about 17 years) and had seen thousands of colleagues lose their jobs. Accompanied by a never-ending sequence of rationalisations and radical plans, all of which resulted in job losses, it was little wonder that many felt the situation to be hopeless. It was just a matter of time, in their minds. Add in a heavy dose of guilt at being fortunate to survive so far, then the overriding emotion can not only be understood but forgiven.

And these were the good guys! A significant minority were bitter and hostile to management and to the company. Whether this was a reaction to what had happened over the years to their beloved Leyland Motors, the old name for Leyland, or more to do with the remnants of the class war which was fought so hard in the 1970s and 1980s, I wouldn't like to guess. The only things I knew were (a) it wasn't healthy and (b) this could be a major obstacle in getting the operation to European levels of competitiveness and thereby ensuring its survival — and, incidentally, mine!

For survival was very much in the minds of the management team. Despite a healthy market at the time and our parent organisation doing reasonably well, black clouds gathered on the horizon. The commercial vehicle market is notoriously variable; any movement in the national economy is amplified in the volatility of truck sales. Since 1989 was a boom year, 1990 could go only one way. We knew things would get tough but little did we know just how tough! Our minds were fixed therefore on coming to terms with a significant downturn in activity, the so-called worst-case scenario. To emphasise the seriousness of what was to happen, that worst-case scenario came to be viewed as best case for several years after that!

However, we weren't to know this, as the company economists, and for that matter the national pundits, were rarely so pessimistic. Nevertheless, even a 25 per cent fall would, we knew, expose Leyland to the dangers of cross-border rationalisation. This was a phenomenon well known at Leyland, as it had been its beneficiary for decades. In times of difficulty, production always gravitates back to the centre. In the days of Leyland Motors and Leyland Truck and Bus, this centre was inevitably taken to be the town of Leyland where the corporate headquarters resided in the palatial Lancaster House. So progressively plants in Bathgate, London, Wolverhampton, Lowestoft, Bristol and many other places were closed and their products transferred to Leyland. However, under the latest configuration, the new centre of the universe was now situated far away in Eindhoven, Holland. Any slip-up on our part could mean the loss of truckmaking in Lancashire forever, and along with it our jobs and livelihood.

The competitive gap between Leyland's current performance and best European practice was considerable. We had problem enough with the timescale involved, so we could ill-afford to be weighed down with internal obstacles. However, the challenges posed by organisational inertia and resistance to change were so in evidence that we had little choice but to tackle them head on. The question was, how? Within the new manufacturing team, I encountered lots of ideas. They all seemed to have a clear view of the problem and an eagerness to tackle it.

However, there was no uniformity of approach. Some believed that the principal instrument of attack should be TQM (Total Quality Management). Leyland had experienced some success with the Crosby approach in the mid-1980s but hadn't gone as far as the author of that technique would have liked. Others believed that one of the key causes of organisational frustration and friction revolved around the logistical uncertainty of the production process. We had too many shortages, too many late deliveries and an irregular weekly achievement of production targets. Despite the monthly miracle of seemingly getting near to programmed outputs, this was achieved with so much firefighting and disruption that everybody suffered. The solution, it was claimed, lay in taking the already Class A level MRPII (Manufacturing Resource Planning) to new heights. By the development of new, bespoke "front end structures", went the theory, we could introduce high levels of predictability and thereby sanity into the world of truck-making.

And, just to compound the difficulty, another group felt that the key causal factor behind our discomfort lay in the world of process conformance. Few of our processes and procedures,

went the argument, had the necessary integrity to ensure re-
peatable success. The only solution lay in a programme to first
ensure the validity and appropriateness of our processes and
then to introduce new levels of conformance. The plan of attack
should therefore be through the recently fashionable Business
Process Re-engineering (BPR) initiative, which claimed to both
streamline and improve conformance.

I would be guilty of gross oversimplification if I claimed
these to be the only three suggestions to address our underlying problem of competitiveness but, as you can see, even they
were enough! We weren't likely to have too many shots at getting this right, given the pressures of time and market, and
certainly we couldn't afford to make mistakes.

It seemed that we had to do all of these things and perhaps
even a few more. The questions unanswered were how to do it
and, equally importantly, how to avoid the organisation disappearing under the weight of several differing initiatives at once.
Over the years, I have repeatedly witnessed the cancer of "ini-
tiative-itis" where entire organisations first become confused
and then disillusioned at the plethora of apparently different
and conflicting priorities being thrown at them from above. The
weakness is usually not workload but disorientation. My personal belief is that organisations can handle a huge amount of
change and variability *providing* it is presented in a manner
which looks coherent and convincing. This belief was to be severely tested as we constructed, very shortly after my arrival,
the unimaginatively titled "Leyland Trucks Manufacturing Strategy" to handle this attack on the organisation's inherent lack of
competitiveness. The strategy involved tackling all the known
weaknesses simultaneously by acting on a number of apparently different fronts. A steering group was formed comprising
representatives from each key operational department and
from those corporate functions which could add real value. A
flowchart was then constructed showing the interrelationships
of the various elements involved. Responsibilities were assigned and, by the middle of 1989, we were ready to go!

Over the coming months we had some excellent work done by the project leaders. The systems manager, Ray Flynn, one of the clearest thinkers I have ever encountered, made rapid progress on developing the IT architecture to match our new requirements. The manufacturing engineering manager, David Spratt, managed to stimulate a radical and visionary examination of how to handle complexity. Very shortly afterwards a number of proposals emerged which had the potential of huge fixed and variable cost reduction. And our new quality manager, Brian Hibbert, relaunched much of the Crosby philosophy with an infectious enthusiasm and energy.

However, despite the progress and an impressive contribution by everyone on the Steering Committee, by about September 1989 it became glaringly obvious that we were on the wrong track again. All the radical ideas and initiatives about organisational systems and structures in the world were going to be of no help at all if the underlying propensity to receive change was still negative. None of the eagerness, determination and urgency of the senior group had conveyed itself to the organisation at large. True, from area to area we had some notable converts, particularly in the middle management ranks, but nothing we did really impacted on the negative, average mindset described earlier. People in general were still fatalistic, still suspicious, and still too mistrustful to embrace either the message or the strategy. In short, we were in trouble!

Everything we had done so far was laudable and needed to continue. But there was now an overarching priority that had to be achieved at speed in parallel with all the foregoing. This was articulated as simply "winning the hearts and minds of the workforce". We had to generate a new culture, one of trust and co-operation at the very least. We could never exploit the potential of these new initiatives, let alone the power of existing ones, if we continued with the overall ambience of hostility, of an extreme "us and them" division. Our ambitions were, in retrospect, extremely modest. We had no vision of the levels of proactivity that characterise Leyland nowadays. We simply wanted to be believed and to be trusted so that everybody, to use the cliché used so often at the time, "paddled together in the same canoe". We had to ensure that all our efforts were expended on fighting the world outside and not dissipated with unnecessary and distracting internal fractiousness.

Culture Shift in the Production Department

The Steering Committee reconstructed its "Leyland Trucks Manufacturing Strategy" to reflect this new reality. Changing the culture of the organisation became the prime objective for everybody. None of the other initiatives were to slow or become deflected; their benefits were desperately needed as well. But each function had to examine critically its own culture and seek to contribute to the whole learning experience.

And they did. The story of the transformation of Leyland Trucks will be dominated by the progress made by the production operation. This is understandable given the numbers involved and the sheer size of the challenge. However, no one should underestimate the contribution made by the "staff" departments, particularly in those early days. Logistics, manufacturing engineering, personnel and so on, all took up the challenge with eagerness and enthusiasm. They all contributed to the organisation learning debate to ensure that the complex needs of the various occupations and specialisms across the company were understood and addressed. This was an important learning point. The world of work means different things to different people. What might be important to one group may be irrelevant to others. We in management had to understand these differences and act accordingly if we wanted to get the best from everyone.

Having said all that, the contribution from the production area was nothing less than outstanding. Led by the most unlikely of characters, John Dwyer — one of nature's rottweilers — production moved at a pace that startled the conservatives amongst us. John's success was even more impressive given his background and his demeanour. Brought up in the heat of Ford

Hailwood, John's training was all about autocracy and directive management. Being built like a small tank also contributed to this archetypal impression, as did the heavy gold rings and the tattoos. Add in language that would shame the barrack room and you have everybody's idea of Genghis Khan at Work. However, John had many other qualities, including the sharpest of minds and a real pragmatism. He knew that, at Ford, only the task-obsessed leader would succeed. So he became exactly that. At Leyland in 1989, a new type of leader and thinker was required and so he changed direction to suit.

I have singled out John here for a specific purpose. Lots of companies going down the Team Enterprise route for the first time wonder if their existing management can cope. Can a leopard change its spots? I doubt whether there are too many examples more extreme than John about, although we've found a few in Optima! Not only was John able to do it superbly; the perception of his conversion on the part of the workforce was equally important. If *their* key contact, who enjoyed their respect, if not their admiration, could change so dramatically, the initiative had to be serious! I often wonder how many old-style managers have been written off in this new world of the so-called knowledge worker when all they were guilty of was simply adjusting to the needs of the time. Change the needs and perhaps they'll change as well. At least give them the opportunity to make the transition, for if they do they'll become some of the most effective advocates of this new approach.

Whilst the Steering Committee focused on the principles of communication, recognition and appropriate employee systems, as described later in the book, the production department emphasised micro-organisational changes. There were two significant challenges here. First, the "track mentality", where a particular attitude or even mystique builds up about working on a continuous process. The perception was likened to this great iron horse grinding away at them every second of the day, reducing individual scope and room for manoeuvre to the realm of the non-existent. No matter where you worked on the conveyer, this feeling of entrapment appeared to be over-whelming. As more that one employee at that time said, to work on a track you had to suspend normal thinking processes and act like a zombie. Clearly, whilst such views prevailed, in-volvement and participation were meaningless. The second challenge arose around the *opportunity* for involvement in the production arena. Very few of the day-to-day problems that bedevilled production and caused so much frustration could actually be solved on the shopfloor. Most reflected weaknesses created by support functions. Root cause analysis inevitably led back to some other area, with shared culpability. To be suc-cessful we had somehow to involve more actively those in lo-gistics, quality, planning, industrial engineering and personnel. Not an easy task at any time, but against the background de-scribed above, one hell of a challenge.

Fortunately, the very first step that John and I took turned out to be exactly the right one. We recognised that beneath John at middle manager level we had a host of strong and influential people. Unless they understood and committed to the initiative, it wasn't going to work. The problem was that neither John nor I had a clear idea of where we were going, let along how to get there. Every other "management" initiative had turned up with action plans, proven paths and project architecture. All we had was a discomfort with the status quo and a vision of a new ethos, hardly what these horny-handed sons of the workshop were likely to appreciate!

We therefore set about debating with them, inevitably after-hours, about the situation, the ambition and the need to de-scribe a coherent route to join the dots between discomfort and vision. We often reflected on the way events had been tackled at work and whether we should have done them differently. At first, these "area managers", as they were known then, reacted adversely, thinking that they were being challenged or even threatened.

After a few weeks, the penny dropped. This was not one of those flavours of the month that could be avoided simply by keeping one's head down. In fact, they were being presented with an opportunity not just to participate but to lead. So in time, scepticism was replaced by curiosity and reluctance by commitment. They not only became involved in management debate; they were also charged with visiting those best practice factories elsewhere, places where we thought we would find one or more of the elements we sought. One such visit to Milliken Carpets by the area managers resulted in the adoption of their suggestion scheme, which in turn evolved into the highly successful Every Little Counts (ELC). After a short while, a critical mass of enthusiasts and evangelists was created instead of the lone furrow ploughed by John and myself. And eventually, after about two years, to my initial dismay but eventual delight, they asked me to step back from day-to-day involvement in factory culture change and leave it to them. They felt confident enough to do it themselves.

Very shortly, however, one immediate threat became evident, with the onset of the fiercest recession our industry had known, certainly since the Second World War. The need to downsize the business became an ongoing challenge as each time we took the "necessary" action, the situation worsened. A succession of redundancy plans and restructuring ensued. However, it is to the credit of the team at Leyland, particularly those at the very sharp end of this constant downsizing, that they never took their eye off the Team Enterprise ball. In fact, it was almost as if their efforts redoubled. Each potentially dispiriting redundancy was also used as an opportunity to move towards the flatter organisation profile demanded by an empowered structure. Supervisory/subordinate ratios were progressively reduced threefold in an attempt to "engineer in" involvement and participation. The times may have been turbulent and stormy, but the vision of this highly efficient and much more socially acceptable world kept us going. The "in" expression became "lean and agile, not thin and fragile" which, despite being somewhat clichéd, summed up our thinking better than anything else.

We also started to make our first steps towards what were then considered to be highly improbable autonomous work groups. None of us, I believe, expected at the outset to get there totally but we all expected the journey to be beneficial. However, the big bonus arrived with the formation of business units. As with most things mentioned above, this will be comprehensively covered elsewhere in the book. The concept of business units was not only new and radical; it also needed the active support and co-operation of nearly every other function to be successful. The manner of this introduction, totally trouble-free and effective from day one, speaks volumes for the multi-functional cohesiveness that follows Team Enterprise. Whilst we still had a long way to go to achieve a *company-wide* unity of purpose, within the management group we had no doubt. Despite the turbulence of the market and its consequent dramatic impact on the organisation, I still feel this period to be one of the most satisfying in my entire career. For the first time I experienced the real potency of a highly professional and highly capable management team acting as one. All I had to do was steer — and take the credit, of course!

More Challenges

By the middle of 1991, the impact on the financial profile of the operation was tremendous. Breakeven points and operating costs had been slashed. Quality, productivity and flexibility had also improved. However, we still had one gap, a glaring one given our stated intention to "win the hearts and minds of the workforce". Things had improved. Employees were now individually more co-operative but, as a group, still highly distrusting and suspicious. Every move that directly affected them and necessitated changes in working practices or conditions was met with hostility and reluctance. The fear of the hidden agenda was still there. Given the trauma of the market-enforced restructuring that had been going on for over a year, this was probably quite understandable.

I have often wondered what would have happened had we not introduced the Change Initiation process covered in Chapter 6. I suspect we would have continued to make progress, but only in an evolutionary fashion. Whether this would have been sufficient to get us through the horrors of receivership in early 1993, I shudder to think. I suspect not. In fact, we may have fallen victim to plant rationalisation, given the pressures on our parent company. Change Initiation lifted the barriers for Leyland, enabling a common agenda to be constructed and the beginnings of a trusting relationship to be established. Real trust to acceptable levels, whatever they might be, probably didn't materialise until two to three years later. Nevertheless, even the slightest improvement in this direction had powerful and positive repercussions downstream.

Progress continued at an accelerating pace after Change Initiation. The creation of teams on the assembly tracks with their individual identities and ability to influence, at least partially, their own destiny, engendered a powerful and welcome side effect. Slowly the "track mentality" described earlier began to diminish as operators discovered more and more imaginative ways of influencing the workplace environment. The introduction of Quality Time helped. Here we shut the tracks down for an hour a fortnight for teams to concentrate exclusively on problem-solving, training or communication. In truth, this was partly funded by the operators themselves but still represented a high risk for the company. However, none of the usual indicators of performance showed any deterioration, demonstrating that, at the very least, the effort was cost-neutral. If you decide to go down this path, be careful about seeking any direct correlation between the practice and tangible, quantifiable benefits. My sole intention in those days was to demonstrate that management was serious about Team Enterprise in general and about the contribution of the workforce in particular. I never anticipated that Quality Time would last as long as it has, and I might even question its appropriateness and effectiveness in a mature Team Enterprise. I would have thought by now that a more gainful and imaginative means of operator involvement would have been developed. However, it appears to work and, being forever a pragmatist at heart, why fix it if it ain't broke?

By far the biggest challenge at that period came from the emergence of the "build-to-order" strategy. The costs of holding stocks between the factory gate and the end customer in a traditional "build-to-stock" environment are colossal. Depending on the market, the cash required could aggregate perhaps as high as the equivalent of six months' production. This was an enormous commitment in terms of both borrowings and expense. The attractions of an alternative approach were obvious, but no one hitherto had shown the foresight or the courage to try it. However a tenacious and talented logistics director in our parent DAF's Eindhoven headquarters called Han van der Sluijs had other ideas. He campaigned and pressurised the company to be more radical and to pioneer a different approach. For an organisation which defined "pioneers" as "those fellows with arrows in their backs", this was a dramatic step. The potential benefits were, however, irresistible, particularly to those in the central treasury who had to daily find the cash to run the business. Han was ultimately given the go-ahead to investigate and to cajole.

The first response was a howl of objection. The sales force initially thought it crazy, the assembly plants absolutely mad and the supply base a further example of Dutch insanity. However, eventually, certainly within the factories, the attractions started to progressively feed through. If only we could get an average lead time of 12–14 weeks down to five . . .

In 1989, this would have been impossible even to contemplate. In those days, we still operated a monthly cycle where virtually nothing was delivered in the first three weeks, followed by an almighty crush in the last week before cut-off. The final weekend of the cycle was not one that any senior manager should witness, as it resembled sheer chaos. However, with the advent of Team Enterprise, we had not just moved to weekly controlled delivery, we were well on the way to daily predict-ability. Even so, to most of us, build-to-order at a five-week lead time was just pie in the sky.

However, Han van der Sluijs acquired a convert in the shape of Leyland's Logistics Manager, John Butterworth. John was an exceptionally bright and very determined young man; once he set his mind on something, it rarely remained unfinished.

John's crusade to embrace build-to-order was so enthusiastic and determined that he took everybody with him. The end re-sult was that the Leyland plant pioneered the scheme and han-dled the challenge magnificently — so successfully in fact that ultimately a "Fasttrack" service was offered which turned ur-gent orders around in just two to three weeks! That such a radi-cal proposal which impacted on all functions could be adopted so smoothly and effectively is testament to the power of Team Enterprise. I have never seen the savings engendered by this switch from build-to-stock to build-to-order quantified, but I would estimate conservatively that the cash saving for Leyland alone to be at least £40,000,000 plus ongoing cost reductions in excess of £4,000,000 per annum. Whether the adoption of a full-blown Team Enterprise is a mandatory requirement in achiev-ing build-to-order is a moot point. However, those at Leyland appreciate that the path was made much easier by the effi-ciency and discipline of our new ethos.

Towards the end of 1992, we were beginning to think we had it cracked. The market was creeping back, sterling was cheap and our new philosophy was working wonders. Fixed costs were down and with them break-even points. Operating costs had also been savagely reduced, with new levels of quality, flexibility and responsiveness emerging. Attitudes, although far from perfect, had improved immeasurably despite the trauma of the recession. We were in good shape, with a shared and clear vision of where we wanted to be. What could possibly go wrong now?

Receivership and Rebirth

We knew that our parent company had been experiencing problems with cash. We also knew that it had taken on a number of commitments that were overstretching it. But we had a new, vigorous and charismatic President in the shape of Cor Baan who talked the right language and appeared open and realistic. But even his best efforts couldn't avoid the worst calamity in the long history of both DAF and Leyland: receivership. On 2 February 1993, Leyland Trucks was taken under the control of Arthur Andersen as they sought to find a solution to probably one of the most complex business situations the UK receivership industry has ever encountered. A book on Team Enterprise is not the place for the story of how Leyland Trucks emerged from this situation. Suffice it to say it needed first class receivers, first class advisors and a first class management team to see it through! And most importantly of all, a huge slice of luck.

Fortunately, that luck was forthcoming and on 11 June 1993 the new company was born. The old organisation was now separated from its former parent, DAF, and split into several standalone, independently owned concerns. Leyland Trucks was formed to address specifically the issue of designing, developing and assembling the 6–18 tonne truck range. Contracts were drawn up with the owners of those parts of the business that had been salvaged, to ensure as best we could a mutual interdependence. It was complex, it was risky, but it had potential! Amazingly, every single part of the old company survived and indeed eventually prospered. Ideally, had DAF not fallen into administration, this would almost certainly not have been the case.

Our new company, Leyland Trucks, was effectively the "hub" of this novel arrangement. The financial arrangements were complex but necessitated a modest equity investment, a somewhat larger preference loan stock and a painfully thin overdraft facility. Aside from our venture capital partners, Barclays Development Capital Ltd., the shares were owned by the fifteen-strong management team. We had no excuses now: a large part of our destiny lay firmly and squarely in our own hands. We could take Team Enterprise to new heights without fear of objection from elsewhere in the corporate hierarchy. It was down to us, and us alone.

During receivership, Arthur Andersen sought not to damage the fabric of what we had established. The communication chains still operated. Even the Weekly Brief continued, despite the terrible circumstances. Further redundancies followed as they desperately fought to keep the operation alive. This included taking out residual line supervision, which accelerated our move to total autonomous work groups. However, despite the pain, one can only admire Andersen for their professionalism, their hard work and their determination to find a solution. I learned more from them, from Eversheds and from Coopers and Lybrand over those 18 weeks than I had done in any equivalent period ever.

One consequence of receivership was that four of the management team — John Gilchrist (chairman), myself, Sandy Morris (finance director) and Stewart Pierce (personnel director) — had to distance ourselves for long periods from the plant as we struggled first to establish the management buy-out and then implement it. Operational management reverted to the other line managers who adapted wonderfully. In many respects, for the next year Team Enterprise stood still in terms of management-driven development as we toiled with more pressing concerns. But to our delight, the momentum established pre-receivership continued to keep it going, helped in no small part by the Dunkirk spirit so evident after the launch of the new company. As everybody knew that cash was now at a distinct premium, spare resources and materials were summoned from every nook and cranny to construct the necessary facilities to help the company trade effectively.

It is difficult to ascribe adequate credit to the ingenuity and goodwill that prevailed over that period. If you could bottle it and use it daily in less taxing conditions, you could transform any organisation out of sight. It really was a wonderfully stimulating period. One small example stands out. As we cobbled together some old tables to fashion the new boardroom, we were approached by one of the lads off the line. He pointed out that this would be the focal point for all the important visitors likely to come to the plant, including bankers, suppliers and customers. We needed furniture to show that we meant business, he said, not the image suggested by the hotchpotch we'd gathered together. He offered, in his own time, to make us a new table and, within a few weeks, presented us with a huge and magnificent construction. The table is still in service today, a testament to the goodwill and commitment of 1993.

Redefining Team Enterprise

Once the organisation settled down, we set about redefining Team Enterprise for the next phase in our evolution. The formation of the new company meant that product engineering and purchasing were now fully integrated into the team instead of belonging to a now non-existent centre. Both departments had witnessed at first hand the potency of Team Enterprise and wasted no time in fashioning their own individual variants of it. We learned a lot from them. Engineering introduced the totally open plan office concept, with no offices for managers. We quickly learned the advantages of open-plan over open-door. Purchasing excelled at internal teamwork, building a professional and coherent department in no time at all. They also exhibited a surprising ability to build relationships with other functions, creating all the benefits of a matrix structure without the impediments of bureaucracy.

However, in our discussions with the new departments, we discovered that a general perception had developed about the "position" of Team Enterprise. It was seen largely as a production initiative that had been "imported" into the support functions, rather than the company-wide philosophy originally intended. In many ways, this was understandable. The production areas had necessarily been the focus of much attention since that's where most people were employed. In addition, the management team there had been extraordinarily innovative in developing and expanding the theme. Unfortunately, this was also accompanied by an impression of the function perhaps belittling the contribution of others. As a result, we often had the "not-invented-here" response when perfectly sensible routines were rejected by others, simply because the idea emanated from the sharp end of the organisation.

In truth, Team Enterprise, like any other initiative, needs constant refreshing. Up to receivership, we were still very much in the initial development stage and hence there was little need for any rethinking or rejigging. However, after a couple of years of steady state, the novelty wore off and Team Enterprise simply began to be seen as part of the furniture. We had, in essence, lost the edge.

Driving for Success

We therefore attempted, in 1995, to put it right by a reformation under the tagline "Driving for Success". Polo shirts endorsed with the theme were given to each worker for use at work. A glitzy, for us, launch was organised complete with music so that nobody could underestimate the seriousness of it all! Behind the propaganda, however, lurked a very serious determination to take Team Enterprise into completely new territory. The stakes were raised.

There were any number of new elements to "Driving for Success", but four stand out as being particularly adventurous. These were:

- The concept of *Zero Cost Growth* — a declaration that the company had to grow significantly to survive but that this growth had to be achieved with zero additional fixed cost and only marginal incremental variable cost. The responsibility for getting there was *everybody's*, not just management's. Pay rises in future had to be earned by overall productivity growth. We spelt out the economics of the marketplace — we had received no annual price increases for our product since 1992 and didn't expect one in the near future. If we wanted pay increases we had to fund them ourselves, *after* we had generated the productivity necessary to assure competitiveness.

- The concept of the *Moral Contract* — an awareness that we all owed a duty of care to our colleagues, not just the company, in ensuring that everything possible was done to preserve employment on the site. If Armageddon revisited Leyland as it had done in 1993, every single employee had to be able to stand up in good conscience and say that they had done their best. This meant moving to genuine *proactivity* rather than simply going with the flow. One measure of this was the number of ideas we submitted each year individually. Accordingly we were all "challenged" to think of two ideas per month in questioning and improving the status quo. There would be no repercussions or criticisms from management for those who failed, just hopefully the peer pressure of "playing the game".

- The definition of *Good Corporate Citizenship* — an attempt to articulate the characteristics of a good employee. This resulted in the Citizenship Wheel, where colleagues would measure themselves and judge whether they really contributed to the new world of work. The terminology may have been clumsy (can you think of better?) but for the first time we made a clear, unambiguous statement of what we expected from each employee. It was no longer good enough simply to turn up, do the minimum required by the job description and go home. Like most other businesses, the world of truck-making was now ferociously competitive and demanded working practices and attitudes far different to those of the past.

- The introduction of the *Tracker Share Scheme* — the attempt by Stewart and myself to create a strong feeling of ownership in the business. We had been less than impressed by attempts elsewhere to improve employee identification by the use of ESOPs (Employee Share Ownership Plans) or their ilk. For a start, Leyland DAF had introduced one that resulted in many employees losing a lot of money at receivership. To ask them to dip once again into their pockets to invest in a business that still had major risks was optimistic in the extreme, if not morally doubtful. Secondly, when employees ultimately off-loaded their shares at a profit, where was the motivation then?

However, I did feel that we needed to do something, so we invented "Tracker Shares". Each employee was awarded a number of phantom or shadow shares through the gift of the owner-managers, the venture capital backer not participating here. This tranche of Tracker Shares was *given* to everybody for one year, and although theoretically non-performers or those with poor disciplinary records could be excluded, they rarely were. The shares had the benefit of paying the actual equivalent dividend that the same number of "proper" ordinary shares would receive. Better still, in the event of a company sale, the ownership of Tracker Shares entitled the employee to a share in the capital gain. At the time we never envisaged the latter provision to kick in, but it most certainly did in 1998!

"Driving for Success" turned out to be a winner. The stark detailing of the realities of working life and the subsequent extra demands on every worker regardless of position came in truth as no surprise to anyone. They all knew it and perhaps wondered why it took so long for us to spell it out. We had little opposition; most welcomed the clarity, the novelty and the challenge. Ideas flew in to such an extent that we targeted the number of suggestions per annum at a maximum as well as a minimum — 22 per year. We feared the consequences of being swamped! It was an absolute delight to witness the benefits of real organisational synergy at first hand. Some of the multifunctional project work was in a different league to that experienced before. Longstanding quality issues were tackled, new product introduction processes streamlined and working practices launched which only a few years earlier would have been confined to the "fanciful" tray. Of particular merit was the introduction of "track-hopping". Our production system was based on a two-track arrangement, each fully manned. However, neither operated at anywhere near capacity with the consequent loss of economies of scale. This shopfloor-based project introduced the concept of assemblers moving from track to track to meet demand. Not only was this quite disruptive for the average employee, it demanded a familiarity with a product mix several times his usual load. However, because the idea came from the shopfloor and was developed by the shopfloor, such obstacles were overturned with ease. As well as the very welcome operating cost savings, this scheme ultimately generated inventory reductions in excess of £1 million per year. Who said only management can make the really important decisions?

Progress continued apace on all fronts. Each process was constantly refined and developed. The autonomous work groups on the shopfloor improved with the emergence of "champions". Material and programme control systems, driven by the combined resources of the purchasing, manufacturing and logistics departments, continued to advance towards best European practice despite the unique handicap of build-to-order. Industrial engineers worked hand in glove with production to effect new levels of productivity and efficiency. Graphs detailing the consequences of all this would be scattered everywhere, particularly in those areas where visitors could see them. All in all it was perhaps the most satisfying and fulfilling period of my working life. The unchallengeable and the unconquerable seemed to be challenged and conquered routinely. There were many examples of such startling success, far too numerous to be recorded here.

The PACCAR Takeover

Sadly, everything in the garden wasn't so rosy. As we said earlier, Team Enterprise is a great philosophy but it is still just a philosophy. The fundamentals of the business need to be in place or capable of being put in place for the organisation to succeed, with or without Team Enterprise. Unfortunately, the Achilles' heel of the new company was the price of product replacement. Engineering a completely new range, which must be done every ten to 15 years, costs a packet. Estimates varied from £70 million to £120 million. At one stage we genuinely believed that we'd manage the lower end, but a sharp reversal of the pound's fortunes against the deutschmark changed all that. Sterling was far too high for UK manufacturing to compete effectively, as agriculture, textile, car manufacturers and so on have found to their cost since.

Alive to the dangers, we set about at an early stage looking for a partner to share the costs of development. Many options came our way but the real attraction appeared in the shape of PACCAR Inc., one of the world's biggest heavy truck manufacturers and at the time owners of our former parent, DAF Trucks. PACCAR could offer funding, volume and the incalculable benefit of being associated with a continually successful and dynamic organisation. The synergies were obvious and the logic unquestioned. In fact, many of my colleagues at the "Meet the Team" sessions had urged me to go for the PACCAR option.

So, in June 1998 the reins of this small, vulnerable but feisty independent operator were handed over to a global powerhouse. However, that wasn't the end of the story. Having been exposed both directly and indirectly to the difficulties of merging two dissimilar cultures, we determined from the outset that the assimilation of Leyland into PACCAR was going to be 100 per cent successful. We wanted our American colleagues to feel welcome, to feel valued and to feel supported from day one. After all, isn't that the Team Enterprise way? If they sneezed, we'd be there with the hanky.

The end result has been an unqualified success. Leyland will take some of the credit because it tried very hard to make it work. However, the contribution of the PACCAR team should be equally recognised. They were incredibly supportive, willing to listen and professionalism itself. Leyland continues to progress by adopting many of the skills and techniques sharpened by its parent over decades. It has taken initiatives like Six Sigma (6σ) and integrated them under the Team Enterprise umbrella, with huge success. It is no coincidence that Leyland won the worldwide President's Prize for Quality in 1999 and the millennium Best Engineering Factory in the UK in 2000. The shareholders of its American parent must view the acquisition of Leyland as one of the best deals they have ever undertaken.

Looking back on Team Enterprise at Leyland Trucks over the period 1989–1998, one cannot avoid a feeling that the impact has been truly remarkable. For the statistically minded, a recap:

- Within two years, a 24 per cent reduction in operating costs

- Within two years, an annualised saving of £10,000,000 per annum

- Within three years, a halving of breakeven point

- Within thirty months, a 35 per cent reduction in warranty costs and an equivalent improvement in build quality

- A significant reduction in absence levels from 8 per cent to 2.5 per cent

- A reduction in customer overdues from around 250 to an average of 10–20

- A much safer working environment with Lost Time Accidents down from 65 per annum to single figures

- Ideas per person per annum increased from zero in 1991 to 14 in 1995 to 22 per annum in 1997

- A step change in measurable shopfloor attitudes and satisfaction levels

- Build flexibility increased to best European practice from a base of rigid demarcation

- A positive and proactive representative structure.

We could go on at length but if you're not convinced by now, you never will be! However the most important contribution by far that Team Enterprise has made to Leyland is simply this: the company's still there. It has survived. And it has prospered despite all the inherent weaknesses of 1989, including lack of access to competitive economies of scale, excessive overheads and a legacy of confrontation. If Team Enterprise can achieve all this with such a generally perceived terminal case, then what can it do for you? The prospects must be mouthwatering!

Chapter 5

Management Leads the Way

Top-down *and* Bottom-up

In the fashionable management lexicon, "bottom-up" is good, "top-down" is bad. With Team Enterprise we beg to differ. "Bottom-up" is still good but "top-down" is just as important. It is no coincidence that the first chapter on implementation in this book relates to management. Without a clear understanding and an absolute commitment by them to active involvement, any participative system will fail. Most endeavours in this direction do fail. We have discussed the most frequent reasons for non-performance in Chapter 3 but now we need to examine the common denominator in all these failures — managerial incompetence.

Life in business today is very different than it was just ten years ago. The key factor behind that difference is *competition*, which comes in many forms and from many directions. Here we will concern ourselves with just two aspects that are rewriting the rules of the game.

Technology is playing a huge part in making the market much more competitive. The fascination for this brave new world of information technology makes company valuations exceedingly difficult and the subsequent volatility of financial markets is well documented. But even for those established companies which may escape the worst ravages of the new economy, careful thought needs to be paid to its impact on internal organisation. The advent of much more sophisticated computer systems working at speeds way beyond our wildest dreams only a decade ago means that more and more power is now vested in the front line of organisations. We are increasingly reliant on decisions being taken with accuracy and rapidity at the most junior level. Pyramid organisation charts are being flattened dramatically. Even in medium-sized organisations up to 1,000-strong, we often see no more than two levels between the Board and the shopfloor or general office. This is not a matter of economics, although the overhead savings are usually quite significant. Rather this is about responsiveness, flexibility and local decision-making. Our old sense of hierarchy is now redundant, being too bureaucratic, too costly and too rigid for the new world.

As a consequence, there is a huge question mark over traditional, autocratic systems. Can we really expect our employees to respond to these huge new challenges if we continue to subject them to autocratic dictates and surround them in an atmosphere of mistrust, suspicion and often fear? The answer, of course, should be a firm "no". You may even feel it insulting of me to pose the question. However, every practitioner in this field, including all my colleagues within Optima, would confirm that the vast majority of companies, in both the public and private sectors, still lie much closer to the traditional model than to modern management practice.

Very often, the culprit is unconscious incompetence on the part of senior management. Perhaps it's because we require a certain single-mindedness to claw our way to the top of the pyramid. Humility is a scarce commodity in the world of top executives. By a process of natural selection, all of us in these elevated positions tend to have rather larger egos than the rest of the population. And as a consequence we don't listen as well as we should and we don't analyse our *own* behaviour, and its subsequent impact on people, as well as we do others'. I am therefore absolutely convinced of the necessity to revisit our conventional thinking about management's impact on the motivation of the people who work for them.

This situation is compounded by another element of the competitive environment, which we will simply call Society. Old fogies like myself, brought up on the disciplinarian education system of the fifties and sixties and subjected to the formalised rigidity of the world of work soon after, find it difficult to appreciate just how liberal society has become in the intervening decades. We have a comfort with the predictability and rigour of autocratic systems. We accepted authority without question, even when logic appeared to fly out of the window. The unreasonable, irrational behaviour of our betters was accepted even when it extended to fearsome aggression or abusiveness because it was . . . well, it was the way of the world. I'm sure a lot of people of my generation look back 30 years and beyond and feel absolutely perplexed as to why we tolerated some of the abhorrent behaviour to which we and others were subjected. It certainly wasn't anything remotely motivational. The fear instilled in the organisation by these practices reduced efficiency and effectiveness rather than promoted them. But tolerate it we did because we felt we had to.

Today, however, society has changed. Even in times of high unemployment, people demand more from working life. They seek to be noticed, to be recognised and to be heard. They need to both receive and give proper communication. They want to be treated like human beings in the same way that they are in other areas of society. In short, they will simply not tolerate the worst excesses of autocratic systems.

If your company fails to recognise this new reality then, in time, your better people will simply walk. They will look for other organisations that can fulfil these new requirements of working life. You will find the quality of your intellectual resources diluting at a time when competition is increasing and it may well be your key competitors that are benefiting from the unnecessary turnover.

So it can be argued very powerfully that the competitive world is now demanding a step-change in organisational culture. And few would argue nowadays that having the "right" culture will generate major benefits in organisational effectiveness, which in turn bestow huge advantages to bottom-line performance. The problem is that few of us know what this right culture looks like. The answer to the question is quite complex and is often presented from the standpoint of academic debate rather than the necessary prescription that most of us seek in our frantically busy and stressed workplaces. At Leyland Trucks, we approached the matter somewhat empirically, or probably more accurately, haphazardly. We often found ourselves, within the team, at odds on both emphasis and relevance, which perhaps wasn't surprising given our very flat management structure. The Steering Committee had at times in excess of 15 members, most of whom shared the same status. This lack of clarity certainly slowed our progress and perhaps conveyed a certain confusion of thinking further down the chain to other key influencers in the company. We needed a clearer blueprint, a better description of this term "culture" of which, despite being in everyday parlance, few people had any real understanding.

Poskett's Law

Fortunately, one of my colleagues, Charlie Poskett, later to become the human resources director for PACCAR UK, started to examine the subject in detail. As befits someone with a lifetime in industrial relations, Charlie was the ultimate pragmatist. He didn't like ambiguity, even less the contrived vagueness of the academic in this area. He sought a practical interpretation of the concept of organisational culture, which could be applied to, and understood by, those engaged in the world of business. His approach was to start at the other end of the problem and simply examine those organisations which were perceived to have the so-called correct culture. His work in Optima also brought him close to numerous companies where the absence of some of the key elements noted below could be seen to be sub-optimising the entire process.

Charlie subsequently distilled seven key factors that make up an effective culture in the world of work. In brief, what he found in these exemplar companies was:

1. **Excellent Communication Systems** — a dedication to providing the right communication to the right people in a fashion that *they* find acceptable.

2. **Enlightened Employee Systems** — Charlie here refers to both formal and informal employee systems. Best practice companies possess first class *formal* systems, ranging from recruitment through induction and on to the panoply of HR techniques designed to keep the organisation at the fore-front of good practice. But Charlie also noticed that in those more effective organisations, *informal* employee systems also had an important role to play in defining the character of the organisation, and in improving affiliation of the individual to the company.

3. **Effective Organisation Structures** — Charlie found that the traditional orthodoxy of organisational thinking had been jettisoned by better practitioners. For example, the desire for greater participation was articulated along the lines of "providing the wherewithal for every single person in the organisation to make more of his or her own decisions". However, when the key constraints preventing this from happening were examined, it was often the design of the micro-organisation which provided the biggest barrier.

4. A clear and obsessive **Customer Focus** — Charlie firstly identified that, in these exceptional organisations, the customer was perceived by everyone, management and managed alike, as the most important stakeholder. There is an understanding that, in today's highly competitive market, customer satisfaction alone will not lead to loyalty and hence repeat business. The focus of the total product offer-

ing should therefore be to delight the customer, not merely to satisfy them.

5. An ongoing ethos and system of **Continuous Improvement**.

6. An appropriate **Management Style** — We will discuss this at greater length later but Charlie noted that each of these organisations, without exception, possessed a range of management styles that were appropriate to the situation and accepted as appropriate by the workforce. And finally,

7. Strong evidence of effective **Teams and Empowerment** — Charlie's research showed a powerful correlation between the effectiveness of an organisation's culture and the presence of empowered teams and individuals.

Now individually none of the above factors will be of any surprise to readers of this book. These issues are well chronicled and hopefully equally well understood. But the value of Charlie's analysis lies in his ultimate conclusion, something that has become known within Optima as "Poskett's Law". Poskett's Law states that:

> **Companies will never aspire to a world class culture, whatever that is, unless they can demonstrate, in both perception and reality, an acceptable situation in all seven of these factors.**

In other words, your company could be independently assessed and find itself "starring" in six out of the seven boxes, but if you fail in, for example, Management Style, then the whole edifice will crumble and you will not achieve the acceptable culture you seek. A successful culture can only be achieved if you have *all seven* factors within the range of acceptability.

The key value of Poskett's Law comes not from its analysis but its application. As will be seen in Chapter 6, the Change

Initiation process, which has proved so successful at both measuring perception and gaining ownership of the need for change, is based on this core interpretation of workplace culture. Without this framework I suspect we would still be switching from yesterday's priority to whatever was uppermost in our minds today, without really getting anywhere.

Some have questioned the completeness of the model and we remain open to suggestions. Often we find a need for greater clarity in the strategic planning process, so this becomes the eighth category. By and large, however, the seven factors are sufficient to cover all those elements that contribute, one way or another, to an effective culture.

Acquiring the "Right" Culture

Knowing what the right culture looks like is a help, but acquiring it is a different proposition. There are many factors that will help generate the culture so essential for an effective organisation in today's world. Many of these will be covered elsewhere in the book but here we focus on the most important element — the role of the "key influencers". The key influencers are those people, usually but not exclusively management, who are seen to exert authority and influence over decision-making in a company. **The way the key influencer group behaves is the key determinant of organisation culture.** The workforce will take its lead from the behaviour of this group and hence create the attitudes, morale, priorities and focus that make up the prevailing ethos of the company.

"Culture" is determined largely by what this key influencer group is perceived to pay attention to, what they measure and what they control routinely. Note the emphasis on perception. The corporate mission statement may well display platitudes about valuing the employee above all else, but if subsequent behaviour does not support this ideal, then the workforce will simply not believe it.

So who is in this key influencer group? In the vast majority of instances, it will be that group of senior management who are believed by the rest of the organisation to take the majority of the significant decisions affecting their lot. In a one-site, medium-sized firm, this will usually be the Board of Management. In a multi-site, larger concern, this could well be local management. At Leyland Trucks in 1989, we deliberately positioned the site manufacturing management team as being autonomous in the eyes of the workforce. To do otherwise would have resulted in some distant, unfamiliar body being seen as the sole arbiters of our fate. Whilst in some respects this may have been true, locally there resided significant latitude to determine many aspects of our own destiny. This is vitally important. The workforce must feel that it is dealing with an influential and powerful local management team so that the necessary *esprit de corps* can be developed. Unfortunately, in many large corporations there is a tendency for the immediate management layer to use referential authority, thus diluting this sense of identification. You have to build ownership for any participative organisation to be effective. And hence the first prerequisite is a perception that the local senior management decision-making body is capable of decisively determining its own fate.

In simple terms, the key questions that must be answered when determining the optimal boundaries for this new culture are:

- Which group of managers are perceived *now* by the workforce to be making most of those decisions that influence local working life?

- Can this perception, in the short term, be changed to a more immediate and junior group?

- Do the actual decision-making processes match your preferred configuration?

But what if we encounter a situation where there are other equally powerful key influencer groups? If one examines the history of the British Leyland empire, for example, you will see that trade unions often occupied that category. The workforce felt a greater sense of identification with the union at both macro and micro levels than it did with local management. The shop stewards would therefore be the major key influencer group, a situation that is dangerous and unhelpful to both sides.

Fortunately, particularly in this new more enlightened age, such examples are not as plentiful as in times past. However, they do happen and the implications need to be addressed from the outset. To be successful, Team Enterprise demands a common agenda, *a unity of purpose*. We cannot achieve this unity if there is no prospect of a natural meeting of interest between managers and the managed. There is no scope for this to be successful if the trade union stands between these two groups in all situations. Trade unions have an important role to play in modern business, but it is not to fill a vacuum created by managerial inadequacy. This particularly applies to communication. My heart sinks when I visit organisations that still communicate routine matters through elected representatives. It is little wonder that the latter assume a significance way beyond their station. Communication is not just words; it is nuance, tone and body language. Key messages cannot be conveyed properly third-hand, especially if the intermediary has a vested interest in applying their own interpretation. My message to these companies is very simple — *unless you are prepared to establish senior management as THE key influencer group, with all the consequences associated with this onerous responsibility, don't even dream about Team Enterprise. It won't work!*

For the avoidance of doubt, let me repeat that I am not undermining the role of the trade union here. Later in the book, I will describe the enlightened and highly effective contribution that the trade unions made at Leyland. They have a vital part to play but, again, they cannot compensate for managerial inertia. Managers are paid to manage and they must do exactly that!

There is one other situation we must consider before we return to the duties of senior management. In many organisations that we in Optima have encountered, it has been claimed that the prevailing, usually negative culture is determined by a traditional, change-resistant middle management strata. I should stress here that the claim is usually made by senior management and often in the context of why their organisation is not performing. Most of my colleagues in Optima would subscribe to the view that the reality is frequently far different. This group has usually become disaffected and disenchanted due to real weaknesses in the leadership of the company from above. Most frequently characterised in organisations with a high turnover of directors or equivalents, the middle management echelon see themselves as being the stabilising force in the world of work. Coupled with a perception of always being the meat in a very thick sandwich, this group tends to hang on to what they know best. And what they know best is the status quo. The common knee-jerk reaction of many senior managers when encountering the situation — wholesale culling — is simply addressing the symptom rather than the root cause. If management leaves a vacuum in its relationship with the organisation, something will fill it. Whether that something is the trade union, middle management or front-line supervision is largely irrelevant. The vacuum should not have been allowed to happen in the first place.

Senior management therefore need to accept their responsibilities as being by far the most important key influencer group if success is to be achieved. They need to lead and to be seen to be leading. The culture of the organisation will be determined by what they are perceived to be paying attention to on a regular basis. The workforce will form its attitudes and opinions based on what they believe these leaders see as important. This will reflect what leaders control and what leaders measure. Leadership behaviour is all-important. How do they reward, recognise and applaud? What do they criticise and condemn? How do they handle the trappings of power and status themselves? As a manager over several decades, it has always amazed me how closely one is scrutinised and how even little gestures can have a completely disproportionate impact on the organisation. At one company I once ran as managing director,

I was confronted by the puzzling accusation that I did not want any female labour in a new factory we were building. The rumour was apparently rife throughout the company and particularly offended the assembly department, where most employees were female. I was totally confused over the issue since the reverse was probably the truth. After a major inquiry, the allegation was traced to a junior manager who had circulated the tale. Apparently, at a project meeting, I had emphasised that all employees in the new factory were to be semi-skilled rather than unskilled. My reasons for this were simple: we needed greater flexibility and greater autonomy to be competitive and hence the need for employees to have a broader range of skills than we had before. What I didn't appreciate is that, in local parlance, "unskilled" was a euphemism for female labour, "semi-skilled" the traditional bastion of the male non-tradesman. Hence my statement about broadening the skills base was seen as fundamentally discriminatory! The hype created by this whole affair really did bring home to me the profound impact that senior decision-makers, consciously or otherwise, can have on organisational culture.

This really reflects the difficulty. Senior management is under close scrutiny all the time to see if the values and principles claimed by them are sustained. The organisation will be particularly vigilant during times of crisis, watching how you react to emergencies or sudden dilemmas. If you maintain your steady-state persona, the organisational will feel assured. If you, in their eyes, revert to type, your much-professed image as a new world, caring, sharing manager will be shattered for a long time. Mistakes in those situations take a lot of repairing. In truth, you are on parade all of the time. Your true character will show through eventually, whether in times of crisis, in the way you allocate resources in constrained circumstances or simply in the way you surround yourself with "your own people". This is really challenging, because senior management are by far the most important drivers of organisational culture in both their conscious and unconscious behaviour. Team Enterprise will therefore stand or fall on your ability to create this right culture. If it fails, it's probably down to you. For guidance on this matter, I strongly recommend you read Stephen Covey's excellent *Seven Habits of Highly Effective People*, particularly his comments on the difference between the Character Ethic and the Personality Ethic. After all, if you're in a similar situation to me in 1989, you'll need all the help you can get!

Getting Started

By now you should be getting the hint that the most important element in establishing an effective Team Enterprise is the senior management team! Hence, Figure 1, which laid out the process for implementation, had as its first step:

Convince and Educate the Senior Management Team

The easy bit here is persuading your colleagues of the riches that lie in the Team Enterprise path. Leyland's experience is now well chronicled and quantified, but there are scores of other similar stories. In my years of lecturing on the subject, I have never had any difficulty in exciting senior managers to the Team Enterprise cause, simply by drawing attention to the paybacks.

The great attractions of Team Enterprise are that:

1. Its success rate, providing a few simple steps as outlined in this book are followed, should be as high as 80 per cent.

2. Your outlay need not be excessive, cash-wise. Change Initiation will be the most expensive element, but this will probably substitute in lots of companies for the periodic attitude surveys, which promise much and deliver little.

3. Done correctly, Team Enterprise will start to generate real returns, financial and attitudinal, within months. If you're not feeling real benefits after three to four months, you're not doing it correctly!

This is a message that appeals to most senior management as we are all charged with growth and improved returns in an increasingly hostile and competitive world. However, I do feel that lots of chief executives, and I was certainly in this category, are guilty of constantly searching for the new Holy Grail, the latest management gizmo which, at a stroke, will transform our fortunes. The zeal with which some initiatives have been applied over the last 20 years, particularly Business Process Reengineering (BPR) and Lean Enterprise, is almost frightening in its naivety. Short-term benefits can be claimed but so often at the expense of longer-term viability. There simply is no off-the-shelf package which can be easily plugged into the organisation and generate immediate and spectacular returns. Team Enterprise is, to use yet another modern cliché, a journey without a destination. It is a journey demanding a colossal amount of hard work (by senior management), a rigorous attention to detail (by senior management) and an ongoing vigilance (by senior management).

Anecdotal evidence tends to support the view that really successful implementations of participative systems are often associated with a distinctive, almost evangelical, leadership. This is nothing to do with any charismatic qualities of the senior executive, although I confess that this occasionally seems to help. The workforce will believe that if the boss is so passionate and devoted to the subject it must be important. There are lots of high-profile examples of this in the UK, such as Ian Gibson at Nissan, John Neal at Unipart and John Egan in his days at Jaguar. However, I have been personally more influenced by some less well-known examples. At Cummins Engine Company in Darlington in the early 1990s, for example, huge progress was made under the guidance of the plant director, Denis Welch. For factory junkies like myself, walking around his operation was a tremendously stimulating experience. His people seemed to live and breathe empowerment. They would talk enthusiastically about their own contributions and how they were improving both quality and reliability. Everywhere you wandered seemed to be stamped with Denis's image. There was little doubt in that company that the workforce knew that their gaffer was not only serious about participation and involvement, but that he would be a passionate advocate for a long time to come. Observing Denis in action taught me two key lessons. First, that passion is infectious. And second, that even in a huge multinational concern, it was perfectly feasible for site management to construct the perception of local autonomy advocated earlier.

There are many other examples where one individual has stamped his mark to wonderful effect. Dick Frost, MD of a small paint manufacturer in Bolton, demonstrated that his zeal to overcome a longstanding inertia can energise an entire company (see Appendix, Case Study 5: Leigh's Paints). He inherited an organisation unaccustomed to change and locked in a mindset perhaps acceptable 30 years ago, but totally inappropriate to this new world of intense competition. By demonstrating that he was both serious about the need for rapid change and equally convinced that the best way forward was through Team Enterprise, the organisation quickly became similarly persuaded.

My favourite example is Bernard O'Connell of Runshaw College (see Appendix, Case Study 1). Having had the privilege of working in a non-executive capacity alongside him for many years, I can truly say that I've never encountered a better example of senior management behaviour begetting excellence. Many observers have noted the astonishing way in which the values and beliefs set by the senior management team are reflected right through the institution. I would strongly urge any readers from the public sector to visit Runshaw to observe the real art of the possible.

Whilst the above examples do reflect individual brilliance, I do not subscribe to the view that this is essential to the success of Team Enterprise. It helps, certainly, but the main ingredients are passion about the subject and the discipline to keep it at the forefront of the management agenda when things get difficult. Changing tack in these circumstances is a sure signal to the or-

ganisation that this is a fair-weather endeavour. Team Enterprise is a philosophy that must be maintained through thick and
thin, feast and famine. It certainly helps to have more than one
passionate advocate within the senior team. I was fortunate in
having a couple of zealots, plus others who soon converted to
the cause. This united front offered by the great majority of the
perceived key decision-makers diluted the need for a single,
inspirational leader.

Don't Lose the Plot!

Consistency and constancy are essential ingredients in the ongoing management of a Team Enterprise. Once a critical point
is reached, which may take several years, the organisation is
quite capable of generating its own momentum. This is both
exhilarating and dangerous. To see a workforce proactively
initiate change as a natural day-to-day activity is an immensely
rewarding experience. At times I have been astonished by the
sheer imagination, ingenuity and fearlessness emerging from
previously considered "junior" ranks. I know for certain lots of
self-started changes have been smoothly accepted, whereas
identical suggestions from the managerial echelons would have
been received with suspicion and mistrust. The barrier of "us
and them" may never be lifted completely, but the consequences can be very much diluted once this natural momentum
is reached.

But I also describe this state as dangerous because there is a
great temptation for management to withdraw and let the organisation "get on with it". Initially you are unlikely to see any
deterioration. In fact, the reverse may be the case, as this gesture, unconscious in all probability on the part of "those upstairs", may be seen as a compliment. But slowly the absence of
managerial interest and emphasis will erode away the founda-
tions of the empowered organisation. Management will lose
touch, its communications not reflecting real issues and its recognition processes missing the right targets. A slow, almost im-
perceptible decline will develop, perhaps evidenced only by

the occasional moan or complaint. This will, however, be unfortunately followed by a rapid deterioration in morale, usually at a critical point in the organisation's fortunes. Such a crisis — for example market changes or the need for restructuring — may mask the underlying dislocation in workforce attitude. By the time the problem is identified, the damage may be considerable. And, unfortunately, the rebuilding timescale is likely to exceed the deterioration cycle by a factor of perhaps five or even ten. The message is clear: lose the plot at your peril!

In my time lecturing on the subject and visiting many companies, I have often encountered tales of the disastrous impact that enforced management change can have on participative structures. In big corporations, management mobility is encouraged, even viewed as mandatory. We often hear of "tours" where plant directors are assigned for periods as low as 18 months to two years. My usual advice in these instances — "Don't do it!" — is impractical. These companies have to fast-track future corporate decision-makers through a rapid career progression, giving the chosen few the necessary breadth of experience needed for high office. But the price cannot be a legacy of disruption and debacle as the whirlwinds race up the corporate ladder.

In these situations, I would suggest that three steps are essential to avoid disrupting the fragile equilibrium of plant morale. First, ensure that a suitable infrastructure is in place to compensate for the turnover at the top. This means greater stability within the local management team, a larger number of Team Enterprise champions and a well-defined monitoring and review process. Second, any new incumbent must be trained in advance to be familiar with the concepts of the philosophy and with the implications of their new role. And finally, forget any idea of rotating plant managers on an 18-month cycle. They and the organisation need a minimum of three years to achieve anything other than a personal development programme, and that's hardly the name of the game.

One can hardly overemphasise the damaging impact that management rotation can have on workplace attitude and hence Team Enterprise. I have seen instances where corporate human resources departments have been totally unaware of the plant's new culture and send in a very able autocrat to replace a visionary. Morale plummets and, before long, performance does too. The autocrat panics, hits home even harder and the place gets worse. Before long, departmental silos re-emerge as the management ranks replay the old game of "who shot John". A vicious downward spiral ensues with the main victims being the workforce, who have tasted a better way of working and doubly resent this return to what they consider to be the dark ages. Even changes in the junior managerial ranks can have a similar effect. A fresh young face in the operating ranks armed with the mechanistic armoury of a business diploma can reek havoc as the subtleties of motivation are discarded in favour of classical industrial engineering. Such damage can often be disguised by short-term efficiency gains but, longer term, the impact is inescapable. Empowerment, involvement and participation are fragile concepts that can be readily knocked off course by managerial ignorance. Unfortunately, the foregoing happens much more often that one might think. Sadly, expediency is frequently irresistible.

The Role of Middle Management

Having established the crucial role that senior management play in both constructing and maintaining a Team Enterprise, we must now turn our attention to the second step in Getting Started (Figure 1):

Convince and Educate the Middle Management Team

We have to focus upon the middle management group, because they are likely to be the most affected. This is particularly significant in traditional, hierarchical organisations. Whilst one cannot be prescriptive generally about the application of Team

Enterprise to differing concerns, it is difficult to see any multi-tiered organisational model surviving the process. In many respects, hierarchy is the enemy of participation, as will be discussed later. Should your organisation be of the classical "tall pyramid" design, then the number of slots in the total management strata is likely to be severely reduced.

If therefore you have the legacy of a traditional structure and, most importantly, do not possess the opportunity to absorb this surplus capacity through enhanced added value, the numbers of occupants in your management pyramid will shrink markedly. There is no hiding this fact. Once your people start to learn about other implementations elsewhere, the consequences will be clear. But the story doesn't end there. The survivors will find their lives very much changed as the pyramid flattens. Management scope broadens, with traditional functional demarcations eliminated. So the surviving middle manager not only has to contend with the disruption and the emotional guilt at being one of the "lucky" ones to emerge from this process; they may well be fearful of the implications of enhanced responsibility.

Our experience here is quite reassuring. Whilst there is nothing one can do to allay the concerns about job losses, unless we can create new added value activities, we can counsel and train to prepare the surviving rump for this brave new world. Properly prepared, there is no reason why the vast majority should not flourish under the new system. At Leyland, we had only one casualty in this area and that was self-inflicted. One middle manager disagreed with the entire philosophy and elected to leave to join another, more traditionally inclined company. The balance, despite some initial nervousness, quickly relished the benefits of a less adversarial climate, enhanced responsibilities and a feeling of making a real contribution to an exciting and radical change of philosophy. None of the managers in the organisation would nowadays vote to go back. Today's world is healthier, more interesting and more rewarding.

Such attitudes are, however, not achieved overnight. One of the key downsides anticipated by this group in advance of introduction is the loss of "natural" authority. In traditional organisations, authority comes as an immediate consequence of position. Moving through the ranks in traditional organisations has this effect. Your status and respect is geared largely to the number of metaphoric pips on your shoulder or stripes on your sleeve. Deference comes with the title and plenty of managers in both middle and senior stations relish the privilege. However, in an empowered organisation, life changes. You may still have the title but the psychological trappings are missing. One has to work across boundaries and across hierarchies. You may occasionally have to take a subordinate role in a project run by a junior. And as a consequence, the respect paid to you in the organisation stems from what you do and how you behave rather than from your job title or grade.

For a traditional, autocratic manager, this can be troublesome. You have to fundamentally change your management style and maintain this new image with consistency and constancy. Revert to type, even momentarily, for no good reason, and your new persona will be undermined. Such a transition is difficult for everybody, but for a middle-aged career autocrat it is doubly so.

We had lots of people in this category but the situation was not all bleak. Their service, experience and capability proved to be a major organisational asset. Our challenge was to find ways of harnessing these talents for the best use in our radically different new world.

The way we tackled this problem may seem to many to be highly laborious, but in the end it worked. We took the view that this was a mutual learning curve, senior management's understanding of this strange new world being little different to anybody else's. Our response was simply to take a series of potentially difficult situations, explore the options and come up with an approach that was both consistent with our new philosophy and also practical. The methodology adopted was to sit down with a small group of key middle managers at the end of the normal working day and invite them to raise their dilemmas, their confrontations and their "delicate" incidents. The manager involved would describe how he had handled the situation and we would discuss it. At first these sessions were resented. They felt vulnerable and "on-the-spot". However, after no time at all, the penny dropped. Senior management knew as little as them. We weren't testing them, we were learning both from them and with them. Ultimately, a healthy debate ensued, yielding a real learning experience for all. As the process developed, the need for formal review disappeared. The structure and form of the above dialogue became a natural adjunct to the way routine business was handled within the organisation.

Once on board, many of these middle managers became key drivers of Team Enterprise. Manufacturing, for example, took great delight in demonstrating to the rest of the company that they were leading the charge. The warehouse function responded extraordinarily. In the old world, this area had been unfairly categorised as the home for the sick, lame or downright lazy. Their latitude for demonstrating differently was extremely limited. However, the warehouse manager, Dave Traynor, quickly spotted the potential within Team Enterprise and set about vigorously effecting improvement plans which soon became recognised as exceptional. Productivity, quality, efficiency and flexibility shot up so much that over the first two years, the warehouse was the star performer in the entire company. Others followed the example and before long middle management generated as much momentum as did the more senior ranks.

The fact that so many middle managers became key players in this process was not unrelated to our "train-the-trainer" philosophy. We elected very early on in this process to avoid external consultant support and go it alone. Our formal training resources weren't great and so we decided to use line management, both senior and middle ranks, as the formal educators. This had a number of benefits, not the least of which was developing a platform for future developments as these "trainer-managers" naturally took ownership of the process.

I am reluctant to recommend this go-it-alone path whole-heartedly as a general guide to other companies, and not just because Optima is in the training game full time nowadays! We were fortunate in having some very good individuals. Leyland was a big company that had shrunk rapidly. Despite its reputation, people enjoyed working there and had a high level of company loyalty. The consequence of this was that we probably had far more talent than our station deserved and, naturally, we made the best of it. If you are to pursue the same approach, you must ensure that the individuals selected to lead the process have both the intellectual and personal qualities to see it through. Workload is an important determinate. My colleagues were no less occupied than elsewhere but desperately wanted to involve themselves in this brave new world. This encouraged them to delegate more, itself a welcome consequence. However, we also had talent beneath the middle management layer, which in turn helped considerably.

My feeling in many other situations I have encountered is that the scope for a similar approach is often restricted by both the level and the quality of resources. However, the benefits are so great that even a partial contribution to the training provided by external agencies can be very worthwhile. If this cannot be delivered, then some other form of active involvement by middle management is essential to gain the necessary ownership. Communication, recognition and audit can be very fertile areas for delegation here.

There are many other opportunities for middle management to both own the process and become constantly engaged. I have also never been against healthy internal competition, as long as it's good-humoured and supportive. Become too aggressive or mechanistic, however, and you can quickly lose the plot! We had major problems in our early days when one business unit acclaimed themselves as the "A-Team" and proceeded to demonstrate their superiority over their colleagues to anyone who'd listen. We had to sharply move in and restore equilibrium before turf wars broke out! This really emphasised the need for everybody to consider the whole organisation as the "Team" and not to have individuals focusing on their own smaller patch. However, in moderation, a little competitiveness can offer some healthy stimulation.

The objective of this chapter was to stress the paramount role that senior management plays in developing a healthy Team Enterprise. Without their active and enthusiastic involvement, the benefits will simply never materialise. Middle management has a different but still equally important contribution. Their personal transformation from the old to the new may well be difficult and this may create apprehension. But not too far downstream, these concerns should quickly be allayed as the higher quality of working life begins to take shape.

CHAPTER 6

TEAM ENTERPRISE IN ACTION: CHANGE INITIATION

We've talked so far about the philosophy behind Team Enterprise, about those common pitfalls which can disrupt even the best-laid plans and about the vital role management plays in achieving our desired state. Over the next nine chapters, we'll explore the detail of the key elements of a modern participative organisation.

We'll start our consideration of these key elements with Change Initiation as, chronologically, this follows "Convincing and Educating the Management Team" as the third step shown in "Getting Started" (Figure 1). Change Initiation is a vital step simply because it transforms the unknowns in organisational perceptions into a battery of evidence which we can learn from. Properly executed, it can also be motivational as *ownership* of the change process is shared throughout the organisation. There are two approaches, both of which will be described later.

The need for a programme like Change Initiation arose in late 1990. Financially, we'd had a great start to our Team Enterprise journey. The benefits far exceeded our initial aspirations. Progress continued to be made but . . . well, it was difficult to describe the "but". We felt a distinct lack of confidence despite these initial successes. It seemed a fragile progression, almost like treading on eggshells. I suppose the major discomfort became really evident through our communication sessions. In order to overcome the inertia and cynicism described earlier, I'd embarked upon a huge and ongoing programme of "meeting the people". I delivered the majority of these events myself, but other senior managers, particularly those in and around manufacturing, did some as well.

The format was relatively simple and straightforward. Two or three times a week, we'd gather together a group of up to 40 employees. The presenter would, in a semi-informal fashion, review Leyland's strengths and weaknesses in a frank manner and finish by posing the challenge: "What are we, together, going to do about it?" Nothing very radical there, but the size of the meetings and the occasionally brutal openness were new to Leyland. Our objective was to undermine the inbred hostility within the company between management and the managed by identifying that elusive Holy Grail — a shared unity of purpose.

Attention spans could not be faulted nor indeed could the questioning. The sessions were usually very lively, if occasionally fractious — plain speaking begetting plain speaking as it were. Given the baggage the organisation carried, the fact that things got somewhat out of hand from time to time was probably an inevitable consequence of the bloodletting. However, despite constant repetition with all the powers of persuasion that we could possibly muster, little real progress seemed to be made.

I use the word "seemed" because that was our clear perception at the time. With the benefit of hindsight, I think we were guilty of basing these perceptions on the negative and vocal minority. Elsewhere in this book we discuss the dangers of listening too much to that bottom 20 per cent element, the ones Jack Black refers to as the "moany-faced sods". Looking back today with perhaps a greater understanding of events, I suspect that we were making a lot more progress than we thought. But as we took our indicators in those days from the more vocal element, we became disenchanted, if not a little depressed at the continuation of such a wide gulf between us.

The matter came to a head at a particularly noisy meeting with the cab paint area, a group rarely short of something to say! At the end of what for me had been a very enjoyable interchange, a shop steward said something that completely flattened me. His argument was simply this: they were fed up being told that the only way forward was to work together because, in our world, that was simply not on. There was "us", and there was "them", and that was the natural order of things at Leyland. He'd heard similar themes from managers over many years and it wouldn't work. Whilst I, in his words, might have been a "decent bloke" outside the factory gates, inside I was just the same as all the others. Slick-tongued, convincing, but not to be trusted. History showed that as soon as the shopfloor let their guard down, the carefully hidden sledgehammer would appear with devastating consequences. No matter what I or any of my colleagues argued, the shopfloor could never allow the class barrier to be breached.

Now, perhaps I shouldn't have, but I took the message very badly, particularly since so many in the room agreed with the steward's depressing conclusion. There was little doubt in my mind that survival would only come if we could achieve a common understanding about the world of work. We had to change comprehensively. But if the workforce wouldn't believe *me*, who would they believe?

Selling a Philosophy

Fortunately I had a meeting that evening with the group personnel director, Stewart Pierce, and I naturally shared my thoughts on the subject. He was less convinced than I about the correctness of the steward's logic but recognised the dangers. Coincidentally, however, he had returned that day from a visit to our sales operation in Oxfordshire where he had been working with a small consultancy which specialised in customer perception analysis. He suggested that perhaps we could utilise the same techniques, except this time focusing on workforce perceptions rather than customers'.

Initially sceptical, I agreed to meet the consultant, one Reg Hardy of HCH Associates. The first meeting did not go well. The techniques seemed over-elaborate and inappropriate for our particular problem. However, I really did not have too many options and, for want of a better alternative, I agreed to give it a try. Despite my fundamental mistrust of "consultants", on this occasion, I relented.

The process, originally called Performance Barrier Analysis but now more usually termed Change Initiation, was certainly cumbersome. However, in fairness, this was the first time it had been used on people at work as opposed to customers. Since then it has been developed and rarefied, of which more later. Reg adopted a five-stage approach.

Stage 1 — Convincing the Workforce

Given the background of Leyland, this was no mean challenge! Reg had to address this by meeting every single employee in groups of 100–150. At these sessions he had to persuade the workforce:

1. That he was truly independent;

2. That he was trustworthy and honest;

3. That the process was effective and beneficial; and finally

4. That everything would be disclosed almost simultaneously to everybody without modification, censorship or spin.

This last point was vital. The workforce had to be convinced that they would see exactly the same information as management in the same timeframe and that nothing would be held back. We agreed wholeheartedly with this approach, and this joint commitment by the external consultant and the senior management seemed to win the day.

Stage 2 — Establishing the Needs

Stage 2 was an enormously complex process and probably, with the benefit of hindsight, unnecessarily so. Reg involved one-third of the total site workforce of over 2,500 in groups of ten and had them establish what he termed the "Needs" of the organisation. In this process, they sat down in a room for about an hour with a consultant. The latter, armed only with a tape recorder (for total objectivity) and a checklist, simply asked them what they would like to see from their ideal job in an ideal company in an ideal world. Leyland Trucks was not mentioned. The checklist was used to ensure that each group dealt comprehensively with the question, commenting on all likely areas of interest.

By analysing the subsequent data, Reg's team was able to establish a list of 50 or so needs, collectively representing the workforce's perspective of an ideal working environment. Each of these needs was carefully phrased in a positive manner to ensure that the subsequent Action Planning phase had the best chance of being handled constructively and amicably. For example, "My manager totally ignores me" might be offered as "I would like my manager to spend more time with me"!

He then took another one-third of the workforce, again in groups of ten, and asked them to "rank" the list prepared by their colleagues. Using a neat, card-based, matched pairing process, each employee was able to determine which was No. 1 for them, which was No. 2, and so on. This gave a measure of "priority".

Once the group had completed this task, they were asked for the first time to comment on life at Leyland Trucks. For every "need", each individual was asked to rate their experience within the company. If they were absolutely 100 per cent satisfied, they were asked to mark it 10 out of 10. For those which registered total dissatisfaction, 0 out of 10. Those in between were graded proportionately. This gave us a measure of "satisfaction".

The whole battery of data was then fed into a computer and scores amalgamated for total company, function and even cost centre. For each significant group, we ended up with three pieces of information:

- **Needs** — what they wanted from the world of work

- **Priority** — how highly they rated each need

- **Satisfaction** — how each need was satisfied within Leyland Trucks.

Stage 2 went a lot better than expected, particularly given the difficulties experienced in the first phase. People seemed intrigued by the process and were willing to air their concerns, usually in a calm and careful manner. A few objected to the use of the tape recorder on the grounds of confidentiality and, in such cases, their wishes were readily accepted.

Stage 3 — Analysis

This simply involved the distillation of the raw data into some meaningful outline. The outcomes were ranked by what the consultant termed USP, "Unsatisfied Potential", which is calculated simply as a product of the ranking and the level of dissatisfaction. The higher the USP, the greater the priority for action. Typical examples of the output from a Change Initiation might be:

- *I have long-term job security* — USP 49

- *My manager/supervisor listens to my views* — USP 34

- *Top management provides clear direction for the business* — USP 32.

Stage 4 — Feedback

Once the data had been collated into a format capable of being understood and acted upon by management and workforce alike, it was then communicated in the same fashion as in Stage

1. Groups of 100–150 gathered to hear the consultant personally feed back the outcome of the Change Initiation Survey. Great care was taken not to lead at this stage, as it was important for the organisation to make up its own mind.

These sessions actually went very well. Reg had by now established his credentials so the audience attention level was generally very much "interested" rather than cynical. The questioning was frank and challenging, with only occasional evidence of the buffoonery which usually took place at these events. For the first time, perhaps, we had been able to tap into the silent majority, reinforcing my earlier view that our perception of events was distorted by placing too much emphasis on the vocal minority. Many managers found the response alarming. We had anticipated much more emphasis on hygiene factors such as wages, working environment, conditions, etc., than on the "softer" side of working life. However, when the results were revealed, we saw that the workforce priorities lay in a completely different direction than we had anticipated.

The top concerns of the Change Initiation process, as ranked by "Unsatisfied Potential", in broad terms, were:

1. Job security

2. Mutual trust/Honesty

3. Fairness of pay systems

4. Involvement/Participation

5. Management behaviour.

The first outcome was totally unsurprising. As my boss pointed out, you did not need to be the Brain of Britain or employ expensive consultants to deduce that the prime concern of the workforce would be job security. After the boom in the UK market in 1989, 1990 saw a fall of a staggering 54 per cent in volume and was not expected to recover much in the foreseeable future. That year and much of 1991 had therefore been characterised by further job losses in a succession of actions attempting to come to terms with the new market reality. It was little wonder, therefore, that this issue was of prime concern.

However, there was an interesting slant on even this entirely predictable conclusion. For the first time, the shopfloor were able to see the perception analysis of senior and middle management as well as their own. And No. 1 for everybody was — job security. This emphasised that we really were in this boat together and that if we didn't co-operate to our utmost to improve matters, then ultimately we would all sink to the nautical equivalent of the dole queue. This may seem to many to be a relatively trivial point but, for us, it was a vital learning experience.

If the No. 1 priority was totally predictable, the second came as a complete surprise. None of the management had anticipated this in their own top five (usually Pay, Conditions, Workloads, Management Capability and Job Security); and yet, as we have seen since in the vast majority of Change Initiations elsewhere, this occurs over and over again. The second most important element for our workforce in 1991 was to work in an atmosphere of *trust* and *honesty*. Downstream, we discovered this to be a complex need. Not only did the workforce desperately want to trust "those upstairs"; they in turn wanted to be trusted *by them*. The same need seemed to apply across functions. Perhaps generations exposed to interfunctional strife had led to longstanding enmities across departmental boundaries. People didn't like it, and apparently had a strong desire to trust their colleagues in other areas and in turn to be trusted by them.

The third point was extremely interesting and had far-reaching consequences. We expected pay to come up but rather as an issue about *absolute* pay levels. Our employees were in fact highly paid in a local context and certainly not badly off with industry comparisons. However, their aspirations had usually been a lot more than the company could afford to pay. That pay came up as the third concern was of no surprise, but its context was. People didn't complain about *absolute* pay levels but rather the *inequity* of the various remuneration packages we had across the company. It was the perceived *unfairness* of the schemes that caused the irritation rather than the *actual* payment level.

Again, perhaps this was yet another case of management gaining their perspective by listening only to the vocal minority. We had communicated intensively in the previous two years on the financial parameters of the business and this, coupled with the ongoing restructuring of the organisation, should have persuaded anyone prepared to listen of the company's limited scope in this area. It seems as if the message had indeed generally got through, *but we had failed to appreciate it.* I know this, retrospectively, makes the Leyland management, and me especially, look rather foolish, but it is by no means uncommon. Reflect on your own situation first before you criticise!

However, our relief on this point was tempered by the severity of the concern expressed on the "felt-fairness" of the pay structures. Some of the demands were mutually exclusive. Track and warehouse workers wanted rises to be made as flat rates rather than percentages, particularly in days of lower inflation. But maintenance, prototype and engineering wanted to see greater differentials to reflect their training, qualifications and status. Even Solomon may have had difficulty in the world of industrial relations! Fortunately, there was one huge area of disquiet which we certainly could do something about — the productivity scheme.

For over a decade, we had in the company a bonus scheme geared supposedly to productivity. The higher the productivity, the higher the bonus — which seems, *a priori*, to be logical and reasonable. Unfortunately, as with so many similar schemes, the real difficulty arises over the measurement of productivity. We had selected a ratio of "standard hours" produced over "actual hours" input. It might have worked had our employees accepted the inevitable fluctuations which occur as a consequence of external factors — market, mix, or material availability to name but three of the many such potential disruptions.

The principle may have been sound — that is, when the company benefits, the employee benefits — however, the reality was that people simply did not understand or accept the inevitable variability in their wage packets.

Nor did I blame them. Imagine a trackworker going home and putting his monthly pay cheque on the table, some £50 down on the month earlier. They would have quite a task persuading their partner that the reason — for example, material shortages caused by a supplier failure — justified such a significant loss of earnings. There was nothing that a trackworker could do about material shortages and they would in turn have major difficulty persuading a disappointed spouse that this was all reasonable and fair!

As a consequence, working life became dominated by the weekly travails of the bonus scheme. Each week, shop stewards would battle for concessions, adjustments or occasionally overt manipulation to keep morale on an even keel. The more militant or mischievous would see the constant and unfathomable pirouettes as a prime opportunity for troublemaking. After ten years of grappling with these wasteful and certainly non-value-added excursions, my colleagues and I had become masters of behind-the-scenes manoeuvring, trying to keep the atmosphere calm. Anyone with the remotest idea of the mechanics of the scheme would immediately spot that the regular and consistent payments which we paid generally just could not be an accurate reflection of reality. But, within certain limits, we were able to do it — at a price. That price was wage drift and an unbelievably disproportionate amount of management time and distraction. When occasionally we couldn't deliver this stability, all hell would break loose.

I had therefore campaigned to get rid of the schemes for years and had, by 1990, persuaded most in management of the total nonsense of it all. The unions, however, had a different view. The bonus scheme was their birthright, their power base. It gave them constant access to senior management, as the latter were theoretically the only ones who could "bend" the rules. But here we had the workforce, out loud and without any ambiguity, telling the world that they didn't like it. The unions, and those lingering conservatives in management, had to accept that change was inevitable and the scheme ditched or replaced with something more effective and relevant to the realities of working life. And that's exactly what happened, with enormous benefits both to the running of the operation and to the general level of management sanity!

All the foregoing was beneficial, but the next two outcomes really opened the door. Here we had the workforce telling us, in no uncertain manner, that they desperately wanted to be involved more, to participate vigorously in the new world of work. This was music to my ears. For years I'd firmly believed it to be the only way forward, but this time it wasn't me that was doing the shouting. It was the entire workforce, articulating it in many and varied ways but still coming down to the same general principle — *"Working life is changing and we want to be a part of it."* However, there was a sting in the tail. They wanted this change to take place with a more appropriate style of management behaviour. We had been told in no uncertain terms that many of our managerial practices did not match the standards expected by our employees in this new world. As you will see later, this was an uncomfortable message, but if we genuinely wanted to improve, what did we need to know? What we were doing well or what we were doing badly? The answer is, of course, the latter.

Stage 5 — Action Planning

For the first time, certainly in my long experience at Leyland, we had before us a battery of perceptions that were both owned and seen to be owned by our employees. The key step now was to make sure that this ownership extended into the Action Phase, Stage 5. The usual management response of taking away the problem, thinking about it and coming back with a solution was hardly likely to work here. After all, they didn't trust us, nor did they particularly like us! Reg suggested that the final stage should be executed in, for Leyland, a very radical manner.

His proposal was to assemble a focus group or action planning group for each key conclusion of the survey. This would comprise a cross-section of interested parties, with particular emphasis on membership from the "lower" levels of the organisation. Volunteers were not sought, as this would have attracted the usual lunatic fringe. The silent majority were still, unfortunately, silent and unlikely to volunteer for such a potentially taxing responsibility, especially if challenged by one of the many barrack-room lawyers about. We therefore sought carefully to "select" influential characters who could play a constructive role in this key activity. Seeking to avoid the "Uncle Tom" or "Blue-eyed Boy" syndromes at all costs, this selection process was risky and difficult but, properly reasoned, could be sold. The fact that these teams were only assembled for a very limited life helped. Their role was to give us our first steer on how to tackle the considerable challenge they had set before management.

The process, even allowing for the inevitable rose-tinted perspective that memory often paints, went extraordinarily well. If what the cab paint steward had described earlier was in fact a huge impenetrable barrier of mistrust and suspicion, then progressively this obstructive edifice was dismantled. I'm not suggesting for one second that we all experienced some grand scale Road to Damascus and that utopia broke out. It took a lot longer to put in place an acceptable level of trust between management and the managed. However, simply breaking through that longstanding blockage was sufficient to get us under way. People came together and offered advice and criticism in equal measures in a clear and comprehensive manner. This allowed us to challenge the status quo for the first time in many years and start gravitating towards our shared objective — *the maximisation of as many long-term secure jobs as possible.*

Subordinate Appraisal

Reg's process yielded one other benefit. Properly constructed and configured, a picture of the perceptions held by a section of the workforce about local management can be drawn. Whilst not as comprehensive as a formal subordinate or 360° appraisal process, within the context of Change Initiation this can be a very powerful tool. For those unused to such exposure, the appraisal stage can be a useful introduction to upward assessment.

This part certainly came as a surprise to me, despite my commissioning of the entire project. I was informed by one of Reg's lieutenants, a very able facilitator named Bob Coutts, that my presence was requested at 3.00 p.m. on Friday in the boardroom. Upon arriving, I found myself facing my direct reports, about a dozen in total. Bob then proceeded to dismantle my management style. Using only the data supplied by these managers where it related to me or to higher echelons, Bob painted a pretty unpleasant picture. I have never viewed myself as a particularly inspiring or charismatic leader but I did think I was reasonably competent. My relationship with these people was, in my view, extremely healthy. We had regular formal and informal sessions on a one-to-one basis where full and frank views could be aired. I had thought that my style was such that, when I invited personal criticism, people gave it without fear or favour. In short, I thought I knew what they thought about me.

I couldn't have been more wrong. Over the next hour or so, I heard that my meetings were viewed by all as pretty useless, my capability at recognising good and bad performance fairly insipid and, worst of all, I was viewed as being autocratic! Me, the ultimate democrat! Now, I know the reader will have as much difficulty with this view as I did. After all, Team Enterprise, which I had personally pioneered and developed, was based on a philosophy of involvement and participation, wasn't it? How could this possibly have been even remotely successful if conducted in a directive or autocratic fashion?

Sadly, in the eyes of my colleagues, I was seen as a "closet autocrat". Someone who plays the democratic game but ensures that, at the death, the most important decisions are those which they had in the back of their minds all the time.

To say I was shocked when this was revealed to general agreement would be a massive understatement. I had no idea that I did this. I genuinely felt that I was involving people in both the process and in the decision-making. I fully accept that this was not the case, but can only plead unconscious incompetence. This certainly wasn't any deliberate Machiavellian or manipulative trait. It must have been a habit adopted out of past experience, perhaps driven by the time pressures of operational management. However, it certainly wasn't acceptable, particularly if it was so evident to all concerned! My mystification still to this day is why none of this ever emerged in the one-to-one sessions described earlier. Perhaps as "the boss", certain behavioural traits are accepted as par for the course. Bosses do that sort of thing! However, my ongoing display of this "closet autocracy" could not have been helpful to the creation of a genuine and effective Team Enterprise. Worse still, given that many of us model our behaviour on our immediate superior, there could have been lots of Oliver clones running around the organisation, all proudly displaying the same profound weakness!

At the time I found the whole idea of having all your weaknesses paraded in front of your direct reports quite disturbing. Whilst no-one thinks that they really are perfect, being told what others think of you in such direct fashion is somewhat challenging. If you are going through this process, therefore, I strongly recommend that you do as I did and have your debrief late on Friday afternoon. Then you have all weekend to soothe your battered ego, wash away all those psychological bruises and, most importantly, learn to resist the temptation to return on Monday morning and fire every bastard in sight for gross insubordination!

Looking back, however, one can see the power of this tool. For the first time in my career, I had a clear appreciation of what my direct reports actually thought of me. If I genuinely wanted to improve, and as the senior man my example was absolutely vital, I needed to know my weaknesses, probably more so than my strengths. A lot of us have an overestimated view of our own self-knowledge. One of my colleagues took weeks to come to terms with the situation. He had to go through the not uncommon mental Denial–Depression–Resignation–Resolution cycle, described by Reg Hardy as the "Valley of Death", before he realised that this was an important aid in self-improvement. The fact that all your colleagues and some of your subordinates have to go through the same contritional process does actually help significantly. Sharing experiences aids the construction of a company-wide ethos of self-examination. Downstream simple audit devices can be put in place, such as brief management style questionnaires, which help maintain an open and challenging platform.

Poskett's Variation

The Hardy process of Change Initiation helped Leyland enormously in 1991. How big a contributor it was to the change in the company's fortunes is debatable. Some may argue it was the biggest single influence. I personally suspect that its main strength was simply in being a powerful catalyst, enabling lots of other initiatives to fire. However, there is little doubt in anybody's mind that Change Initiation was for Leyland an indispensable tool in the fight to achieve competitiveness.

However, there were downsides. Doing it in the fashion described is a big, complex exercise. The welter of data emanating from the surveys can in some situations be overwhelming and occasionally confusing. And despite the high level of participation in at least some part of the programme, it still doesn't involve 100 per cent of the workforce.

Accordingly, the Optima Change Initiation process, as opposed to the Hardy Change Initiation process, was developed and introduced to both Leyland Trucks and many of Optima's client organisations. Based on Charlie Poskett's extensive experience in working with companies going through a culture change process in order to achieve greater competitiveness, it was felt that the key parameters of each of the elements covered in Chapter 5 under "Poskett's Law" could be defined by a number of well-chosen questions. These questions, the "Survey", became the heart of the Optima process.

There are seven stages in the latter:

Stage 1 — Design of the Survey

For each of the elements needed to describe culture, one of our colleagues, Dave Sherliker, has established a number of statements which have proven to be effective in extracting workforce perceptions. Each of these statements is phrased positively to convey from the outset a sense of determination to improve and move forward. Many questionnaires or attitude surveys simply become major opportunities for whinging, moaning or general complaining. We emphasise from the outset that we are interested only in the past as a reference point from which we must improve. The sense of positivity must therefore be established from the outset.

However, there may be additional issues that are not covered by the standard format. Hence the first stage is to sit down with local management and flush out any unusual characteristics of the organisation which may need addressing.

This stage should take no more than a few hours once the senior management team has been appraised of the process, particularly in understanding what is likely to happen downstream.

Stage 2 — Communication of the Survey

As with the Hardy version, this stage is best conducted by a third party in order to gain trust and belief in the process. The external facilitator acts as the honest broker in persuading the workforce that this is an exercise which will ultimately have benefits for everybody in the affected group. They will give assurances of both the confidentiality and the integrity of the process. Commitments will be given for as near simultaneous communication of the outcome as can reasonably be managed. Stage 2 is therefore an absolutely vital step in obtaining an effective Change Initiation. We are looking for participation rates of over 65 per cent, as a minimum, and hence the credibility of the facilitator is all-important. Group size is controlled, usually limited to 40 or so attendees to ensure that even the normally bashful have an opportunity to challenge or simply to ask questions.

Stage 3 — Release of the Survey

Immediately after the completion of Stage 2, the survey will be released to the entire workforce. The survey will contain:

- The list of statements agreed in Stage 1. Although they will each apply to a specific category of culture, the statements are mixed up to aid objectivity. Sample statements for one category, Management Style, are shown in Figure 8. Participants are asked to grade level of satisfaction on a scale of 0–10.

Figure 8: Management Style

Management Style
5.   I am happy with the way I am managed.
8.   My manager says thanks for good work and effort
14. My manager shows me respect and consideration
30. The employees get on well with management
34. Managers listen to my views and suggestions
39. Mutual trust exists between managers and employees
54   The company understands when people make mistakes.

- A second written section where participants are asked to detail their views on the Strengths, Weaknesses, Opportunities, Threats and, temptingly, Frustrations of the organisation. This dilutes the prescription of the survey and allows participants to vent all their opinions, both positive and negative, on the company. We always find this section to be of immense value in "fleshing out" the quantifiable data. Of particular power is the invitation for individuals to express their "frustrations". This tends to be the busiest section.

The surveys are issued to each individual and are coded for the benefit of analysis, although it is emphasised that this code will never be seen by any company representative. Sealed ballot boxes are placed around the workplace to emphasise security and confidentiality. Between seven and 14 days are sufficient to allow for most to complete the surveys, usually with the help of ongoing local prodding to ensure that everybody plays their part in fashioning an agenda for the future. The surveys are then collected and shipped back in the still-sealed ballot boxes to the Optima head office.

Stage 4 — Analysis

The data is then analysed by Optima consultants. By reference to the quantified responses and the anecdotal commentary of the Strengths, Weaknesses, Opportunities, Threats and Frustrations sections, the analysts can draw out issues for further investigation in Stage 5.

Stage 5 — Validation

Stage 5 is a vital stage in the process, which enables the consultant to take the indicators from the written submissions and to validate their relevance, importance and priority. This is done through a series of in-depth validation interviews with 10–15 per cent of the workforce, either individually or in small groups. Sessions with the members of the senior management group can be particularly effective here.

Stage 6 — Feedback

A report is then constructed by the consultant, comprising two elements. First, a full set of quantified data relating to the survey questions is generated, usually categorised into four or five groups. These groups could be, for example, Senior Management, Middle/Front Line Management, Shopfloor and Support Areas or any variation applicable to the organisation under review. An example of this is shown in Figure 9.

Figure 9: Management Style — Strength of Agreement

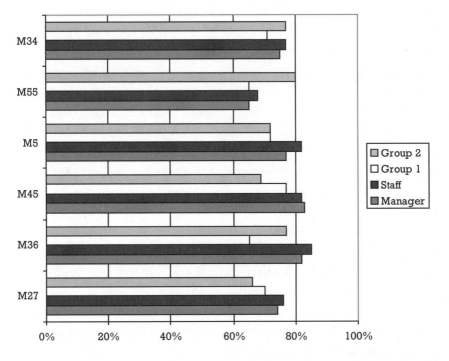

Second, a factual report will be produced, highlighting concerns raised by the written submissions and further investigated by the validation interviews. The report writer will not conclude but merely state the opinions of those who have participated in the exercise. This is vitally important. We do not want any premature concluding at this stage. The report should be factual, objective and impartial.

The report will be fed back to all participating groups in the same manner as Stage 2. Logistics, convention and logic dictate that the Senior Management group gets to see the report slightly ahead of the rest of the organisation. This is not to allow them to censor the outcome but to give them a little time to prepare themselves for the consequences. The facilitator will stress the importance of not reacting impulsively to any conclusions that seem to be emerging, however self-evident they might appear to be. The success of the downstream stages, which in turn determine the success of the entire programme, depends on everybody involved thinking carefully through the issues and establishing a measured response. The last thing needed is managers jumping the gun.

A similar session may also be required with middle managers in some exceptional circumstances. More usually, the facilitator will go straight into mass communication. He will convey the conclusions verbally with visual aids but will not normally circulate any written output. This is a delicate phase and needs to be executed with care and due deliberation. Reflection is the watchword here, not action.

Stage 7 — Action Planning

Stage 7 will follow on quickly from Stage 6 and replicates exactly the same format as that described in Stage 5 of the Hardy process. Small "Focus Groups", perhaps named in a manner that suits the culture of the organisation, will be assembled to look quickly at each key problem area and report back on recommended action plans. As before, membership will be nominated by management, the group will be facilitated by outside support or by skilled internal facilitators who are viewed as objective and independent, and the group will last only as long as is needed to conclude and report.

However, the Action Planning stage will probably extend over months, if not years, and therefore it is vital that a process is put in place to manage it effectively. If everything goes to plan, what will ensue will be a whole train of Action Planning groups and Continuous Improvement initiatives, which will drive the organisation forward from the bottom upwards. There is therefore much to be gained in managing this carefully and professionally. We have tried in the past not to be over-prescriptive here, feeling that organisations must find their own feet. However, experience tells us that the following model is useful in most applications in maintaining control, enthusiasm and priority. It also has the benefit of ensuring active senior management involvement for the duration of the "project", the latter being a lifetime if we've done it correctly!

Downstream Management

In most organisations, the range of concerns, issues and improvement opportunities emanating from Change Initiation will be vast. To get the best from the goodwill, commitment and enthusiasm which will ultimately flow, we recommend that the architecture detailed in Figure 10 is put in place and maintained as a long-term proposition. Throughout this book we have stressed the need for senior management to be visible, committed and even evangelical. Here is a prime opportunity to do just that! At the head of this infrastructure we recommend that a Senior Management Steering Group be established.

Figure 10: Action Planning Architecture

MFFG = Multi-Function Focus Group

The key prerequisite is that this steering group, however named, should be populated almost exclusively by the members of the senior management team. I say "almost" because in some instances a secretarial function operated by someone like the quality, continuous improvement or culture change manager may be appropriate. But to be effective, *all* senior managers have to sit routinely on this body. Otherwise, the organisation will soon become lop-sided, with the missing functions left behind as others charge on. The role of this group is threefold:

1. To design and maintain the architecture of the change process

2. To monitor, measure and review the work of the subcommittees

3. To ensure active senior management involvement in all aspects of the change process.

What this group cannot do is handle the broad range of actions representing the entire gamut of the change process. It would rapidly become immersed in far too much detail and waste the time of those sitting in attendance who may not be too interested in some of the topics. The emphasis in this process should be to keep meetings to the point, interesting and as short as possible! Nothing kills initiative faster than bureaucracy. It is much better therefore to take the outcomes of the change initiation process, whether the Hardy or Optima variant, and split them into discrete groupings. We recommend at least three different categories:

- **Culture Change**, examining areas such as communication, recognition, attitude, development, management style and teamworking;

- **Employee Development**, examining areas such as training, pay systems, career progression, organisation structures and employee systems;

- **Corporate Strategy**, examining areas coming from the survey such as business planning, cascading objectives (journey-boarding), systems effectivity and product introduction.

These committees will be staffed by a combination of senior and middle management plus key influencers relevant to the particular category. Within the limits prescribed, the groups should exercise a significant level of devolved authority. The overall Steering Group will have ample opportunity to review progress but, given the level of empowerment which will be expected further down the chain, these key committees must be seen as decision-makers and change initiators in their own right, not merely conduits from above. They will meet to discuss each of the issues arising from the project relevant to them and decide how best to pursue them to resolution. The preferred model of resolution is the creation of multi-functional, multi-hierarchical problem-solving groups. Our objective is to release all those talents and abilities hidden in the body of the workforce. We should never forget therefore that our task here is not just straightforward problem-solving but, much more importantly, motivating and inspiring everybody in the world of work. We want to actively involve them in the amelioration of the issues they themselves helped to identify. Properly constructed and facilitated, this should raise no fears. If the management agenda is correct, then taking the group logically and calmly through the review process should result in exactly the same conclusion. If it doesn't, then perhaps the management agenda may have been somewhat flawed to start with! However, in our experience, there is little evidence for concern. People react positively to being entrusted with these key responsibilities and are highly unlikely to let you down. If we were to predict a difficulty, it would be that management might struggle to keep up with the rate of good advice and ideas arising from these multi-functional groups. In other words, as ever, management is usually the problem, not the workforce!

Summary

Change initiation is a powerful and perhaps mandatory tool in the change agent's armoury. If you are to be successful in your culture change journey, you need to establish the real perceptions of the workforce and ensure that they both recognise and own the downstream correction processes. The Hardy and Optima variants described here can do precisely that.

We therefore have two variants of a powerful change initiation process, which we would recommend to the vast majority of organisations. The question is often posed: which one should I choose? The answer, I think, is relatively straightforward. For most workforces, you should elect to take the cheaper and quicker Optima process. The simplicity of the approach, alongside the ability for every single person to participate fully, will outweigh the complexities and cost of the Hardy process. However, some management groups may reject the prescription of the Optima survey and wish to go back to first principles when analysing *their own* concerns. In these situations, it appears that they are comfortable with using the Optima process with the general workforce but demand greater detail when it comes to analysing senior, middle and often front-line management issues. This can be a valid concern. In many organisations, there are deep-seated stresses within the management hierarchy which should be sorted out before moving on to the general staff and shopfloor areas. A more reflective and detailed process like the Hardy approach seems to work better here.

However, whether you elect to adopt a change initiation process or not, if you are to be successful in your culture change journey you must find ways of:

- Establishing the true perceptions of the workforce

- Establishing a recognition of the need for change in the workforce

- Establishing an ownership of the change process within the workforce.

And if you do find a cheaper or more effective means of doing it than described here, then give me a call, because I'd love to hear about it!

CHAPTER 7

TEAM ENTERPRISE IN ACTION: COMMUNICATION AND RECOGNITION

COMMUNICATION

Good communication practice underpins all management activity. But what exactly is good practice? After all, very few companies would put their hands up and readily admit that they were hopeless in this area. Most companies actually believe that they are "doing alright" in communicating to their employees. Yet in nearly all of the companies studied by Optima, the reverse is found to be the case. Why? In a nutshell, it is simply that very few senior managers understand the need for effective communication or the way to go about it.

Back in late 1989, it became fairly self-evident that our existing communication systems at Leyland simply weren't working. We had to set about rebuilding them from principles established by the workforce in our biennial Attitude Surveys. In these surveys, employees told us repeatedly that they didn't like our conventional instruments of communication. They didn't want corporate videos, company newspapers and mass "state of the nation" briefings. They wanted their information to be timely and ongoing. If something of significance happened, they wanted to hear it there and then from their supervisor, not later from the grapevine or, even worse, in the local newspaper. They emphasised that the preferred mode of delivery was from their immediate supervisor or manager, certainly not the managing director, the personnel manager or the shop steward. We had to completely rethink our entire approach to the whole subject of communication.

It wasn't easy. Suffice to say that, even up to five years later, local management devoted at least ten times their previous level of resource to the development and implementation of new formats for communication, and still hadn't got it right. But it was a lot better in terms of effectiveness and acceptability. The bad news is that the solution is definitely not simple and straightforward. Workforce needs for communication are many and varied. There is no single answer, but instead a whole gamut of devices, all of which need maintaining. One must also be careful in assuming that there is a universal template here, suitable for all companies. Sadly, there isn't; you need to design your communication system around your own circumstances. Structures, local cultures, geography, working patterns and even presentational capability need to be accommodated if you want to get it right.

In no particular order, listed below are the key devices for effective communication used at Leyland:

1. Weekly Written Brief

There is a definite need for information at a "macro" level to be conveyed routinely in print. The questions to be raised are, firstly, exactly what sort of information; secondly, how frequently; and thirdly, in what format. To answer the first, we have to examine what the workforce seek from this form of publication. To focus entirely on factual information here is, in my view, a gross oversimplification of the need. I believe that the requirement is as much about *access* as it is about information. If we accept that it is the behaviour and attitude of senior management that establishes the culture of the organisation, as discussed in Chapter 5, then any written communication must provide some illumination on these areas if this basic need of the workforce is to be addressed. The Written Brief needs to emphasise as much *opinion* as it does *detail*. The workforce has a requirement to understand management thinking on a range of issues so that they can take their own cues as to how to behave, how to react and how to move forward. If there is a managerial vision, then this is one of the key places to communicate it. If not, then I suggest you'd better devise one quickly!

Over the years I have seen many attempts to communicate through company briefs and newspapers, and few impress. Frequently, opinions are only conveyed when it's time for admonishment or exhortation. There is no ongoing attempt to maintain an awareness within the workforce of management's responses to strategic challenges or change. Quite often, the defence is commercial confidentiality or, patronisingly, a claim that the shopfloor or general office "simply wouldn't understand the issue". I find the latter very frustrating. When disaster strikes, these same managers are the first to use strategic challenges as the excuse for action. The workforce is expected to understand it then.

The capacity for understanding complex issues within the workforce is surprisingly high. For years at Leyland, one of the key macroeconomic pressure points was the relative exchange rate between the deutschmark and sterling. Given our dependence on a mainly UK supply source and a market dominated by continental competition, even the slightest shift had enormous implications for the business. We regularly communicated all the factors which impacted on the deutschmark/sterling rate, we forecasted likely consequences and we added our own opinions. As a result, nearly every single employee knew exactly where we stood and could comment intelligently on the issue. When rates changed, the consequences came as no surprise: they already knew.

Understanding what management thinks on key issues is all-important to the workforce, but it has to be done routinely if it is to have any credibility. Occasional forays in times of crisis will only raise the spectre of manipulation or propaganda. Familiarity helps enormously here. If the readership sees the opinions and attitudes of their leading group flow week-in week-out, they will become comfortable with the process. They may still harbour suspicions, but constant repetition and consistency, backed up by experience, will lead them towards a more supportive comfort zone.

In terms of frequency, we believe that in most organisations, operating in a complex and volatile market, weekly dissemination is necessary. Too big a gap between communications renders the news out of date. However, if you have a simple business or a relatively small number of employees, you may get away with less. As a rule of thumb in Optima, we recommend:

- More than 500 employees   —   Weekly
- Between 250–499 employees   —   Fortnightly
- Fewer than 249 employees   —   Monthly

In small organisations, other forms of communication are probably more effective, which reduces the need for such frequent circulation.

The format of the brief should be seriously considered. Many organisations simply cannot resist the temptation to have their internal communications in a pseudo-magazine layout with glossy pages and nice photographs. I have no particular objection to this, provided the editorial team can guarantee issues at the prescribed time. If you say that the brief is to be issued at 3.00 p.m. every Tuesday, then you must issue the brief at 3.00 p.m. every Tuesday without fail. You need to establish what my colleague Charlie Poskett calls the "6 o'clock News" syndrome. There is enormous comfort in switching the BBC on at 6.00 p.m. every night and seeing with total predictability the "News". To attain the same level of credibility within the organisation, a regular, dependable routine is similarly required. The workforce expects to see it at a certain time and therefore you must meet that deadline, week-in and week-out. Having a complex glossy edition can make this difficult so if anything needs to give, make sure it's not the deadline!

The Leyland Trucks format is a simple A4 piece of coloured paper folded in half to give four sides. Apart from headers and a few desktop-produced "characters" to break up the monotony, its content is simply a series of typewritten articles. Page 1 contains the lead article by a senior director or manager; pages 2 and 3 are devoted to articles from other functional heads and page 4 is exclusively social content. The last item is important but care should be taken to ensure that it stays in proportion. Twenty-five per cent is quite enough!

In the early days, persuading people to prepare copy was difficult. Even when it finally arrived, it wasn't always written in the right style. Accordingly, I had a habit of writing all the articles for each edition. The first would be printed under my name and the rest offered to my colleagues as their efforts! All they had to do was add their names. Fortunately, nobody took umbrage at this presumption. But it served a purpose. Firstly, it demonstrated that this was a serious initiative, as demonstrated by the senior site executive's interest. Secondly, it demonstrated the style and the content which I felt was important. Since then the Weekly Brief has been issued every week at the appointed time without fail, even during the dark, despondent days of receivership. Many of my colleagues became highly proficient at putting together short, sharp pieces which combined fact, opinion and humour in the requisite proportions.

In summary, therefore, if you already have a written brief, ask yourself the following questions:

- Do people read and appreciate it?

- Does it support the managerial communication agenda?

- Does it contain sufficient indicators of management attitude and opinion to lead to the creation of the "correct" culture?

- Does it minimise factual data?

- Is it written in clear English and in a user-friendly style?

- Is it issued with the right frequency?

- Is it released consistently at the requisite time?

2. Daily/Weekly Briefings

The Attitude Surveys mentioned earlier clearly indicated that for day-to-day, routine information, the preferred source of delivery was the immediate line supervisor. We must therefore consider how to get supervision into the loop effectively. The key word here is "effectively", because there will be few readers who haven't at one time been involved in well-intentioned efforts to communicate that have collapsed due to the sheer effort in maintaining them. This form of communication needs to be brief, relevant and pertinent to normal daily activity.

At its simplest level, we have the "five-minute morning meeting" which takes place in many office areas. At the start of the shift, say 8.00 a.m., everybody gathers together. The manager will briefly indicate the priorities of the day, convey any relevant information and invite comments. A quick interchange follows. Perhaps someone is particularly stretched that day and may ask for assistance. At 8.05 a.m. precisely, the meeting disbands. It is swift, specific and totally relevant — lean engineering at its best! However, it works very effectively. Often called the "Hill Street Blues Meeting" after the American police series which started each shift with a similar gathering, this form of briefing has the key benefit of bringing everybody together for a few minutes before the trials and tribulations of the working day. A good manager will keep their contribution to a minimum to allow others to participate. In some instances, the manager doesn't lead but leaves it to a rota, thereby enabling everybody to play a key role.

As well as a useful vehicle for routine, detail communications, the five-minute meeting has other benefits. The simple coming together as the first act of the day serves to bond the team together. I have seen a very fractious group of individuals become a strong, supportive team as a result of a few months of doing this routinely. In addition, it also helps on timekeeping. We noticed a significant improvement in people being at their desks at the appointed time. The embarrassment of attempting to sneak past all your assembled colleagues and their clear disapproval becomes a sufficient incentive to get to work on time!

To my surprise, not all departments adopted this model. Some felt that the information conveyed happened informally in their areas without the need for such devices. I was less than convinced, feeling that the rejection had more to do with "not-invented-here" attitudes. Nevertheless, in the spirit of democracy, I had to resist the inclination to intervene and prescribe the model, although the temptation was certainly there! However, these other departments did adopt their own variants which all received a high level of employee satisfaction.

The purchasing department model, for example, was to meet as a group on Fridays from 9.00–10.00 without fail. The format was simple. The agenda comprised carryover items from the last meeting plus anything that others wished to raise. However, the point of departure from convention was that the chairmanship of the meeting rotated each week, the director only getting his turn when it came up. The net result was a highly satisfied and closely knit group who decided themselves what information they wanted and made sure they got it!

The above models are fairly straightforward and simply require the discipline to attend them regularly and the common sense to respond quickly to any reasonable request for information or clarification. In suitably sized functions, they have the great advantage of easily getting everybody together. Once the group size exceeds, say, 16, it was felt that some sub-division into coherent, self-recognised subgroups was necessary. The trick here is for senior functional management to ensure that they appear even-handed and give each group similar attention. However, when the department is just too big, for example in manufacturing, another model altogether is required.

There are numerous suggestions for widescale daily communication formats around today. I wouldn't want to discuss their merits and disadvantages here, as I believe you need to tailor a structure suitable for your own circumstances. The following describes how we at Leyland handled our manufacturing area, but use it only as a guide or as a reference point.

The dayshift at Leyland starts at 7.30 a.m. At this time, the manufacturing manager would meet his direct reports, the business unit managers, and a few peripheral key influencers. He would have prepared himself the night before, perhaps after attending a meeting with his peers or with his immediate boss. He would go through the priorities of the day, highlighting any events which needed care and also indicating those which needed downstream communications. This meeting would take approximately 15 to 30 minutes. The meeting would disband and then at 8.30 a.m. the business unit managers would meet their key operators (known as "team leaders" elsewhere, see Chapter 10) and appraise them of the main issues of the day. They in turn would raise and discuss problems they or other team members were encountering. Again, the meeting would last a maximum of 30 minutes. The key operators would return to their stage and appraise their colleagues to finalise the sequence. If the day's message was particularly complicated, the manufacturing manager may well have prepared a written brief as an *aide-memoire*.

This "cascade" provided an important part of the Leyland manufacturing culture. In its early days, there were lots of mistakes and the occasionally false start, but progressively things improved. The constraints of time made it important to ensure that key issues were emphasised and irrelevant items quickly discarded. The whole routine guarantees that the final interchange in the chain is the one desired by the workforce, i.e. the information flows from their preferred "conduit".

In summary, therefore, the following are the key questions to be answered in relation to satisfying the need for daily or weekly communication in your organisation:

- What formal mechanisms do you already have in place?

- How effective are they rated by the target audience?

- Do they allow for upward communication?

- How are unresolved issues handled?

- Does local supervision play a key role in final dissemination?

3. Senior Management Access

In Chapter 3, we touched on the merits of Managing By Walking About. This can be a very effective tool if carried out correctly, but getting it wrong, for example by overemphasising the negative minority, can at best neuter its benefits and at worst even cause damage. But if properly forewarned, most managers can satisfy at least one element of the requirement for *access* by routinely walking the floor and listening to the genuine concerns of the majority.

However, in many instances, what will be achieved will be little more than "flying the flag" and demonstrating a genuine interest in, and concern about, people. Whilst both are valuable and highly desirable, it isn't enough. If we genuinely want everybody in the organisation to become proactive, they have to have the opportunity for greater in-depth evaluation of the company's strategic issues. We achieved this at Leyland through "Meet the Boss" and "Meet the Team".

Many managers who come along to Optima courses find the time commitment, the regularity and the challenging nature of the proposal to be too onerous. However, I firmly believe that, done properly, "Meet the Boss/Meet the Team" can turn out to be one of the most powerful tools in your culture change armoury. It is certainly worth the effort.

The format is simple. Once or twice a week, the chief executive/managing director or equivalent goes into a room with approximately 16 chairs. Those chairs are occupied by people either selected at random from across the organisation ("Meet

the Boss") or from a specific group or team ("Meet the Team").
All are volunteers, except of course the managing director.

The latter has no formal agenda. He simply asks those present to raise any issue, frustration or criticism which may be
troubling them that day. They can raise whatever they like. In
Meet the Team sessions, the attendees often meet beforehand
to prepare questions and then put them through a spokesman to
guarantee anonymity. The MD needs then to respond and, after
replying, invites further comment to ensure the matter is answered satisfactorily. The session takes 45 minutes to an hour.

A number of Optima clients have introduced Meet the Team
at my suggestion and have rung me back after the first few
weeks in absolute horror. In many traditional, autocratic regimes, this may be the first time that the workforce has had the
opportunity to get their frustrations off their chest. It should be
no surprise therefore if you get it with both barrels. Despite
forewarning these eager change agents that the first few
months, let alone weeks, could resemble a bloodbath, the in-
tensity still comes as a major shock! The organisation has to get
comfortable with the process and it is fairly predictable that the
first phase will be littered with questions relating to the "hygiene" issues in the world of work. So you will get everybody's
pet hates on holidays, pay, pensions, as well as car parking,
canteens and, almost inevitably, the state of the toilets. Your response has to be first to listen carefully and then point out gently the proper avenue for such issues, which normally means
line management, not you! There may be longstanding subjects
where your intervention could be beneficial. But generally, be
patient, be polite and be attentive. It will pass!

Eventually, the level of debate shifts. Instead of raising the
hygiene factors, the audience progressively becomes more
concerned with higher level strategy. I used to marvel at some
of the debates I had at shopfloor level about marketing strategy, product development strategy or even corporate financing. The level of interest and enthusiasm often matched that
shown in the boardroom. And this would not be unusual. After a

couple of years, one would rarely get the minutiae from most areas but rather an intelligent discussion of the factors that really influenced the fortunes of the company.

I am a passionate advocate of Meet the Boss/Meet the Team. Spending an hour or two each week, in medium-sized organisations, is well worthwhile. In large organisations, the load needs to be spread to other influential directors. Unquestionably, the benefits are huge for such a modest investment in time. They include:

- Giving the boss a real perspective on workforce perceptions, priorities and concerns;

- Allowing regular access, at least twice a year, for every employee, to the key decision makers to discuss matters of importance;

- Establishing a greater understanding of each other's situation;

- Providing a routine safety valve on matters of potential controversy.

My advice is therefore unambiguous: give it a try for a year and you'll never look back!

4. Noticeboards

The value of noticeboards in communicating detail information is, in my view, completely overstated. At Leyland, the noticeboards were the pride and joy of the manufacturing group. They were tidy, brilliantly presented and totally false. To the outsider, particularly the visitor, things looked mighty impressive. Graphs were drawn immaculately and kept up to date, elaborate training matrices detailed the status of operator flexibility and everything was arranged in neat parallel lines and equidistantly spaced. In other words, few operators had been anywhere near the place! All the work had been done by either the business unit manager or one of his support staff. Excellent PR for visitors to the factory but hardly adding value for the manufacturing function.

In general, I find most noticeboards fall into this category or else are neglected, with out-of-date information and dog-eared posters — until, of course, the boss comes around and raises Cain. We shouldn't really be surprised. How many of us managers work in offices where our daily operating information is pinned to the wall? The only time I have been impressed by factory notice boards was on a trip to Milliken Carpets in Wigan. The notices were filthy, dog-eared and smeared. The writing was almost indecipherable, with both the grammar and spelling atrocious. But it was real! The information was up-to-date and obviously used regularly by the process team. The nature of their specific manufacturing operations made this form of measurement and presentation appropriate. That it would never win any awards from the Advertising Standards Authority is irrelevant. The key criterion was that it added value for someone.

For most operations this is not the case. Noticeboards should therefore be used only to support the idea of an "optical" factory. We all need constant reminding of our purpose, our mission and our objectives. At Leyland, after the traumas of receivership in 1993, I had large boards hung from every aisle reminding us all as we wandered around or worked in the factory. On the boards, we printed the three key core objectives of the company — one relating to financial return, one geared to what to do to avoid a repetition of receivership and the final one a blue sky ambition to ensure future viability. Noticeboards work fine in this area and they are also highly effective in promoting recognition processes. But that aside, don't waste your time!

5. Business Reviews

Many organisations rely on a quarterly or half-yearly business review as the main means of communicating to the workforce. We often find within Optima a completely distorted view of its effectiveness. On being introduced to a company, management can often wax lyrical about these elaborate routines where employees are treated to a sophisticated overview of company fortunes from the proverbial soup to the proverbial nuts. This favourable impression continues when one is shown the incredibly detailed and spectacular coloured PowerPoint packs that are used to convey the message. But then we talk to the workforce and unfortunately a completely different picture emerges.

The fancy diagrams may be appreciated and the facts understood but so often the mode of presentation causes the event to fall flat. In one company, management was mystified when a number of employees described their pride and joy as "bollocking sessions". It turned out that the production manager used the data to routinely castigate his subordinates for their continuing abject failure to perform and regularly finished by threatening Armageddon if things didn't shape up. This had gone on for years with the net effect that many people didn't even bother to turn up and the ones who did took hardly any notice. Not exactly the stuff of leading-edge communication!

Business Reviews can be a useful additional tool to paint a short, general picture of business prospects. Detail should be kept to an absolute minimum, in line with people's ability to absorb it. The key benefits are exposure of the senior decision makers to a wider audience, essential in the absence of Meet the Team/Meet the Boss, and a greater appreciation of the broad parameters of the factors impinging on the company's livelihood. But why anyone should feel the need to do this more than annually beats me. It's a very big sledgehammer, which will probably miss most of the walnuts needing cracking.

6. Other Devices

There are many other communication devices around and you must decide on their appropriateness or necessity. The only tests are whether the recipient finds it useful and whether the exercise justifies the effort. It is relatively easy to measure this effectiveness and one should do this frequently to ensure that you are not wasting your time on *any* communication activity. We in management are, sadly, past masters in self-deception. Care should be exercised to ensure that we are simply not wasting even more time.

RECOGNITION

Writing this book has given me a rare opportunity to reflect on my experiences over the past 30 years. Some of the conclusions I have reached will be viewed as subjective, with others seen as opinions, open to dispute and challenge. However, there is one issue about which I have an absolute certainty and this is:

> **Recognition systems are one of the most powerful, and least used, tools in the management armoury.**

I didn't always think so. Our attempts in the late 1980s at Leyland should have been enough to put anybody off the idea for life. Some bright spark decided that an "Employee of the Year" would be a good idea. The first successful candidate, an unassuming conscientious setter in our machine shop, had a dog's life as a result of being singled out. The lunatic fringe condemned him for being a management lackey; his immediate colleagues resented the disproportionate attention he commanded; and local supervision seemed intent on demonstrating that he didn't deserve the honour anyway. The second successful candidate left the company not too long after receiving the award. It seemed that individual recognition simply didn't work in our culture.

Team recognition was perhaps not as disastrous, but it had its moments. One key breakthrough happened in the Fabrication Shop where a team of boilermakers, hitherto not known for their co-operation, came up with a wheeze to save thousands of pounds a year. Our Dutch masters at the time had their own ideas on recognising good performance and instructed local management to reward the team in the manner established in the Netherlands. However, the boilermakers had been led to expect a microwave for their "brew" area — not an outrageous demand, you might think. Instead, imagine the scene when these horny-handed workers were confronted by a deeply embarrassed manager carrying, of all things, a tray of fairy cakes. I believe the manager is still in dispute with the company over the dry cleaning bill!

A similar lack of common sense was exhibited each year in the selection of the company Christmas gift. Whilst a classy portable barbecue might have gone down well with the outdoor lifestyle of the Dutch, it was certainly inappropriate to the workers at our Albion plant on the Clyde. A great majority of the latter apparently lived in tenement flats in Glasgow where the opportunities for lighting a barbecue were limited, to say the least. Word has it that the skips placed on the way out of the plant were full to bursting that day with metal grills, the plastic case being retained as a lunch box.

Even worse, the same demented selection process the following year came up with garden lamps, fuelled by methylated spirits. It was rumoured that our Glaswegian colleagues threw out the lamps and drank the fluid — but I'm sure that was a bit of mischievousness on the part of their English colleagues!

It was therefore no surprise that my colleagues and I were more than a little sceptical about formal recognition routines. We had, of course, read the books which extolled their virtues with great enthusiasm. But they were all American texts and, as we all know, America is a foreign country with an alien culture, much different to us reserved Brits. In the mid-1980s, with the introduction of a Crosby-based Total Quality Management programme, we had flirted with his ideas on recognition but without success. We found them too "in your face", with too much razzmatazz for the northwestern personality. We became embarrassed about the whole affair and felt that the only end products were jealousy and envy. In short, not suitable for the more introspective British worker.

However, as we progressed down the Team Enterprise road, we began to notice that there was something fundamental missing. As we attempted to shift workplace motivation away from simple monetary interest and job security into areas such as pride, self-esteem and straightforward satisfaction, it was evident that management needed devices to acknowledge progress. In short, we lacked the recognition processes we had so disparaged earlier. But as these had all failed in the past, we had to go back to first principles and work out where things had gone wrong.

The culture of our workforce, as has been said many times already in this book, was certainly not conducive to a textbook approach on recognition. We had too much resentment, too much mistrust and too much hostility for these classic mechanisms to work. The centre of our own particular universe was the shopfloor, where culture dictated the atmosphere in the rest of the company. To be successful, we had to find ways to improve the empathy between the trackworker and the company. This wasn't going to be easy.

"Hello?" — Individual Recognition

Once we started to analyse the situation, however, we became almost instantly aware of the profound forces at work engendering this negative atmosphere. Take, for example, someone working on a stage on the conveyor belt for the first time — someone who was newly recruited into the company and therefore without the scepticism and cynicism which seemed to bite in within weeks! Coming towards him is the business unit manager who hired him. Seeing a familiar face in this sea of strangers, he shouts out a greeting. However, the manager is preoccupied. His first job in the morning has to be to quickly count heads to ensure that we have enough people to run the tracks. He is therefore counting and counting quickly. He has no time for pleasantries and swiftly carries on, totting up the numbers.

The effect on our newcomer is somewhat sobering. He might even try it again the following day but, if he does, he won't do it again. He retires to his shell, convinced that here the workers are very small cogs in a very big wheel. He is a worker, not an individual with a personality.

When we explored this proposition, we found scores of other situations where local management simply didn't acknowledge the presence of others. Perhaps it was the pressures of time, perhaps it was characteristic of all factories with moving conveyors, but either way, we had created a huge impersonal vacuum where one existed as a worker, not as a person. We probably gave the mobile cranes more attention.

The problem was mainly down to local management behaviour rather than that of the senior team, which probably accounts for the latter being so unaware of its ramifications. However, I wouldn't want to single out the former here as being totally culpable. We should have known and we should have done something about it earlier.

We started immediately discussing the importance of interpersonal relationships in the workplace with the business management team. In particular, the importance of a simple "Hello" or "Good Morning" each day. We even persuaded Cranfield School of Technology to lay on a five-day training course for us, one key element being awareness training in this very area.

And this was just "Hello". Can you imagine how difficult "Thank You" was? It struck me that if we had caused so much damage by not acknowledging the presence of our workforce, how much more had we done by not acknowledging their efforts? How could we expect people to give more, to daily challenge the status quo and to stretch their imagination and creativity if we didn't tell them that we valued their contribution? The implications were frightening. We had to create an ethos of appreciation, quickly.

I am, by nature, impatient. Whilst I was prepared to spend time cajoling my colleagues into doing more in this direction, I wanted a quick reassurance that they were really changing their behaviour and not merely paying lip service to the latest Oliver flavour of the month. The following really does illustrate both the limitation of our ambitions and the slowness of the shopfloor culture to change. I arranged for something we termed "Informal Individual Recognition Tokens" to be purchased. Our first was a plastic travelling clock, made in Taiwan, costing all of £2.10 and embossed with a Leyland Quality logo. I called the middle managers in and instructed them to distribute these tokens to 25 per cent of the working population over the next year. In other words, within the next 12 months, I wanted each manager to identify where 25 in every 100 of the people who reported to them had done something above and beyond the usual call of duty. They would in turn give the recipient one of these fine examples of Taiwanese engineering as a simple "thank you" for their efforts.

There are two things to note here. First, the paucity of our ambition. From a standing start where virtually no one received any gratitude from management at all, perhaps 25 per cent of the population doing so in any one year may have been a significant improvement. But in relation to a healthy situation where this should be happening probably a hundred times more, this is, in hindsight, acutely embarrassing.

But it's where we were, so I can't change that. Second, the value of the token was incidental. We have found throughout our explorations into the practical world of recognition that monetary reward is a totally ineffective means of motivating people, as we shall see later. The fact that the clock cost £2 or £20 was irrelevant, the benefit was in the physical act of a manager expressing gratitude. A feeling of worth was our desired reward, not a financial trade-off.

It took a full four to five years to make the simplest act of recognition, saying Thank You, totally acceptable at Leyland. There is no evidence anymore of cynicism or jealousy or envy. Just a nice warm glow at being appreciated. I would not hazard a guess at how much that's worth to the bottom line, but it must be considerable. Certainly it's more than worth the hassle and the effort.

Today, individual recognition is a much more relaxed affair. We still have recognition tokens, the latest being a Leyland quartz clock which looks rather splendid, despite costing less than £3. But tokens only play one part in a healthy spectrum. People are now much more comfortable with giving, and receiving, a simple thank you. Familiarity has certainly not bred complacency but more a sense of unity. One device we "borrowed" from a visit to Milliken Carpets was the Thank You Card. This is a purpose-designed card which looks like a birthday card except it says "Thank You" on the front and inside has space to say who it's to, who it's from and why it's being sent. These are available to everyone.

To summarise, individual recognition should be part of the culture. Informal recognition, defined in Leyland's Guide to Team Enterprise manual as *the acknowledgement of individual presence, role and contribution* should be a major part of every managerial portfolio. Employees should be encouraged wherever possible to see themselves as *significant* contributors to functional, multi-functional and company-wide teams. The most effective form of individual recognition is shown by experience to be a simple "thank you", but tokens, flowers for inconvenienced partners or thank you cards can be used very effectively, alongside probably hundreds of other devices. The key is to emphasise the sentiment, not the value.

Team Recognition

The saga of individual recognition at Leyland may have put you off going down this road. That would be a mistake. Individual recognition is difficult, but it is a vital part of establishing the correct culture. Team recognition for similar reasons is also important, but the good news is that this is much easier. We were often mystified why our approach as teams seem to work so well and yet we struggled at an individual level. I am sure that the psychologists will have a reason for it; perhaps the security of being in a group overcomes a lot of the personal concerns of being "exposed" individually.

Having said it's easier than individual recognition, one must also counsel that it is not too difficult to get it just as wrong as well! Perhaps the following description of our experience at Leyland might help.

The first danger, as with all other forms of recognition, is placing too high a perceived value on the reward for a deserving team. Looking back on the story earlier about the boilermaker team's hopes for a microwave, actually satisfying their expectations may well have been an equally big mistake. Other groups could react adversely, particularly if they think that the achievements have been overblown. Attracting controversy here satisfies no-one. It will damage the concept, damage inter-team relationships and ultimately damage the group. Perhaps the right course of action would have been to dampen down expectations before the fairy cakes arrived! My belief is that the effort should go into the recognition process rather than the value of the token. We are trying to awaken collective pride, a feeling of achievement and a healthy camaraderie. Throwing as much money as you like at it will never achieve these ends.

At a very early stage, we decided that we wanted to encourage the formation of effective multi-functional teams — teams which would come together either under management direction or, even better, spontaneously, to solve a problem and then disband. Each quarter we asked for nominations from the management group for examples that had exceeded the usual bounds of duty and achieved an exceptional outcome. We would then evaluate the contribution of each using a predetermined set of criteria. The criteria would include:

- Clear objectives and agreed goals

- Clear evidence of achievement

- The extent of multi-functional involvement

- The use of company-prescribed problem-solving techniques

- Teamworking in the group

- Indicators of behaviour "beyond the call of duty", and so on.

A small committee, including myself, was formed to undertake this quarterly review. At the end of the evaluation, each team would be formally recognised by the presentation of a certificate with the "best" team having their name inserted on a shield, as well as receiving their own certificate.

Due to the numbers involved, we kept the recognition ceremonies brief and simple. Participants from the teams were invited to a lunch where a brief description of the project was given by the managing director or equivalent. The teams would then step forward to receive their certificate and a photograph taken to mark the occasion. These photographs would be plastered all over special notice boards in the middle of the factory. Descriptions of their achievements would be written up in the *Weekly Brief* so that everyone could hear about them.

Occasionally a celebrity might visit the plant and we rarely missed the opportunity to incorporate the inevitable guided tour with a recognition ceremony. At the end of the VIP's tour, we would assemble every employee in a part of the factory big enough to hold a stage. After a few brief speeches, we would invite each qualifying group to step forward and receive their certificate from, amongst others, Prince Charles, John Major and Michael Heseltine. The distinction of being applauded as a team in front of all their workmates seemed to be highly satisfying to most participants. It was definitely chest out, head up in a display of pride and personal achievement which I always found inspirational. Throw in the glamour of a visiting VIP with the sense of ceremony, and the feelings of achievement were enhanced.

Suggestion Schemes: Every Little Counts

So we have individual recognition and we have team recognition. Is this enough, we asked ourselves? It isn't. Both these ideas have management influence and control at their core. We may ask for nominations for teams from peer groups but we know that this will be the exception rather than the rule. Individuals and team recognition only work if all management levels engage proactively and lead the initiatives. This need for management action could therefore be seen as a constraint. Success would be a function of management effort or management interest. To create the organisation we aspired to, we needed another mechanism which *employees* could control. Something to enable them to contribute, irrespective of management intervention or interest.

To a certain extent, our ambition to have spontaneous, multi-functional teams at the heart of the organisation forming automatically as problems arose met this requirement. But only in part. We needed a much bigger-scale initiative, which would characterise this spirit of ongoing individual contribution.

The textbooks pointed to suggestion schemes, but we'd had enough of them. No matter how sophisticated or enticing the system, suggestion schemes at Leyland had always ended in vast unmanageable bureaucracies or employee indignation or both. And the more we looked elsewhere, the less convinced we were of ever finding a suitable model.

Once we reached this conclusion, we decided to go back to first principles and ask ourselves what we really wanted from suggestion schemes. We concluded that what we wanted was simply *suggestions* and *ideas*! We were not overly concerned about cost reduction, quality improvements or higher productivity in the first instance here. If we got the ideas generation right, then those would surely follow. Since ideas generation is surely a reflection of motivation, then the more ideas, the greater the reflected motivation. Our real ambition was to create a veritable snowstorm of ideas floating around the organisation, which could be used to trigger a chain of bigger and better improvement activity.

If we were correct, then perhaps all we needed to concentrate on was ways and means of motivating our workforce to come up with loads of ideas on a regular basis. It also seemed eminently sensible to reward at the point of submission rather than implementation, as the latter could be so long coming. And wherever possible, we should involve the initiator in the development of any idea requiring further work.

This is how the Every Little Counts (ELC) scheme was born. It is a very simple scheme, arranged in three easy stages:

1. An employee thinks up an idea and fills in an ELC form, which is printed in duplicate.

2. They submit the form to their manager. If the manager accepts that the idea, however trivial, has been submitted in a spirit of constructive support, a £1 voucher for Argos or Marks and Spencer will be handed over. This is the formal "thank you".

3. The idea is either:

   ♦ Given back to the initiator who is told to investigate it further or to simply get on with it, or

   ♦ Given back to the initiator alongside support for further investigation or implementation, or

   ♦ If the idea has nothing to do with the initiator's range of responsibilities, it is passed on to the appropriate department. A first response is expected within 48 hours.

The reward system for an ELC is symbolic. The £1 value of the token is incidental; it is just a means of expressing gratitude, of saying thank you. Some companies after a visit to Leyland have been so impressed by Every Little Counts that they have adopted a version for their own use. However, inexplicably, they have increased the token to £5, where the financial value now becomes perceived in the organisation as significant. The objective of the scheme therefore becomes once again maximisation of earnings. And so the cycle of decline, of jealousy, envy and sheer self-interest begins again. To nobody's benefit.

The £1 has been chosen deliberately so that nobody is going to view the financial reward as anything other than incidental. At Toyota in Japan, I believe, they simply give out a few yen for each idea so that the financial considerations are minimal and all the emphasis is on appreciation and gratitude. There are no significant rewards to be had further down the line under the ELC scheme. An idea might save £40,000 per annum, as happened with a suggestion to improve the packaging of an export product. Another saved £1,000,000 in inventory costs. However, the value of the saving bears no relation to the recognition. All ideas are equal under Every Little Counts if they have been offered constructively with good intent.

There is, however, a bit of fun downstream. The Every Little Counts initiative is managed by a committee operated mainly by shopfloor and general staff representatives. They are charged with:

- Maintaining the volume of ideas

- Improving the average quality of ideas year on year

- Keeping the whole theme fun and enjoyable.

In turn, a budget of about £30,000 per annum is given to them to achieve these objectives and, of course, to pay for the tokens. One of their more successful innovations was to pick, each quarter, the best five ideas across the company. The winners are then invited to a local hostelry where a dinner-dance is held. Food and drink are provided in abundance so the participants can enjoy themselves with abandon, usually without the prying eyes of any management being present. The only stipulation made is that someone takes a camera and places the resultant pictures on a special display just inside the factory. This, incidentally, appears to be the most popular noticeboard in the company!

As was stated earlier, for the past seven years or so, Leyland has averaged 22 ideas per employee per annum. We don't aspire to any more as we don't think we can handle them. Of course, there will be the occasional criticisms and abuses, but care has to be taken not to come down with a heavy hand. It is best, in most instances, to seek guidance from the committee. They will usually sort matters out!

I am often asked how much we save each year on our ideas generation scheme. People are taken aback when I say I don't have a clue and have no intention of finding out. To do so would undermine the whole foundation of the programme. Our objective is to motivate everybody in the organisation to constantly challenge the status quo. The one single measure I do insist upon is counting the number of ideas. As long as we continue with 20–22 ideas per employee per annum, I am content, because I know that all the other benefits, such as cost reductions, quality improvements and so on will flow automatically. Measuring these absolute benefits would result in bureaucracy, which in turn would kill the spirit of the scheme. Have faith; it really does work!

There are probably many other aspects of recognition systems which we haven't covered in this brief overview. My advice is just to keep looking and seek best practice elsewhere. Try not to reinvent wheels. Best practice probably results from years of trial and error, so it's best not to replicate mistakes. Make sure that recognition is kept at the top of the management agenda. I chaired the three-man Recognition Committee for my entire duration at Leyland Trucks. It's that important. And never forget that you are dealing here with motivation, pure and simple. Lose sight of that and you'll lose the plot completely.

CHAPTER 8

TEAM ENTERPRISE IN ACTION: ORGANISATION DESIGN

In Chapter 3, "Six Pitfalls of Team Enterprise", we emphasised how Team Enterprise is mostly about cultural change rather than systems or structural change. Here we are going to discuss a subject which more than any other is purely identified with the latter. Examining the "organisation" from a cultural perspective will, in most instances, result in some significant alterations to existing structures. Unfortunately, we cannot avoid that if we are to achieve our objective of an effective Team Enterprise. It will not be surprising if most readers are by now groaning, or if they aren't, they jolly well should be! I suspect that most of us in business, commerce or even government could write a book on the subject — or more appropriately, a book on how *not* to do it. My heart sinks when I hear companies announce, "We are delighted to announce the following organisational changes . . .". Rarely is anybody delighted apart from the corporate bureaucrats who fashioned the initiative. The rest of us fear the worst and usually get it.

The following must therefore be read with caution. Perhaps I should stamp every page with a warning:

> **Remember, changing your organisation can damage your health, and a lot more besides!**

We will discuss three areas of restructuring:

- Macro-organisation change

- Micro-organisation change

- Project organisation change.

In each, we will strongly counsel that the problem be approached slowly and deliberately. With the first, changes in the basic framework of the company which we have termed the "macro-organisation", we urge you to proceed at a rate no faster than *dead slow*. With the second, which examines the ramifications for structures at the base of the organisational pyramid, you might be able to go a little faster, but not much! Project structures are more relaxed affairs but still need caution and deliberation. All three are areas where we want to get our thinking right first time if we can. We will not be perfect; there are too many variables at work here, but we must ensure that the general fabric of our final recommendation is sound enough not to necessitate anything other than minor adjustment after implementation.

THE MACRO-ORGANISATION: THE PROBLEM

Traditional organisation structures are not compatible with the fundamental philosophies of involvement and participation. If one takes an extreme example — how extreme I'll leave you to judge — such as the Leyland Trucks manufacturing organisation in the 1970s, the weaknesses are self-evident. Ultimate responsibility would rest with the managing director. However, he would have little to do with day-to-day matters, as this task would rest with his works director. But between the works director and one of the poor chaps at the sharp end, there would be no less than six intervening levels. And this does not include the pseudo-supervisory roles, at least as perceived by the operator, of the setter and the inspector. The average shop floor worker's shoulders must have been very bruised carrying this lot!

Such structures have a number of inherent weaknesses, and these are described in the following pages.

The organisation might be the problem!

Suppose an executive near the top of his complex pyramid — either the managing director or the works director — attends a Tom Peters seminar or similar and becomes totally convinced of the merits of an empowered organisation. Now fired and enthused, he goes back to his company, gets his management team around him and excitedly evangelises the new revolution. Conscious of the need to set an example, he hurriedly devolves himself of lots of responsibilities which, in the past, he had jealously kept to himself. His management team are discharged with a strong admonition to do likewise.

However, his direct reports didn't have the pleasure of several days in the guru's company and have to satisfy themselves with a copy of the video or one of his books. Understandably, therefore, the urge to delegate is less emphatic. But the boss says "Empower", so that's exactly what they do but without the clear enthusiasm of their superior.

Down the organisation goes the instruction. However, none of the intervening layers have had the opportunity to attend a seminar, or study the book and video, so the only motivation is senior management instruction. As the message progresses, it gets weaker in both theory and practice. At the bottom of the pyramid, the shopfloor and general office see only drip-feed and tokenism. It makes little sense and the initiative simply drifts away.

However, it can and often does get worse. The man at the top suddenly realises the need to communicate, so that's what he does with gusto. The company magazines, newspapers or even videos are full of him chattering excitedly about this brave new world which is happening, as he speaks, all around them. The mystified workforce glance around, see nothing different and mutter darkly about the ignorance or worse of their leader.

There is little doubt that a multi-tiered organisation will constrain empowerment due, if nothing else, to the physical barriers of management hierarchy. The more levels you have, the more difficult it is going to be to create an effective Team Enterprise. Within Leyland, we coined Oliver's Law (Poskett had one, so why shouldn't I!) which stated:

> **The effectiveness of empowerment is inversely proportional to the number of management levels in the organisation.**

If you therefore have an organisation that is based on traditional hierarchical principles, you have a simple choice to make. Either stay as you are or, if you wish to develop a Team Enterprise, start flattening the pyramid!

There is only so much delegation to go around!

If one examines how organisations develop in the first place, the key factors for expansion are usually activity level and the need to control. Most traditional models take their cue from autocratic, Tayloristic regimes where control is effected by management. As one tier of management outstrips their capability, usually described by a theoretical span of control, then another is added to maintain the equilibrium. Eventually, the classic pyramid emerges, characterised by a high number of managerial echelons and these closely defined and restricted spans of control (Figure 11).

However, these structures are self-justifying and self-sustaining, even when workloads shrink. Intermediate management levels will simply absorb more decision-making and become increasingly bureaucratic as their most precious resource, their own availability of time, needs to be satisfied. Such organisations will be characterised by lots and lots of meetings, numerous reports, painfully slow decision-making and a general inertia. Ring any bells yet?

Figure 11: Traditional Pyramid Structure and Added Value

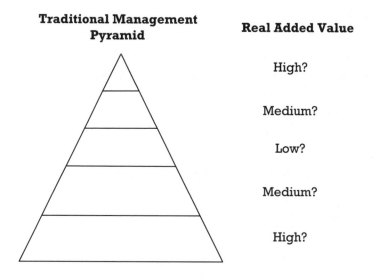

If, however, we do indeed change the philosophy of the organisation and adopt a Team Enterprise approach, we need to introduce two basic principles: the maximisation of effective delegation and an emphasis on added value. The only constraint to delegation should be capability. If someone can be trained or developed to undertake responsibility in the short term, then immediate plans should be put in place to do just that. Medium- and longer-term possibilities should also be investigated for action later on.

The act of delegation will release huge tranches of non-value-added activity. All those seemingly important management meetings will now be redundant. The interminable reviews, reports, agendas and so on will likewise disappear, as they and delegation are mutually exclusive. The net effect is that the mid-ranks of the management hierarchy will have nothing to do. However, given the organisation's infinite ability to invent new, non-beneficial activities, unless the profile is restructured, you'll end up with the added value profile of Figure 11. The only answer is to progressively flatten the pyramid as the opportunity is released.

The view from the bottom of a traditional pyramid can be very cloudy!

Sitting at the bottom of a traditional hierarchy can be a confusing experience. The ability of the various elements of the pyramid to establish their own indispensability by creating mystique about their purpose and by developing major edifices of self-protectionism is well known. For someone in line management who has to make scores of decisions each day in the tightest of timeframes, this opacity can be confusing, restricting and generally very frustrating! In the late 1970s, for example, I was put in charge of the company's component operations, a huge mishmash of fabricating, forging, machining and assembly. The operation had been the poorest performer within the Truck and Bus empire for donkeys' years. Industrial relations were dreadful, as the area became dominated by Luddite shop stewards who controlled the shop with cynicism, hostility and not a little mischief. It was obvious to me that using this group as the key conduit of communication between management and shopfloor was worse than futile. Not only were the messages not getting through, completely different agendas were being created which had nothing in common with the real needs of the company.

I decided therefore to bypass the shop stewards and communicate directly myself, using, at first, a written brief. The initial reactions from the shopfloor, and even some of the more reasonable representatives, were very positive. They valued the directness and the immediacy of the contact, which could be reinforced on my constant MBWA. However, I was quite staggered to be called in at a very senior level by corporate personnel who informed me in no uncertain terms that I was trespassing on their turf. They made it clear that, first, only they had the competence to communicate, line management apparently not having the subtlety to understand the nuances of trades union issues. And second, even more emphatically, that if I continued I'd be out of a job!

This is not an unusual situation, although it may be extreme. The point here is simply that we cannot expect people at the lowest echelons of the organisation to make more of their own decisions and to act in a more proactive fashion if they feel surrounded by confusion, uncertainty and bureaucracy. Unfortunately, traditional management hierarchies all eventually gravitate to this state.

The Macro-organisation: The Solution?

The good news is that the solution is self-evident and well proven. The bad news is that the transitional process from old to new is fraught with difficulty and needs to be handled with kid gloves to be effective. The prospect of insidious internal subversion may sound dramatic but it can be absolutely crippling if it is allowed to materialise.

Theoretically, the solution comprises three elements. First, we delegate responsibilities as far as we can practically do so. Second, we enlarge managerial spans of control so that each manager can have greater control and influence within their own patch. And third, we flatten the pyramid to reflect the realities of the new situation.

Our end objective in any sizeable operation (say 250–750 employees) should be to have no more than two managerial layers between the key decision-maker (the MD, the board or the site director) and the shopfloor and general office. The very act of restructuring releases lots of the non-value-added activity described earlier. After all, there is little point in having a management meeting if there are no other managers to talk to! But be prepared for the consequences. At Leyland, moving to delayered structures took out 42 per cent of all senior and middle management positions within two years. Within four years, the number had risen to 56 per cent. In other words, for the same deliverables, only 44 managers out of every 100 remained after just four years. The problems in transition are therefore fairly self-evident if you have the sort of traditional structure that we at Leyland inherited. Nevertheless, the financial attractions, as well as all the benefits of increased efficiency, are equally obvious. The temptation to rush things may prove irresistible.

But it must be resisted. There are many examples of delayering where the blunt application of the theoretical resulted in horrendous repercussions as the business fabric was damaged and management morale badly holed. Some companies saw no alternative but to reverse the process, losing credibility and money in equal measure. How you should go about it depends on your own situation. If your business is suffering short-term dislocation due to unaffordable overheads, you will have to move quickly. If you are in steady-state and looking to progressively improve margins and profits, then a more cautious approach may be beneficial. Within Optima, we would suggest the following seven-stage process:

- **Stage 1: Evaluate the Need**. Review your business structure, margins, profitability, etc., against stakeholder/shareholder requirements and benchmark best practice. Establish a timeframe for change, recognising that a longer implementation process is likely to be less risky and more robust.

- **Stage 2: Evaluate the Desired End Product**. Take a view of the "ideal" shape of your business, post-implementation of Team Enterprise. Working from a zero base, use best practice elsewhere to build a model reflecting your aspirations.

- **Stage 3: Compare the "Ideal" with Current Reality**. Quantify the potential savings available to you if you can achieve your aspirational model. This will help you "sell" the exercise upstairs and keep you motivated when things get tricky. Follow this by examining the key bottlenecks in getting to the ideal.

- **Stage 4: Draw Up a Plan, Including Timescales**. This depends on the outcome of Stage 1. If things are serious, then you may have to go big-bang. If not, you can construct an "aspirational plan" where you define the shape of things to come but you consciously take your time and wait for opportunities to implement the programme in sections. Decide how to communicate your intentions. Include in your plan a detailed proposal of what, how and when you intend to communicate.

- **Stage 5: Implement the Plan**. This stage includes communication, training, education, redeployment, succession planning, redundancy and, where appropriate, piloting.

- **Stage 6: Monitor and Review**. A vitally important stage which is often missed out. There is no merit in the common practice of "allowing the organisation to find its own feet". Establish an effective Steering Group which includes a hefty representation of line management.

- **Stage 7: Change the Plan!** Accept from the outset that you will not have all the detail right, even if the principles are pretty untouchable. Be prepared to change based on experience and let your subordinates appreciate that this is not a mistake-intolerant zone.

Redeployment of surplus resource is a key concern. Optima, for example, arose from an appreciation that the sizeable human resource function that had served Leyland so well had outlived its usefulness. When the opportunity emerged to develop a new added-value stream, as described earlier, the ideas, resource and motivation were all in place. The net result is a win–win outcome all round. The company benefits in many ways from having Optima and the employees gain not just from job security but also from the tremendous intellectual satisfaction of building a reputation for excellence in the world outside the factory gates. Had we not been open-minded or prepared, perhaps the opportunity may have sailed by. Thinking laterally and positively can often have huge benefits.

In summary, the attractions of delayering the macro-organisation are often simply irresistible. The end product, if you get there, is a streamlined lean machine where involvement and empowerment flourish. The journey is not an easy one, but for many companies, it remains the best opportunity for medium-term profit improvement.

THE MICRO-ORGANISATION: THE PROBLEM

The objective of the micro-organisation in Team Enterprise is, as stated before, *to provide the wherewithal for every single person in the organisation to make their own decisions.* To achieve this, it is management's task to ensure that any constraints or bottlenecks are removed, thus enabling devolved decision-making to be carried out effectively. One significant obstacle can be the design of the organisation itself.

Let's examine the dilemma of "Fred" in a fictitious but unfortunately fairly typical brownfield operation (any resemblance to Leyland here being purely deliberate!). Fred is a conscientious soul who, like so many of his colleagues, actually gets enormous satisfaction from getting the job right. Despite all the turmoil in the workplace, Fred's first loyalty is to the customer and, irrespective of causality, Fred endeavours to ensure that all defects are rectified before his bit of the product is despatched. Fred's job is a straightforward assembly operation. One day he finds himself short of components. He does some basic investigative work but is unable to establish that the problem lies with the design of the job as described and prescribed by the planning department. The production planner, perhaps in a rush to finish one busy Friday afternoon, has designated the component to be one-off when it should have been four-off. Accordingly, Fred is not only short of components, having only a quarter of the necessary quantity; he is also short of time. The system demands that the industrial engineering synthetic standards are derived from the Planning Sheet and hence Fred is only given 25 per cent of the appropriate time to do the job.

Fred is therefore struggling. As well as the component shortage — which he partially resolves by badgering the storekeeper to give him more despite the computer — he is now having difficulty in keeping up with the job. He tells his chargehand, who realises immediately that it could be serious, so he in turn tells the foreman. The latter reacts quickly. He instructs the storekeeper to quadruple the supply of the offending components to the line and tells Fred to do his best while he sorts the job out. The short-term fix is in place, even if it does require Fred perspiring more than normal. Recognising that there could be difficulties to come later if the root cause isn't resolved, the foreman puts it in his report to his boss, the senior foreman.

The senior foreman meanwhile is handling dozens of shortages and a similar number of quality problems and manning imbalances. Fred's little problem at least has a fix, so it's not the top priority on today's agenda. He waits until the following day's production meeting before he informs the works superintendent. He in turn reacts aggressively and bawls out the production control representative for yet another example of their gross inefficiency. This escalates to the logistics manager who gets the system checked and takes great delight in informing the works superintendent that the shop control processes are working exactly to the computer instructions, and he makes sure that the production manager knows as well. Tempers become frayed.

The whole vexed issue bounces around the organisation until the stores department finally runs out of components and assembled units begin to come off the production line incomplete. This is now very serious and the production director gets involved. He eventually establishes that the planning of the job is the real culprit and launches into a fierce verbal attack on the planning director. He in turn drags in his direct report, the planning manager and rails at him. Ultimately, the problem comes to the notice of a red-faced planner who takes all of 90 seconds to fix the problem, permanently.

The foregoing can take days or even weeks, depending on the degree of disruption. The reason it takes so long is that communication on vexatious issues follows the organisation chart, up the production ladder until it is eventually transferred across to the support function. And then down the support function ladder all the way to Eric, the planner. Sometimes the response has to follow the same tortuous process, in reverse.

Now Fred, to his knowledge, has never met Eric. Planners to Fred are those office-wallahs who live a quarter of a mile away in that plush office block furnished even better than his front room at home. And he's never seen any of them sweat like he had to on that job! But the quickest way to resolve the problem would have been to have Eric talk directly to Fred or vice versa. The issues would have been sorted in minutes, not days.

If this were an isolated example, this wouldn't matter. But these minor disruptions occur all the time in busy workshop or office functions and affect all the support activities. Just imagine the non-value-added activity generated as a result of aggregating the entirety of these issues. It is colossal. Delayering the organisation would help to an extent, but it's not enough. What we need is a supportive micro-organisation which allows the Freds, the Erics, the Janes and the Bobs to investigate and resolve such minor issues themselves without having to resort to higher management.

Business Units

At Leyland, we had suffered from these issues for years. I well remember running a sizeable operation (500+ employees) as production manager. My support staff, who did not report to me but instead to my functional equivalents, lived up to three miles away. For the production engineers or planners to visit my shop, they had to catch the 9.30 a.m. taxi, which got them to me just before 10.00 a.m. At 11.20 a.m., they had to get their taxi back for lunch. The same process happened in the afternoon. My "envelope" for access was less than three hours a day. And we wonder why we had problems!

By 1989, a lot of these issues had been resolved. We had partially delayered and we had situated the support functions more conveniently. But the characteristics of Fred's problem noted earlier were visible in abundance. Something radical was needed to overturn the horrendous inefficiencies of the workplace.

Our old organisation model, in relation to manufacturing, was basically as shown in Figure 12.

Figure 12: The "Traditional" Organisation (1989)

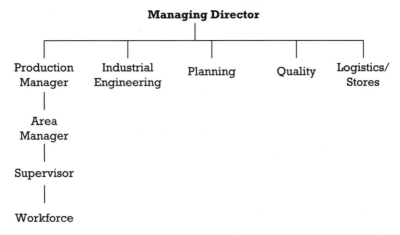

We decided on two fundamental changes: the introduction of teams and "business units".

The idea of business units was simple. Based on the belief noted earlier that the most efficient location for problem-solving was at the workplace itself, we began to restructure around that process rather than functionality. This necessitated a representative from each of the relevant support activities being placed permanently with each significant production entity, the newly termed "business unit". They would be positioned on the shopfloor alongside the workforce and work exactly the same shift pattern. If the tracks ran, then they'd be there! We also expanded the range of responsibilities of the old area managers and made them accountable for all the day-today activities that impacted on production. They became Business Unit Managers. This resulted in an unfortunate acronym that needs no elaboration here!

Our new organisation chart is shown in Figure 13.

Figure 13: The New Structure (1991–93)

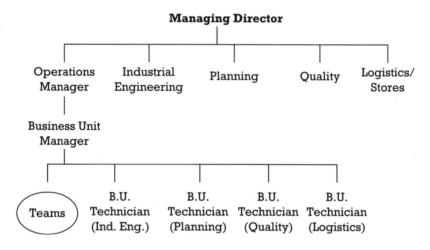

As this was new territory to all of us at Leyland, our level of confidence in its success was not high. We therefore persuaded each of the support functions to "donate" three likely candidates temporarily to the three new business units. All agreed willingly, aside from the industrial engineering manager, who was concerned, and quite rightly, at the size of his ongoing workload. The idea of losing three of his key people to go and "play" with manufacturing, to quote him at the time, did not particularly appeal. However, we persuaded him to take a watching brief for three months to see if it worked. Only then would we revisit residual manning levels.

We eventually got our "volunteers" and they were sent on a training programme designed to equip them for this new world. We did not immediately leap into autonomous work groups in one bold step, but instead adopted a halfway house where supervisory–subordinate ratios were reduced threefold. Within a few weeks, the experiment was underway. Its introduction was characterised by a surprising lack of issues. Nobody complained, nobody seemed to struggle. The shopfloor, always cautious if not cynical about management-inspired change, adjusted to the new arrangements very comfortably. There was little or nothing to report.

The Results

Progressively, a noticeable improvement in performance ensued. The absence of the usual knockabout, internecine strife soon seemed to be taken for granted. I began to get worried because there didn't seem anything to worry about! However, after a couple of months, the industrial engineering manager asked to talk to me about his manning levels. Not being the best of listeners, I quickly assumed he was campaigning for his replacements, so I immediately put my foot down and told him the three months wasn't up yet. There could be no question of headcount review until we understood the full ramifications of our new structure.

He persisted. He didn't want to talk about increased *headcount* but merely to pass on some observations. At the start of the process he had ten engineers who were fully stretched. With three disappearing to manufacturing, he anticipated a significant overload for his seven remaining staff. However, the reverse had happened. He was now running *short* of work. We puzzled but couldn't work it out. There had been no significant changes in new product development, engineering change or any of the other key drivers to justify a *reduction* in workload. The planning manager was called in and asked for his observations and he reported the same phenomenon. As did the quality manager.

It seemed that the workload of the support functions depended in no small part on problems being raised from the shopfloor. As these wound their way through even our new delayered hierarchy, they gained in complexity. Meetings, reports, minutes and so on all generated a hefty workload. However, with the new business unit organisation, apparently a sizeable majority of these problems (estimated by some at 80 per cent) were now sorted out between the operator and the new business unit technicians without the intervention of any third party and without too much in the way of paperwork!

The key benefits of the approach appear to be:

- It provides the wherewithal for people to make their own decisions in an informed way.

- It promotes multifunctional teamwork, right across the organisation, by setting an example at the "sharp" end.

- It destroys huge tranches of non-value-added activity.

- It makes manufacturing a more attractive place to work for aspirant young people as a greater variety of positions are now available. Visibility is high.

- It improves problem resolution time very significantly.

- It helps erode the "us and them" attitude that exists in most conventional manufacturing areas.

For Leyland, therefore, the adoption of a business unit approach has been highly successful and continues to be so after ten or more years. For you, this model may not be appropriate. I certainly wouldn't automatically recommend this approach to other manufacturers, let alone other businesses or institutions. But the principles are transferable. You have to ask yourself if the design of your organisation at the coal-face, whether that be your general office or your service deliverers, is sufficiently flexible to allow people both the inclination and the resources to make their own decisions. If this answer is no, as I suspect it will be to some degree in all non-Team Enterprise organisations, then the basic principles embodied in the business unit model should be able to guide you to a better framework.

THE PROJECT ORGANISATION

For a Team Enterprise to be truly effective, an extensive multi-functional project ethos needs to be in place. This may not have the immediacy of the other two forms of organisation discussed earlier, but it does not lessen its importance. A well-designed project infrastructure will both break down the natural tendency of organisations to succumb to excessive functionalism, otherwise known as the "silo effect", and will improve added value by tracking processes rather than functions.

Multifunctionalism

Some might argue that this is best addressed by structuring the whole organisation around processes or by a hybrid, matrix edifice. However, one of the basic requirements of any model, in our experience, is that it should be clearly comprehensible to everybody in the company. The designs I have seen using this more radical approach usually fail heavily here. We have seen segmented concentric circles, three dimensional spheres and complex interwoven ladder frames which might be as clear as day to their designers but they mystified me! Even if the poor participants managed to understand its features on day one, there is every chance they'd get totally lost downstream. So whilst I firmly believe that people have to follow *processes* across the organisation, I think this can best be achieved by focusing on *behaviour* rather than company *structure*. In many respects the "70 per cent culture, 30 per cent structure" argument equally applies here. We want to establish the habits and attitudes within the company to take us down the path of multi-functionalism rather than rely on impersonal organisational models.

If the recommendations suggested in Chapter 6 are adopted and a Culture Change Steering Committee established, one of its first tasks must be to establish the concept of working *across* departments as a natural means of solving problems. It is vitally important that all senior management plus any functional heads not represented on this body are both fully conversant and committed to this philosophy. There is going to be enough difficulty with middle management worrying about others trespassing on their hallowed turf without concerning ourselves about those at the top. Even moderate levels of protectionism or self-preservation will destroy any hope of creating the right ethos, so have your antennae finely tuned to open or surreptitious hostility. This isn't as easy as it seems. As we often find when Optima goes through its Change Initiation Process, every manager we talk to seems to be convinced that they themselves are totally open-minded and open-armed! Whether they are deluding themselves or trying to delude us is never very clear. But the fact remains: such errant management behaviour is invariably the key obstacle to progress.

Step-by-step Approach

If your organisation is not comfortable or familiar with a multi-functional approach to problem-solving, then start by designating projects to be resolved by this process. Ideally, the subjects selected should be of interest to a broad cross-section of the workforce, as you are essentially piloting the concept. A major systems change, for example, embraces everybody and is therefore highly suitable to a genuine cross-functional approach. The key outcomes of Change Initiation, directed by the Culture Change, Employee Development and Corporate Strategy Groups, are also ideal, as these are issues raised and "owned" by the workforce. However, there is a science to delegating in this fashion, particularly in the early days. Get it right and the application will spread of its own accord. Get it wrong and it'll be doubly difficult to resurrect it. The following steps may be found useful:

- **Step 1: Define very carefully the terms of reference.** This needs to be done by all the departments who are directly involved in the project outcome. Their commitment should be publicised by each "signing off" the agreed terms of reference.

- **Step 2: Appoint a project sponsor.** A project sponsor will ensure that the project group stays within its terms of reference and gets the necessary resources as and when required. They will help the group decide how and when to report back. Ideally, the project sponsor should be a member of the senior management team, especially in the early days when multi-functionalism is being tested. A natural authority may be needed from time to time to deal with any unwanted obstructions.

- **Step 3: Identify the project team.** A cross-section of abilities and personalities is needed, ensuring a careful balance between functions. Avoid the organisation cynics or politicians at all costs! As the process develops, the same old faces seem to be nominated on a disproportionate number of teams. Ensure that a steady supply of new team members is maintained.

- **Step 4: Train the project team** in project management skills and in teamworking, preferably using internal resources. This particularly applies to new members to ensure they play a full part from the off.

- **Step 5: Define the project carefully**, including expected outcomes, resources, timescales, constraints and consequences of failure. The last mentioned may seem harsh, but the team need to be aware of the commercial realities of the situation. The company is going to some lengths and expense to launch this project and the team need to know its significance.

- **Step 6: Arrange the meetings.** We always found in projects of any significance that it was best to have a skilled internal facilitator at the initial meetings(s). They can iron out any interpersonal difficulties and ensure that the team remained focused on their brief.

- **Step 7: Report back and recommendations.** Whilst it is fashionable for an audience with the senior management group to be commissioned for this purpose, I think this introduces an element of artificiality. There is nothing worse than presenting to an obviously disinterested senior management team who are clearly going through the motions. Those genuinely involved in the project would have been fully briefed in advance anyway. I recommend a written submission to be reviewed by the appropriate senior group and reported back to the project team by the project sponsor.

- **Step 8: Recognition.** All-important — use the techniques recommended in Chapter 7. Regular and genuine recognition should become a characteristic part of this process.

- **Step 9: Review.** The project sponsor should call the project team back at a suitable time post-implementation to review progress. If necessary, an additional report can be generated and submitted to the senior management group for further action.

A nine-step process for such a small initiative may seem to be cumbersome but this is far less onerous in practice. After a while these steps will be second nature and take very little in the way of time and resource. However, miss a step and you could well find yourself looking at an embarrassing mishmash. This will be particularly damaging to the participants and may discourage future involvement. Time spent in preparation here is rarely wasted.

Our end objective is for this process to occur almost spontaneously across the company. Someone picks up a problem, decides they need help and commissions assistance from the relevant functions. They meet, using the disciplines noted above, conclude and report back. Their job done, they then disband. Used in conjunction with a sophisticated continuous improvement initiative, this could be a powerful means of establishing a natural internal momentum. Empowered people really working toward mutually beneficial objectives!

CHAPTER 9

TEAM ENTERPRISE IN ACTION: MANAGEMENT STYLE

In Chapter 6, we learned from Poskett's Law that an appropriate management style was prerequisite for success in a Team Enterprise. He gave us few clues about what could be defined as *appropriate*, aside from indicating that best practice organisations seem to exhibit a range of management styles which were *deemed* appropriate to the situation and which were *perceived* as appropriate by the workforce. However, such is the diversity of management style across apparently successful practitioners that it is impossible to be totally prescriptive about what's right and what's wrong. We could avoid the debate altogether and simply say: "The best management style is one which is continuously assessed and challenged by one's subordinates and which is constantly modified according to circumstances and perceptions." In other words, we simply adjust our behaviour to suit the situation, taking into account the reactions of the people who work for us. This dynamic model might be fine if we have an accurate and ongoing means of gauging real subordinate perception. However, I suspect that whilst the sentiment is laudable, it simply isn't practical.

In our early days at Leyland, the guidance given to our middle and front line managers was equally vague. We would simply explain that there is a range of management styles available to us all. Figure 14 was used to demonstrate how we should use these styles:

Figure 14: The Range of Effective Management Styles

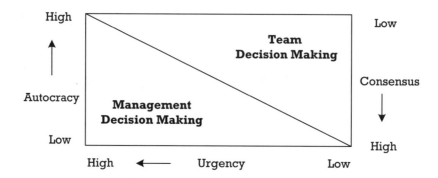

The horizontal axis is used to denote *urgency*. Very urgent situations, such as a major safety problem, lie to the left, more leisurely situations to the right. The left-hand vertical axis indicates the level of *autocracy* needed, whilst the right hand vertical axis the level of *consensus* required.

We have to accept that, in certain situations, an autocratic manner may be mandatory. If I'm sitting in the boardroom and I smell fire, then I don't think I'd be thanked for having a debate and suggesting a secret ballot on what to do! The obvious and quite acceptable behaviour would be to instruct everybody to get out immediately and have the debate on the wisdom of the instruction in safety at the Fire Assembly point. At the other extreme, if an issue arises, for example, about when people can take their holidays, in the absence of any clear business need, a decision can be arrived at by pure consensus.

In between these two extremes, there are a range of behaviours which are appropriate to certain situations, all indicated by the diagonal line. Next down from autocracy is *persuasion*, where we attempt to convince people that the management line is the right one. Beyond that we may try and *consult* with our subordinates, hearing what they have to say, before we decide. We may even go further and *jointly decide* the outcome.

All we did with our managers in our early days was to indicate that these options existed and that they should make their own judgements about which ones they should use, depending on circumstances. However, we stated quite unambiguously that, wherever possible, we should move into the shaded area and, as a general principle, the nearer the right hand side the better. To emphasise this, Figure 15 may be deemed more appropriate to our philosophy, where the shaded area is increased to reflect our commitment to involvement and empowerment.

Figure 15: The Preferred Range of Management Styles

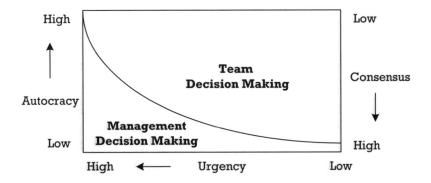

Whilst the foregoing may seem sensible and rational, it has one significant weakness. Few managers have any idea of how they are perceived by their subordinates, as Change Initiation repeatedly finds out. Management egos also vary enormously and this will heavily influence subsequent behaviour. Having had the opportunity to work with a number of different operations and companies in this area, I would point to four types of manager where difficulties can be anticipated: the Natural Autocrat, the Squirrel, the Pedant, and finally the Appeaser.

The Natural Autocrat

This is the most difficult category to deal with, especially those who are autocratic because they genuinely believe that their own judgements and opinions are infinitely superior to their subordinates. The other type of autocrat, the Reluctant Autocrat, adopts this style through fear, conformance or ignorance and can, eventually, be persuaded to change. However, Natural Autocrats have such self-centred egos that to defer to any perceived inferior would be total anathema to them. Paradoxically, they can often accept that *other* managers have to operate in this fashion as these unfortunates lack their intellectual characteristics and personality. This makes them somewhat difficult to spot!

To compound the problem, many Natural Autocrats have almost a split personality. With their subordinates, they are tyrants. With their supervisors they are deferential, supportive and helpful. This behavioural paradox doesn't seem to trouble them, as it is probably a natural trait rather than a political manoeuvre. Many readers ascending the career path must have had similar experiences to myself, where tyrannical bosses have puzzlingly become pussycats when overtaken in the hierarchy. I have also often been staggered to find out that some of my managers, who in my eyes appeared to be well-balanced and reasonable, have been seen by their subordinates as raving egos on legs. And invariably, their perception is much more accurate than mine!

What do you do with these people? This is a difficult question in most situations, particularly if their behaviour comes as a shock to their line manager. There is, however, one test. Can the organisation survive with these people carrying on as they do at present? Will the empowerment/involvement initiative, in other words, be successful even with this, now established, errant behaviour?

If the answer to the question is no, you have two simple choices — change their personality or get rid of them! Quite often, the latter causes great crises of conscience with senior managers.

There is often a strong bond between the Natural Autocrat and his boss. I have heard expressions used like "salt of the earth", "my right arm" and "the firm couldn't operate without him" used in passionate defence of their favourite son. Frequently there is a blank refusal to accept the conclusions and we have to re-trawl through the outputs and add substantial additional interviews to verify that the initial perception was indeed reality. Even then you will hear arguments about vendettas, mischief and individuals "carrying the can for organisational weaknesses elsewhere". Where this happens we have to emphasise that Optima is simply the messenger. What you do with the message is down to you!

In 99 per cent of instances, I believe that efforts should be made to persuade the incumbent to change their behaviour. Most people are pragmatic and will, ultimately, accept the criticism. Ultimately, however, can be a hell of a long time! A programme of behavioural change should be developed jointly with the manager, perhaps with the help of a neutral mentor to speed things along. Observation and facilitation of departmental meetings by the latter can be a huge help here. However an ongoing programme of measurement, possibly with the use of a management style questionnaire (see later), is essential to avoid a reversion back to the previously unacceptable style.

If 99 per cent indicates to you that my abiding faith in human nature is too optimistic by far, then draw your own conclusions! Unfortunately, there will always be the occasional example, the 1 per cent, where whatever you do seemingly makes little difference to their behaviour. In these instances, the injury caused to the subordinates in the Natural Autocrat's department is probably too deep-rooted to justify any salvage operation. You have no alternative but to move on the offending manager. Whether this is out of the door or into another role is down to you and the range of options available. If you do decide on transfer, my advice is to avoid other managerial roles at all costs. You will simply be digging another hole, and the chances are you'll have enough of them already!

The Squirrel

The Squirrel works on the principle that all knowledge is power and therefore the more knowledge they keep to themselves, the stronger their anchor will be in the company. Squirrels appear all over the organisation but seem to have a particular penchant for the "professional" support functions, notably legal, finance and personnel. These people are the stuff of nightmares for Team Enterprise. The first stated ambition of an empowered organisation is to get people to make their own decisions, but how can the Squirrels allow this without eroding their power base? They will use all sorts of devices to protect their position. They'll claim confidentiality, they'll claim statutory or regulatory obligations and they'll argue about skill levels and capability. Their department may be characterised by political manoeuvring, by resentment and by joylessness, but they'll still vigorously defend their patch.

Such characters are often found in quasi-governmental organisations, as this seems a fertile ground for secretive non-decision-makers. Fortunately, the problem in many instances is relatively easy to solve. Quite frequently the Squirrels are those technically expert individuals who have climbed the promotional ladder due entirely to their professional competence. At no stage has anyone ever raised the issue of managerial capability, let alone trained them for the transition. The solution may be to encourage them to seek a broader view of the world of work through education and the types of facilitation noted earlier. And then use the management style questionnaire to ensure that the improvement is tracked.

The Pedant

The world of business today is fast moving. Decisions have to be taken quickly, often armed with incomplete information. Making the occasional mistake is now an occupational hazard. Making no decision is the worst possible scenario in this rapidly changing, helter-skelter climate.

Enter the Pedant, the scholarly senior executive who, either through insecurity or sheer bloody-mindedness, will not make a decision until every "i" is dotted and every "t" crossed. Their biggest concern in life is never to make a mistake. Their disdain for those they consider impulsive can be detected at distance.

Their subordinates cannot help but be affected. They will fear error and therefore avoid making any significant decisions. They will know the consequences of their mistake-intolerant zone and act accordingly. Other functions will hate dealing with them, being frustrated by their indecisiveness, their refusal to accept deadlines and, worst of all, by a perception of pompousness and arrogance.

Whether the Pedant can ever be converted is open to question. I am doubtful whether people like this should ever be given significant managerial responsibility, such is their natural lack of empathy for both the demands of people and of business. However, given my previously stated faith in human nature, you probably need to try. Remedial action is as before: education, facilitation and measurement.

The Appeaser

The Appeaser will welcome Team Enterprise with open arms, but for all the wrong reasons! They will see it as a relief from seemingly being obliged to play the heavy-handed manager, even if only occasionally. They hate conflict, fear being unpopular and dislike being forced to arbitrate. Unfortunately, Team Enterprise provides the opportunity, in their eyes, to operate permanently at the extreme right-hand side of Figure 15, Management by Consensus.

It is easy to spot when you're in the company of subordinates of the Appeaser. Their frustrations will be voiced with expressions like "abdication not delegation" and "laissez-faire management". Quite often the area will seem anarchic, a situation the Appeaser will put down to the complexities and volatility of the world around them. In many respects, the Appeaser is as big a threat to Team Enterprise as is the Natural Autocrat, the Squirrel and the Pedant. This new philosophy demands high levels of self-discipline, which generate a far "tighter" regime than even that developed by autocracy. However, the driving forces are peer pressure and self-motivation, both of which can get horribly mangled by the Appeaser's incompetence.

Fortunately, the Appeaser will be easily identified through the management style questionnaire, his subordinates having no compunction about shopping him! Whether the Appeaser can change his spots is a difficult question. But as before, you can but try.

Lessons from Covey

The above tells us a little about what management style shouldn't be, but that isn't helpful to the vast majority of aspiring team entrepreneurs who want to know how best to present themselves to their subordinates. This is difficult, as different companies seemingly pursuing Team Enterprise in the right ways can have very different management styles. The key determinant of success is often the behaviour of the senior decision-maker. As nobody is daft enough to suggest that we have to clone a specific style and prescribe it to all companies adopting this philosophy, we have to accept differences. But what we can do is identify bands of *acceptable behaviour* and perhaps draw out some common traits.

Looking at the history of Leyland Trucks over the past 30 years, one can see clearly how this senior management influence has set the tone for the rest of the management hierarchy. In the late 1960s, the company definitely had a specific style, which I suppose one might describe as "paternalistically authoritarian". The directors of the company saw themselves as gods, and were treated that way. They operated clinically and autocratically but still had traces of the benevolence of earlier times. Leyland Motors, as it was, became the first manufacturer in the country to have its own health and safety officer. Its Social and Athletic Club was also highly unusual in the quality and breadth of provision. This helped maintain a family atmosphere despite the remoteness of the managing team.

In the early 1970s, this was replaced by a highly aggressive, macho style. The cosy comfort of the gentleman-director was replaced by hard-bitten professionals who usually operated with foul-mouthed aggression, using fear as their principal instrument. I say "usually", because not all were foul-mouthed but they were, not infrequently, raving and offensive autocrats!

My colleague, David Graham, tells a story of one of these individuals who shall remain nameless — but, for ease, here we'll call him Bill. Bill's motivational techniques were based purely and simply on fear. He didn't swear or curse or even rant and rave, except when he felt it necessary. But he perfected the art of questioning to a weakness. With the most penetrating stare, no doubt practised for hours in front of a mirror, Bill would attack his managers on every conceivable occasion by firing questions until the unfortunate recipient of his wrath failed to give a satisfactory response. To quote David, "It didn't matter whether it took one or 20 questions, the sod would interrogate you until you screwed up — and then you got your hiding." Bill would despatch his miserable subordinate with a warning to sort things out by the next morning, or he'd be back. And he always was.

After a while, the penny dropped with those unfortunates. They were going to get a good hiding anyway so why not take it early. Even better, why not take it on an issue you knew you could solve or perhaps even had the solution tucked away in your back pocket already. So with game on every morning, this ridiculous ritual was played out. Bill is probably convinced to this day that his motivational technique was successful, but the truth was that the whole sordid affair was a pitiful charade. True, he scared everybody to death, but not to any benefit. The main consequence was a massive sub-optimisation of the company with no imaginations being stretched or creativity unleashed.

A few years later, it was deemed necessary to have all managers and potential managers subjected to a psychological assessment. I personally have nothing against the "psychs", as they did me no harm and have often been useful since. However, some bright spark decided that line management needed to be populated by a certain breed. To be successful, we all needed something of the "psychopath" in us. Sadly, I'm ashamed to say, I passed with flying colours. Now, of course, they didn't use the term "psychopath"; that was just our interpretation of their requirements. If I recollect correctly, the expression used was "task-focused", which meant that we were prepared to break down walls if it meant getting the job done. Perhaps this was exactly what was needed at the time, as some still argue emphatically today.

However, it is more likely that this was a knee-jerk reaction to the symptoms of ongoing under-performance rather than the true causal factors. But whatever the intent, it created a fashionable management style that persisted for many years and was known colloquially in the factory as the "Rottweiler brigade".

By 1989, therefore, we had inherited at least three decades of widely differing management styles, none of which seemingly had any merit aside from giving us a clear steer on what to avoid. As we embarked on Team Enterprise, the only guidance we could give management was a vague generality based on "winning the hearts and minds of the workforce" and a list of things *not* to do based on past experiences. However, we never at any stage defined positive behavioural traits of good management practice.

It was only after I gave up the role of chief executive in January 1999 that the penny really began to drop. As part of my role in Optima, I was asked to devise a programme to teach management on how they should behave in a Team Enterprise environment. This seemed an interesting proposition so I researched numerous books and articles on the subject without much success. There were lots of anecdotes and lots of pointers but nothing of any real use to my brief. I nearly gave up but then I came across Stephen R. Covey's *The Seven Habits of Highly Effective People*. Interestingly, this book was not specifically directed at management behaviour. It was much more to do with personal development on an individual basis. However, the further I delved, the more convinced I was that these principles or "habits" held the key to good management practice in Team Enterprise.

I will not dwell too long here, as no doubt many readers will already be familiar with Covey. His books are worldwide bestsellers. However, there are two specific learning points emerging from his work which are of immediate interest.

The first concerns the style of management we should adopt. Covey draws a clear distinction between what he calls the Character Ethic and the Personality Ethic. The Character Ethic deals with what he describes as more *basic* principles of effective living which must be integrated into one's character for success. In this category he includes things like humility, integrity, courage, patience, modesty and fidelity. The Personality Ethic relates to a view of success geared to personality characteristics. So our success is what we project — the right "personality", our public image or our air of positivity, etc. Whilst there are many benefits from the Personality Ethic, they will never sustain us in the longer term unless they are genuinely supported by the inherent strengths of the Character Ethic. Politicians are classic examples of this. We elect them primarily on their public image, the creation of the spin-doctors. However, once in office, the intense scrutiny of political life exposes their deeper underlying traits, the Character Ethic. We may then see them as being manipulative, not faithful, as egotistical rather than humble, or as timid rather than courageous. No amount of spin-doctoring can then rectify the damage in time. We see them *for what they are*.

In management, we are, on a smaller scale of course, subjected to similarly intense scrutiny. Our undoubted ability to communicate alongside a positive and energetic personality might establish a strong initial influence. But as time goes by, if we cannot support that image with strong character traits, our credibility will decline. Given one of the main themes of this book — that management behaviour is the key determinant of a successful Team Enterprise — the implications of Covey's theories are far-reaching. If we wish to be successful in management over a long period, we need to ensure that our toolbox of slick conventional managerial attributes is reinforced by these key characteristics. We ideally need to be seen as fair, patient, modest and to possess humility, integrity and courage. But what will ultimately undermine our effectiveness is if we are perceived to be *lacking* in these traits, i.e. we are unfair, impatient or immodest.

Very little of our management training focuses upon the Character Ethics. Most of conventional personal development activities will be geared to the "Personality", as witnessed, for example, by Leyland's emphasis in the past on communication skills, recognition skills, teaming and positive thinking. All of this is highly creditable and needs to continue, but we have to recognise that success will only come if our management team has either these more fundamental characteristics or can be trained to acquire them to a level of acceptability.

Measurement — The Management Style Questionnaire

Measuring the effectiveness of your own management style is not an easy task. After all, what you are attempting to gauge is perception or, specifically, other people's perception of your performance, style or character. Change Initiation can give a first fix on where you stand, as can more targeted tools like a formal 360° feedback or one of the many "teambuilding" courses which include elements of upward and peer appraisal. However, such measures are taken at a point in time. Perception is a more dynamic beast and can vary dramatically over very short horizons. We need, therefore, a technique to at least give us a more frequent indicator of change.

Within Leyland Trucks, we submit ourselves to redoing Change Initiation every two years and have annual "Training Needs Analysis" where upward appraisal is encouraged on a one-to-one basis. However, these devices are not frequent enough to effectively detect change, nor flexible enough to really assist in implementing corrective action. For this, we rely on the Management Style Questionnaire, designed to reflect all aspects of management behaviour.

The Management Style Questionnaire initially consists of around 20 questions, which can be modified subsequently to reflect new concerns and nuances. We encourage each manager in the Leyland hierarchy to do this quarterly until a steady state is reached. Thereafter, the frequency can be reduced to three times or even twice a year. I used to employ it in the following fashion:

1. Each quarter, an unmarked questionnaire would be sent to each of my direct reports. (You may wish to extend the circulation to others who perhaps don't work directly for you; for example, anybody who has a "staff" rather than "line" responsibility). The questionnaire is designed to evaluate the boss's performance in the eyes of the subordinate.

2. Each recipient would complete the report, marking their satisfaction on a scale of 1–5. As this is confidential, there is no signature or identification code.

3. The reports would be sent to a third party (in my case, my personal assistant) who would aggregate the responses to each question and give a range and an average.

4. This consolidated report would come back to me and I would compare the latest version with its immediate predecessor, and from time to time several other past submissions. I would mark up any areas of noticeable deterioration or improvement.

5. The consolidated report, along with my comments, would be circulated to each participant.

Where we went from there depended on the severity of any decline. If it represented a slight alteration to previous marks, I might write asking for comments, or get two or three colleagues into a room and have a discussion. If more serious, then I would have had one of our internal facilitators, usually a senior personnel professional, find out for me.

You have to be flexible and open-minded in digesting the information generated by the exercise. The feedback can be challenging, puzzling and often unexpected. One question — "My manager recognises and celebrates the success of others" — once caused me no end of consternation. As you will have gathered, from the early 1990s I have been obsessive about the benefits of recognition and played the leading role in its development in the organisation. Lots of the successful elements of recognition at Leyland Trucks arose from my ideas or my adaptation of good practice elsewhere. I was not proud of many of my traits as a manager but in this area I most certainly was! However, over a period of about a year I noticed a steep decline in the marks I was given on this point. I couldn't understand it; if anything, my efforts in this area were redoubling and were met with increasing success. And yet I was being marked down. So I sent out my most recent assessment with a plea for a little illumination.

It was the manufacturing engineering manager, Allister Butler, who put me right. He suggested that my colleagues had marked me down because I didn't, apparently, take recognition seriously. This staggered me. I felt that I took recognition very seriously indeed. Didn't my attention to, and leadership of, the initiative indicate so? Apparently not. Allister explained that when I took a recognition ceremony, I laughed and joked all the way through, making "fun of people". My colleague, Stewart, who alternated with me in taking these recognition events, evidently handled things differently and obviously more acceptably. He was serious, didn't make any jokes and maintained a much higher level of decorum about the whole affair. According to Allister, Stewart handled the ceremony correctly whilst I . . . well I was seen as going through the motions and generally taking the mickey!

Nothing could have been further from the truth. I wouldn't dream of challenging Allister's comments about my behaviour — after all, they were reinforced by his colleagues — but the analysis of my intentions was completely wrong. My motivation was simple: I personally find being recognised myself a bit embarrassing. I feel uncomfortable and want to get it over with as quickly as possible. I don't like being singled out.

I have always thought, obviously mistakenly, that most other people felt the same way. So when it came to my turn to recognise publicly the efforts of others, I was acutely aware of this potential embarrassment. So I would attempt to make them more comfortable by playing down the occasion and by making jokes. My intention was to relax people. But, in reality, I was doing something completely different. I was perceived by them to be undermining their achievements. I was diluting their sense of fulfilment and the sense of loyalty and pride which they felt for Leyland. Stewart, on the other hand, although no doubt recognising the potential embarrassment, also understood that the sense of occasion was the most important aspect of the day and that any discomfort was at worst tangential. So he did it right and I screwed up.

I relate this story not simply to expose yet another weakness in my seemingly moth-eaten reputation, but to indicate the power and necessity of constantly testing the perception of oneself in other eyes. I could have gone on for years doing exactly the same under the mistaken impression that I was helping people when the truth was that I was achieving the opposite. How many other aspects of unconscious incompetence do we constantly exhibit to the detriment of ourselves and the organisation? The Management Style Questionnaire at least gives us a chance of finding out. There may be those who question the statistical validity of the approach or the framing of the questions or indeed the whole methodology. They may be correct, scientifically. But this is not an absolute science. It is a tool, and just a tool, for helping us see through this difficult area of perception. You need to work on the technique, recognising potential weaknesses. I have seen, for example, some people getting top marks for every question. I fear this reflects sycophancy rather than objectivity and, if this happens to you, the challenge is to resist the ego massage and encourage your subordinates to be more critical. The end we seek is continuous personal development, not a rosy glow of attainment.

The absolute marks are of no significance whatsoever. You cannot, except *in extremis*, compare a set of marks for one manager with another. There are too many variables at large to make it significant. The only use of the data is to compare for yourself the marks for one question against the other questions and to see how the markings change from quarter to quarter. Do not be tempted to read anything more into the exercise. All we are looking for are hints and pointers. It's up to you to follow them through.

Time Management

The Management Style Questionnaire can give you a set of useful indicators in terms of your effectiveness across a range of variables. One other useful tool is to analyse from time to time how you spend your working day, week or even month. If we are doing the Team Enterprise thing correctly, one would expect to see a progressive but distinct move away from operational detail into broader managerial activity. For example, before implementation, the profile may be dominated by chasing shortages, firefighting and general crisis management. As you progress, you should see greater focus on strategy formulation and on constructive person-management. If you don't see this change, you may have to review whether you are adapting correctly to this brave new world or even whether the whole initiative is off-course.

My predecessor at Leyland asked all his production managers (who were later to become business unit managers) to quantify the time they spent on each division of responsibilities. This proved a useful comparator later on. One of the managers carefully computed his activities, as illustrated in Figure 16. As much as 40 per cent of his time was spent on the shopfloor solving detailed problems. He is a bit generous in describing the activity as ". . . and communications" as he really means talking *at* people about organisational minutiae. At least 20 per cent of his time was spent simply chasing shortages and arguing with chasers, storekeepers, materials men and all the other rag, tag and bobtails one finds in complex assembly activities. He describes it as "Logistics" but there was little logical in those days. Quality problems took a modest 5 per cent of his day and most of this was spent in rectification and in making sure that no-one could blame his direct boss or him personally for any defects as vehicles left the factory. Industrial relations and industrial engineering, unfortunately in those days never far apart, took a massive 20 per cent of his day. One of the measurement criteria for managerial effectiveness used to be how many employees had been warned, suspended or sacked for errant behaviour. He had to make sure he kept his end up there as well! And finally, around one-sixth of his time was spent in meetings, perhaps either talking aggressively to people or being the butt of a similar tirade from above.

Figure 16: Typical Time Allocation — Pre-Team Enterprise

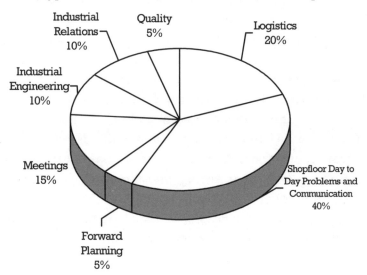

Or that should have been "finally" — except that when the business unit manager in question took the chart along into his secretary for compilation, she pointed out that forward planning was not mentioned anywhere on the slide. His response was along the lines of "You'd better stick 5 per cent in for that then", despite his real activity sample having not identified any noticeable effort in that direction. And that's how the pie chart aggregated to 105 per cent. Fortunately, nobody noticed!

Fast forwarding about seven or eight years, the exercise was repeated and the results are shown in Figure 17. As well as noting that the total is now exactly 100 per cent, you will see other differences in terminology. His role was now that of business unit manager and that accounts for some of the difference. He was now truly multifunctional, having line responsibility for day-to-day production planning, industrial engineering, quality and some logistics. A fifth of his time was spent talking *and listening* to his people. One key new feature of his day became the working lunch as break times were used to meet his subordinates in a forum where ideas and opinions could be exchanged frankly and co-operatively. Another fifth was spent in "management" meetings, reflecting his new broader role, now not defensively arguing about "who shot John?" but actually co-operating with other functions to ensure best practice. Being able to delegate detail enabled him to spend 20 per cent of his time forward planning, looking at the implications of new products, new working practices and new projects. In the past, this would have been done extremely sketchily at the last minute. Now he could think ahead. Another chunk of time was spent *auditing* processes and products. Much of the detail on problem identification and resolution had been delegated to others. His new emphasis was on ensuring that the basic processes conformed to the necessary specification. And finally, the balance of his time — up to 20 per cent — could be applied flexibly at his own discretion, depending on priorities.

Figure 17: Typical Time Allocation — Post-Team Enterprise

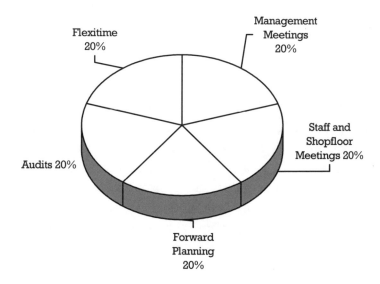

Flexitime 20%

Management Meetings 20%

Staff and Shopfloor Meetings 20%

Audits 20%

Forward Planning 20%

The actual statistics on how he distinguished core time spent on his four main categories rather than the "flexitime" he had at his discretion need not concern us here. The main learning point from the manager's experience is that his view of working life had changed fundamentally and that this was reflected quite vividly in the way he spent his time.

Workplace Discipline

One of the most common questions asked about Team Enterprise, when traditional organisations encounter it for the first time, usually revolves around discipline. Taking away the sanctions of autocratic management exposes the operation, in their eyes, to massive opportunities for the malingerer and the mischievous to wreak havoc. They see microscopic management intervention as being the only effective mechanism to guarantee delivery. Such thinking is not unusual. Many large corporations operate on the belief that an obsession with detail right through the chain of command is the only means of effecting control.

However, this ignores the ingenuity of people to work around those control systems which they find oppressive or threatening. Take clocking in and out. These are theoretically very effective mechanisms in ensuring that the bulk of the working population put in the hours they are supposed to work. But the bulk of the working population would do that anyway under far less onerous strictures. Those who want to manipulate the system will find a way of doing so, clock or no clock. Constant, oppressive managerial attention has similar downsides. The majority will find it stultifying and counter-productive. The errant minority will in time use their ingenuity and mischievousness to work around it. Their agenda can often be simply to mess up the system, irrespective of any personal benefit to themselves. There is little evidence anywhere to associate tight autocratic management control with productivity, efficiency and innovation.

One of the surprising characteristics of an excellent Team Enterprise installation is, however, how disciplined it all is. The usual indicators of poor performance, labour turnover, absenteeism, lateness, etc., are markedly better in empowered organisations than in their traditional counterparts. Misbehaviour of any sort is far less prevalent and far less tolerated. A former manufacturing manager at Leyland once commented how easy it was to fire people under the new philosophy. He wasn't, I hasten to add, talking about any Machiavellian exploitation by management but merely a reflection that misbehaviour was not acceptable to anyone in a team environment. Whilst in the old world, somebody bucking the system would be viewed with tolerance or even admiration by the rank and file, such behaviour would be instantly condemned in the new.

The forces at work here are teamwork, pride and self-esteem. Empowerment offers huge opportunities for those who have felt oppressed by the strictures of orthodox management control to play a much more proactive role at work. Once a critical mass of like-minded souls is created, then anything that disrupts this new harmony will be fiercely resisted. Whether this be errant management behaviour or shopfloor delinquency is immaterial; the workforce will see it as a threat to their new-found levels of job satisfaction and resist it.

The best speaker I have ever come across on this subject is John Spragg of Rolls Royce Cars at Crewe. John is now a tour guide who flirts from time to time with presenting his views on the world of work. His style is very endearing, being that of an old-fashioned stand-up comic. But his message is so vivid that one cannot resist the argument he puts forward. And that argument is equally balanced between the iniquity of the old management style and the potential of the new. John's time at Crewe has been spent mainly as an operator on the conn-rod line in the Rolls' machine shops. For 20 years, he had the mind-numbing experience of being tied to a machine, with no opportunity to think. He talks about how in his early days he used his own initiative to develop a little jig to prolong tool life by a factor of several lifetimes. He could have kept his innovation to himself and used it to have a very easy time, particularly on nightshift where he frequently worked and where it would have been easy to exploit it. However, he shared his innovation with his foreman, only for the jig to be thrown in the bin and for John to be warned that he was "paid for doing not thinking". John never submitted another idea for 20 years.

Two decades later, however, cell working was introduced within the factory and John, although initially sceptical, became a firm advocate. He talks enthusiastically about how this simple innovation touched the lives of all of his colleagues much for the better. And the company benefited enormously as well. If you ever get the chance to hear John, I strongly recommend you take it. Once you've been "Spragged", you'll never forget it!

Summing Up

In summary, therefore, there is no prescribed format for the "right management style". However, there are certain behaviours to avoid and certain behaviours to adopt and adapt. The key route for success, like so much else within Team Enterprise, is measurement. Use Covey's basic principles as your guide, repeatedly measure your effectiveness and learn from the experience. It sounds easy but it isn't. It takes courage, persistence and commitment. But get this element right and you'll be well on your way.

CHAPTER 10

TEAM ENTERPRISE IN ACTION: TEAMWORKING

Background

It probably seems strange that a book devoted to Team Enterprise does not discuss the subject of teamworking until two-thirds of the way through. This is quite deliberate, despite the reasoning being at odds with much current thinking. We believe that, chronologically, teamworking should be one of the last elements you think about when you construct your empowered organisation. I appreciate that most initiatives in this area actual *start* with teams as the smallest building block. However, most such initiatives fail and perhaps it is this flawed thinking which represents the key causal factor behind these failures. I would go further and say that the principal indicator of *success* in empowered organisations is always the strength and coherence of the supporting *infrastructure*, rather than the team itself.

A study of "Innovative Approaches of Self-Directed Work Teams" by Bekaert-Stanwich consultants on behalf of the European Foundation for Quality Management found that experience of Total Quality Management (TQM) was a common denominator in all their good practice organisations. We might debate whether TQM is an *essential* ingredient in predicting

success, but I don't think we would be able to draw any defini-
tive conclusions here. The key learning point, arising from the
fairly considerable experience of Optima's practitioners in this
area, is that success in empowerment reflects a holistic view of
the world of work, not the microscopic one pursued by those
who focus simply on teams. The common feature of these good
practice institutions may have been their ability to operate on a
broad front, a discipline fostered by TQM. Fortunately, therefore, you don't have to delay your introduction process by first
spending three or four years implementing TQM! However, you
must give a lot of thought on how you are going to integrate the
key principles of a TQM-type approach into your own programme. These, I would suggest, are a recognition of the importance of management commitment; a structured approach to
problem solving; and, finally, the importance of ongoing continuous improvement. Miss out on any of these elements and
your chances of failure are likely to be depressingly high. Fortunately, we have covered all these areas elsewhere in the
book; in the final chapter, "How to Get Started", we will seek to
prescribe a route to embrace them all in a co-ordinated and
coherent programme. However, only you can dictate the pace
of change, as this depends on just how much your company has
to do in terms of getting these key principles established.

At Leyland Trucks, this philosophy was reflected to a degree
in what was called the "Five Key Principles of Team Enterprise". In Figure 18, the key principles behind the whole theme
of culture change are explained. I should hastily add that these
were the *original* principles drawn up in late 1989 and reflect
both the thinking and the priority of the time. Were they to be
redrawn over a decade later, I think that both the phraseology
and the content might differ, particularly if we attempt to con-
fine our intentions to just five principles. However, they do give
a flavour of the challenges facing the management team. This
was not just a reshaping of the average perspective of the
workforce but, probably more importantly, the acquisition of a
whole new mindset for management.

Figure 18: The Key Principles of an Empowered Organisation (1989)

---

1. Decisions must be delegated to the lowest practical level of the organisation.

2. Communication must be natural and ongoing at the supervisor/subordinate level.

3. Demarcation lines should only be drawn on capability.

4. Consultation is not enough — we must educate and train to exploit and develop the individual talents and expertise of the workforce.

5. No one should feel more/less an employee than any other.

Why Have Teams?

Anybody who has worked extensively developing teams, particularly empowered teams, would have to accept that the whole area can be an absolute minefield. It is fraught with risk and inevitably demands a seemingly disproportionate amount of management time. So why bother? If you can't answer this question sufficiently clearly to at least convince *yourself* of the irresistibility of the case for teams, then you certainly shouldn't bother! You cannot go down this path with anything other than total commitment and absolute enthusiasm. Any half-hearted gestures will inevitably founder. So the very first step is to convince yourself unequivocally that teams are not just nice things to have from a standpoint of social engineering; they are also vital instruments in achieving your business's necessary competitiveness.

Lots of reasons are advanced for having teams. These range across:

-   Productivity, quality and efficiency improvement;

-   Involvement, participation and ideas generation;

- Lead time, cycle time and inventory improvements;

- Flexibility, added value and process reliability; and

- Motivation, satisfaction and empowerment.

Teams can generate all of the above, but the lower down the list you go, the greater the perceived benefit. If we ignore, incorrectly, the last on the grounds that this is in the "nice to have but of no direct value" category, the key savings are going to come from enhanced flexibility, improved organisation, added value and increased process conformance/reliability. The financial benefits here can be colossal. If you remain unconvinced by this, then get on your bike and visit best practice companies where evidence can be seen at first hand. Only if you and the rest of your management team possess an unquestioning conviction that Team Enterprise equates to quantum improvement in bottom line performance will you have the stamina to see it through.

Types of Teams

There are generally supposed to be four types of team:

1. Directed Teams

2. Lean Teams

3. Self-Directed Work Teams

4. Project Teams.

Directed Teams

These are the traditional teams, such as department or functional groups, which operate under a strong sense of hierarchy and centralised decision-making. Some limited latitude may be allowed but generally the term "team" is used to distinguish their group from others. The motivational force, aside from the usual autocracy, is the camaraderie and comradeship obtained by being part of a specific group.

Lean Teams

Lean teams are usually found in high-volume, short-cycle manufacturing. They are a natural development of Tayloristic thinking, as usually their use is encouraged by their greater efficiency over other models of workplace organisation. In some businesses, a degree of empowerment or involvement is allowed at the margins of their activity, but generally they are far too busy to do anything other than address the direct needs of the process.

Self-Directed Work Teams

Self-directed work teams can be found in any area of business, industry or commerce. Their key characteristic is the extent to which they are responsible for much of the detail decision-making undertaken on a daily basis. Also know as "autonomous work groups", they feature an avoidance of hierarchy and high levels of interaction within the group. In industry they will usually be found in staff/support departments or in production areas where high cycle times dominate.

Project Teams

Project teams can be found anywhere and are usually constructed for a specific purpose. The team will be created around a task which, when complete, will result in the group disbanding. In Leyland "multifunctional project teams" were used extensively to promote involvement and to expedite the problem resolution process. This area was covered extensively in Chapter 8.

Whilst project teams are important to Team Enterprise, we will concentrate in the rest of the chapter on the difficulties and benefits of self-directed work teams (SDWTs). They exhibit many of the characteristics that we seek to achieve through Team Enterprise. Successful implementation of such teams probably equates to success on a wider front, as all the infrastructural prerequisites described elsewhere will need to be in place to achieve this end. We will not discuss the first two categories, as they do not figure in a Team Enterprise.

Team Structures

There are three key factors which merit consideration when examining team structures: size, leadership and deployment. As far as size goes, we can say with some confidence that the maximum practical composition is probably no more than 16–18 workers. Beyond this, it is difficult to be prescriptive. There are some obvious determinants, including:

- Nature of process

- Geography

- Nature and cost of the chosen leadership model

- Flexibility, both desired and current

- Commonality.

There is little point in attempting to superimpose a one-sized group on an organisation, as it is hardly likely to make a natural "fit". You need to examine all the factors noted above plus any specific to your own situation. Of particular importance will be the choice of the leadership model. If you choose a conventional team leader who is 100 per cent devoted to "management and co-ordination", financial considerations will dictate the size and nature of the group. Consequently, some of the "ideal" conditions may have to be sacrificed on the altar of pragmatism. However, if you choose a model where the time assigned for "management and co-ordination" is less than 100 per cent and can be adjusted to suit the specific circumstances, then in theory there is no minimum size. The model selected for trackwork at Leyland Trucks simply consisted of dividing the production line into logical chunks, which were typically between 14 and 18 employees. The line had already been subdivided into "stages" for the benefit of industrial and production engineering. It was therefore not too difficult to use these natural break points to develop the new groups, occasionally by simply aggregating more than one stage. In other staff and indirect areas, the need to establish self-directed work groups was generally not thought to be worthwhile. All of the benefits, it could be argued, were available by extensively empowering people without the formality of new structures. For the tracks and some other areas, the formation of these new groupings was not simply all about greater access to a wider range of employee talents and expertise. It was also a clear signal that the autocratic and direct regimes of the past were now finished and that the way forward was dependent on a different, more enlightened vision. I doubt very much whether we could have achieved anything like the benefits described earlier if we'd persisted with old structures. But your establishment may be different and probably only you can make that judgement.

Of crucial importance is the selection of the leadership model. Current practice across industry tends to reflect three alternatives:

- The retention of a traditional supervisor newly trained in empowered practices;

- The creation of a "team leader";

- The creation of a "key operator".

It is difficult to see how you can generate a self-directed work team with all its emphasis on local autonomy and still retain traditional supervision. This seems a contradiction in terms. Even the title "supervisor" implies that people will be monitored, controlled and directed — the exact opposite of what the new model is trying to achieve. It may be perfectly feasible to retain the old configuration and still attain limited empowerment. That in essence may be the limits of your ambition over the short to medium term. However, as a long-term proposition, the two are incompatible.

Most companies give a clear signal that life is changing by appointing a "team leader" instead of the traditional supervisor. The differences between the two in some instances can be more theoretical than real, but most try to establish a clear differentiation by removing the onus of anything resembling discipline from the new man or woman and also ensuring that a fair proportion of the new incumbent's time is spent "on the job". This is vital to cement a proper working relationship between team leader and colleagues. For the team to work efficiently, there must be no sense of hierarchy, as any hint of this, whether direct or implied, will undermine the essential dynamic you are attempting to create. Perhaps a better title may be "team co-ordinator" to emphasise that this new role is about co-ordination and facilitation and not simply a play on semantics. Remember that many of the workforce will have long memories and need more than job titles to convince them that there is anything fundamentally different in this new arrangement. Having been through "leading hands", "chargehands" and "foremen" before the relatively recent introduction of the term "supervisor", most will think this to be yet another new tune on a very old fiddle. All the above had one thing in common: they were the "bosses". Not big bosses, perhaps, but carrying the smack of authority nonetheless. Once this perception of hierarchy creeps in, there is every danger that you'll revert back to square one and all the disadvantages of formal supervision.

When we created our teams at Leyland, we sought to eliminate all traces of even pseudo-hierarchy. We eschewed the term "team leader", as leadership implies authority and hierarchy in traditional situations such as ours. Instead, we appointed "key operators" who were expected to perform all the duties recognised by team leaders elsewhere but who had one important difference: they are paid exactly the same as the operators they work with. My personal belief is that, in the UK, any financial differentiation in these circumstances automatically creates a psychological barrier. It doesn't seem to matter whether this differentiation is a few pence or a few pounds. The very fact that someone is paid more than others makes them stand out as being more responsible than the rest. The sharing of workloads in a constructive and mutually supportive fashion becomes that much more difficult.

Today, this approach seems highly ambitious. Back in the early 1990s, against a background of perpetually getting "something for something", it seemed impossible. But we had to try. We knew that, although such an arrangement may not have been sustainable in the long term, the creation of this position under the terms explained would send the clearest of signals that we were looking for something completely different and completely radical. We tried to establish a post where the motivation was definitely not financial, as there were no monetary rewards. Instead, we looked for a purer form of incentive as people took on the position for pride, self-esteem or simply job interest. The fact that the greater visibility of the role would possibly support future career aspirations was not missed either. But generally, the applicants who took on the job were mostly inclined to do so for the interest and satisfaction. The issue of remuneration, or lack of it, was discussed in detail with those applying for the positions and, remarkably, was received with an unexpected level of sympathy and understanding. They knew that this was not about economics but more an attempt to break down some of the most destructive barriers which were generally perceived to have crippled Leyland for decades.

The notable success that ensued with the introduction of group working was due, in no small measure, to both the commitment of these key operators and, equally importantly, to the healthy relationship they were able to enjoy with their peers. Funnily enough, although we anticipated that this lack of financial reward would perhaps last, at best, only for a few years, it has been sustained well into the new millennium. For when the issue was taken up each year with the key operators, they themselves repeatedly decided that the likely increment was never going to be sufficient to justify the loss of the close camaraderie they enjoyed with their colleagues. I honestly wish that someone could devise some form of financial reward to recognise their considerable efforts, but no one has been able to do so without endangering the key dynamic which makes it so effective.

Our initial experiments with group working were remarkably successful but not without the occasional weakness. And one such area increasingly seemed to be capable of undermining the whole initiative. Ironically, difficulties arose with the role of the key operator, our pride and joy, and it appeared that the more successful the latter were individually, the greater the potential for disruption. As the group developed and absorbed more and more responsibilities, it became increasingly difficult for the key operator to retain his image as just one of the team or, as somebody put it, "first among equals". His increasing "distraction", trying to get to grips with the heavy administrative workload, virtually created the same perception as that of the supervisor he had replaced. Figure 19 illustrates the effect. Instead of being the cohesive force *within* the group, the key operator was, through no fault of his own, being progressively positioned *outside* the team.

Figure 19: The Consequences of Greater Empowerment

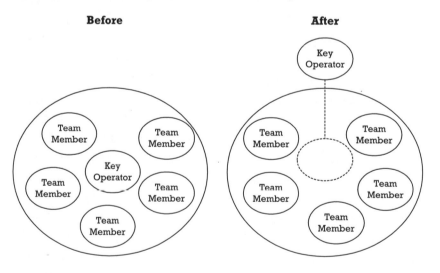

This had all the hallmarks of an impending disaster. The team felt cheated as the brave new world progressively seemed to move back to the old model. And the key operators became even more stressed as they struggled to cope with a role which was way beyond their training and expectation. We had, to be truthful, got it wrong.

As luck would have it, about this time, John Dwyer, the manufacturing manager, and myself were invited down to Rolls Royce Cars in Crewe by Christine Gaskell, their personnel director, to view their attempts to go down a similar path. They had achieved some success within their teams but struggled with infrastructural support to the philosophy. The visit was therefore an interchange of ideas to see if we could help each other. I'll leave the management of that prestigious organisation to judge whether they got anything out of us. However, as soon as John and I got to the shop floor and started talking to their teams, the penny dropped. We couldn't wait to get back to Leyland!

Basically, our mistake was in expecting too much from the key operator. With hindsight, it is obvious that if traditional supervision couldn't hack it, then there was little reason to suppose that the key operator wouldn't equally struggle given the same load under much the same conditions. Our basic model was flawed. We didn't need *one* key influencer in the group — we needed a *bunch*! Inspired by the Rolls experience, we set about creating a "critical mass" within each team. A team member was assigned responsibility for health and safety; another might take on training; a third, housekeeping; and so on. By subdividing the responsibilities and spreading them across the team, we improved the critical mass of team members who were actively involved in managing the process. Figure 20 illustrates.

Those members with enhanced responsibilities were called "Champions". Don't ask me why; the deed was done way before I had a chance to intervene! In retrospect, I doubt that it did us any harm, but I would strongly urge you to avoid overelaborate nomenclature. Terms like Champions or Good Citizenship could be a turn-off in the wrong circumstances, so don't take the risk. Think of something far more sensible and undramatic. Despite this clumsy title, the approach worked a treat. Responsibility was shared and the key operator became drawn back into the group. He, after all, had to "cover" for the champions when they were called off the job to undertake investigative or reporting responsibilities. The champions responded well too, seeing the opportunity for their limited involvement as a tentative stepping-stone into this new and uncertain world of work. Group Working Mk II has survived almost intact to this day.

Figure 20: Group Working Mk II (After Rolls Royce Cars)

The selection of the champions was a fairly arbitrary process usually left to the team. Occasionally, the business unit manager or a functional specialist might spot a likely candidate and press for the appointment. However, this was unusual, as the voluntary system seemed to work effectively enough.

Recruitment of Key Operators

The selection of key operators was certainly not left to chance and great care exercised in ensuring that only candidates who could demonstrate the capability of handling this difficult role were picked. The process was relatively straightforward:

- **Stage 1**: Advertisement placed around the factory inviting applications.

- **Stage 2**: First shortlist developed by standard interviews.

- **Stage 3**: Written tests based on psychometric and intellectual evaluation.

- **Stage 4**: Identification of second shortlist

- **Stage 5**: Second shortlist given to group for final selection.

The written tests were vitally important. To ensure success, we had to screen out those who possessed neither the interpersonal skills nor the intellectual capabilities for the role. However, provided both these hurdles were cleared, the company should be relaxed about who actually assumed the role. Handing over responsibility to the group was not just an exercise in overt democracy; it also recognised that the group had a more intimate knowledge of the candidates and would be likely to gravitate towards the natural leader. We rarely encountered any difficulty or controversy. Occasionally, the group might be undecided and allow the candidates to rotate the position. This again posed no difficulty for the company and hence was perfectly acceptable. On very rare occasions, the group might express a strong wish for a candidate who had not passed the psychometric hurdle. This proved to be quite a dilemma, especially in one instance where no one had successfully qualified for the role. However, where we bucked the system and went with the popular choice — not, I add, a frequent event — on every occasion the successful candidate became a resounding success. So much for science!

Support for Teams

Given the difficulties that all team members, including key operators and champions alike, will have in getting to grips with the brave and bold new world of autonomous working, it is important that responsibilities and accountabilities are fed through on a progressive basis. A big bang approach will render precisely what the name suggests and little else. Empowerment should be released in line with the growing capability and capacity of the team. Over-delegating will create unwanted stresses and strains which, like the example quoted earlier, can endanger the whole process. Patience is the key watchword.

With that in mind, it is of little surprise that the supportive infrastructure around the team is all-important here. Somebody has to judge pace, somebody has to be vigilant and monitor progress and someone has to decide when to release more of the rope.

Since we now only contemplate demarcation on the grounds of capability, it is vital that authority and freedom to act are balanced by ability and responsibility. This balancing act is generally carried out at Leyland by a combination of the business unit manager and the business unit technician. Figure 21 shows the entire configuration. Each business unit manager will have around 120 direct operators working for them. Obviously their scope to intervene, guide and counsel is very limited and hence the role of the business unit technician becomes increasingly important.

Figure 21: Teams and Their Infrastructure at Leyland

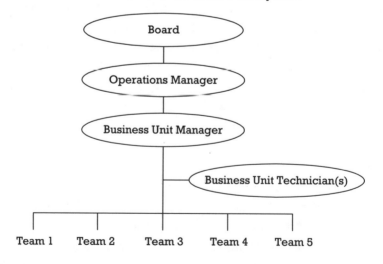

The specific responsibilities of these business unit technicians are designed to generate a multifunctional support to the various teams in their domain. Our ideal skills matrix would be a balance of quality, tooling, people management, method improvement and logistics.

The technicians are always physically within the vicinity of the teams and carry radio telephones for instant contact with the key operator. The necessary support is therefore available immediately.

We were very fortunate at Leyland in securing talented candidates to become technicians not only in terms of these specific skills but also in terms of their outstanding creativity and enthusiasm. For example, shortly after their introduction into this new regime, they felt that being classified as the *expert* in one professional attribute was unnecessarily restrictive. At their own initiative, they used whatever free time they had to "buddy" up with each other with the end objective of becoming multiskilled. This *"Jack of All Trades, Master of One"* approach yielded enormous benefits. It meant that 85 per cent of day-to-day problems occurring on the tracks could be addressed by all of the technicians with only the remaining 15 per cent necessitating the attention of the technical "expert".

Your own organisation structure may not be compatible with the model described here. Prescriptions are inappropriate, as business needs will vary. However, if the approach doesn't fit, then your challenge is to create the same dynamic and unlock the same synergy with whatever concoction you develop. The relationship between the team, the key operator and this "external" coach/facilitator will dictate the success or otherwise of your Team Enterprise in the workplace. Any trappings of hierarchy have to be discarded, but please don't think that the adoption of superficial signals such as uniforms will help here. Cosmetic add-ons will eventually be seen as merely flagging up an intention. If reality doesn't support that intention, credibility will not ensue. Communication and recognition have to be genuinely felt and embraced by at least the key players involved. Your supporting infrastructure needs to be seen as enthusiastic, helpful and focused on the same common goals as those shared by the team.

Whilst the business unit technicians, or equivalent, are vital to the development of the preferred culture, other areas have to adopt a likeminded approach. All departments that have major interactions at workforce level need to be educated in both the objectives of Team Enterprise and how they are expected to behave in supporting them. When we started in 1989, due to all sorts of internal problems, we couldn't get either product development or sales and marketing to join with us to launch a co-ordinated initiative. The geographic and functional distances were simply too great. As a consequence, our progress from time to time limped along instead of racing, due to conflicting signals. Had we been able to act in concert, I estimate that our pace of change would have been at least 25 per cent faster. Unfortunately, within the companies Optima works with, we see history repeating itself time after time. An enlightened manufacturing supremo may embrace the philosophy with great energy but decide to go alone, for perhaps unarguable reasons. However, there always comes a point when the full potential cannot be realised due to this clash of priority or beliefs. Bringing other functions on board "after the event" can be problematic. An element of "not invented here" is inescapable and may be based on a degree of logic rather than simple emotion. A system designed purely around one function is scarcely likely to be appropriate for the entire organisation.

In summary, therefore, the team can only be as good as its infrastructure. Your education, training and even exhortation must take a broad perspective and include all the so-called supporting players. This will not surprise those who take the holistic view that Team Enterprise includes everybody and excludes no one. But even the most well intentioned often drift into the trap of seeing the shopfloor as the centre of the universe. The temptation is understandable, particularly as most people are usually employed at the coalface. But myopia is still myopia, no matter how you tart it up. In every circumstance, you must always see the broad perspective. Otherwise, you will simply, as they say in more cerebral management texts, sub-optimise.

Communicating with Teams

We examined the general subject of communication in an earlier chapter. Here we detail the interactions that the team has with the organisation to make sure that it is "fuelled" adequately to undertake the responsibilities delegated to it. In Leyland, at a basic level, daily needs are addressed by cascaded team briefings through the key operator to ensure that immediate priorities are known and understood. Every month, the tracks are closed down for a fixed period (up to two hours) where each team gathers to review, sort out priorities and solve problems. This "Quality Time" has to be facilitated somehow in all organisations. The Leyland model may not be ideal or appropriate for everyone. However, it is vital that the teams adopt a mindset that all problems need to be addressed systematically down to *root cause* and that the status quo is, to quote one visitor to Leyland, "a mountain full of opportunities just waiting to be mined". The Meet the Team sessions discussed earlier can also be useful in reinforcing this philosophy.

The appropriateness and relevance of team efforts in the direction of continuous improvement is vital. The team needs to feel that it is using its energies in pursuit of objectives that tie in directly with those of the company. Care needs to be taken with the deployment of responsibilities and challenges to reflect real needs and real priorities. Figure 22 illustrates the process adopted at Leyland, one no doubt recognisable in many institutions. I am a great believer in promoting the key elements here by the adoption of visual management techniques. Your factory and offices should be adorned with posters, pictures and billboards prioritising in plain English your principal aspirations. Whilst care needs to be taken not to be seen as mere purveyors of propaganda, we can learn a lot from the advertising industry. A focus on key messages, frequently changed and adapted, alongside regular repetition can keep the organisation from straying into peripheral areas of little importance.

Figure 22: The Team Enterprise Deployment Model

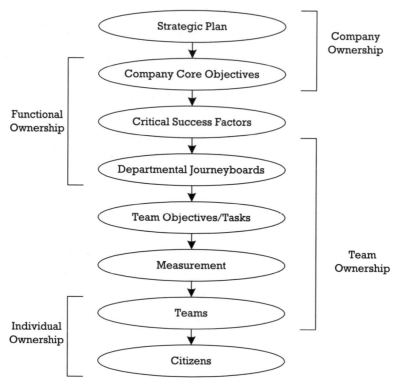

Each team should be encouraged to keep its own communication centre, comprising a Nobo board or flipchart, a notice board for their own measurement criteria and a desk where manuals, guides and training notes can be stored (unless of course you have a fully functioning intranet, which would make this redundant). Despite my comments earlier on the use of notice boards for *management* communication, *teams* can find them very useful for their own purposes.

Good communication is essential in terms of progressively increasing the empowerment of teams and individuals. I see no benefit in trying to adopt a bureaucratic or finely detailed mechanism for achieving the latter. Effective Team Enterprise stems from a balanced "loose–tight" approach, particularly relevant where prescription can constrain innovation and creativity. Each function should determine targets or even broad limits of what it hopes to see through empowerment. However, each team, alongside those responsible for coaching and facilitation, should decide on their own rate of progress. Only by focusing on the problems of the team, rather than the problems of management, can the "right" pace be established. This demands a high degree of sensitivity on the part of the business unit manager or equivalent. They should learn to focus on creating a supportive learning environment, which may be somewhat difficult in the "muck and bullets" of everyday grind. However, people need to feel comfortable in identifying problems to work on and experimenting with different approaches without fear of retribution if things go wrong. Command-and-control management styles often beget a blame culture where a mistake inevitably results in a search for a culprit. The American phrase, delivered with crossed arms and index fingers extended, "Who shot John?" sums up the mentality perfectly. If this emerges, perhaps even momentarily in the heat of crisis, people will retire to their bunkers, keep their heads down and simply wait for this latest "flavour of the month" to pass over.

Mistakes, it is said, should be celebrated if we are to learn. I see the spirit and intent, but practice is far more difficult here than theory. I remember an occasion when we were trying to adopt Jack Black's positive approach to everything (Chapter 14). There were no "problems", only "challenges" and we had to accustom ourselves to welcoming them as learning and development opportunities. We were having a main board meeting in the presence of our non-executive director and investor representatives against a backcloth of a particular nasty problem, sorry, challenge. All of us on the management side were feeling anxious and vulnerable. So when the door burst open and the manufacturing manager strode in beaming from ear to ear, we gave a collective sign of relief. "Great news," he said, "the issue's far worse than we thought. What an opportunity for us to show our real worth!" And then, to our mortification, he added little else. Even those of us who were confirmed Jack Blackites were left speechless. The non-executives simply grimaced, convinced that we had collectively gone mad.

While it may be beyond human nature to embrace failure as a friend, we have to learn organisationally to use mistakes as vehicles for getting it right next time. We must also be consistent across all employees in applying the same criteria. Turning understanding on and off dependent on the audience or the circumstances will convince no one. It's also management's job to delegate properly, an art that few of us do adequately. It is not just dishing out responsibilities; it is also a matter of clearly defining expectations, of parameters, of resources and of deliverables. And you need to make absolutely clear the consequences of failure. There is no responsibility without accountability, so don't shy away from making sure that all share the burden of non-achievement. Performance failures should be faced openly and constructively. Only in these conditions will the maturity to develop a supportive learning culture emerge.

Measurement and Training

Good management practice involves measurement. "What gets measured, gets done" applies just as equally to team performance as it does to more familiar operational parameters. The teams should be exposed to relevant measurement criteria reflecting daily and periodic performance, particularly those issues where the team directly impacts on output. The trick is to focus on measures of interest and consequence without overburdening to the point of boredom. Many managers, used to gauging progress constantly in this way, fail to appreciate that only a few in the organisation find quantification a turn-on. Be patient, be selective and be relevant.

However, periodic examination of progress on the "softer" side of management is also vital to sustain focus on this broader view of working life. Issues such as management style, housekeeping and effectiveness of training should all be given credence by measurement. These measures and the measurement process need not be scientific or elaborate — simplicity suffices in most instances. This is a motivational tool, not one to satisfy the intellectual cogitations of the statistician. If it works, it's good enough.

Similar logic must be applied to training. One of our first mistakes was in adopting the egalitarian "training everybody on everything" approach. Difficulties arose almost immediately with raised expectations. People expected to instantly apply these new skills and got frustrated when the opportunities didn't emerge. A more mature approach is to develop a portfolio of the necessary skills and expertise around teamworking and provide a series of packages to be used as and when required. So, for example, the modules developed on "Listening Skills" and "Working in a Team" may be given immediately to everybody whilst "Problem Solving" or "FMEA" would be delivered to a group of representative individuals. The latter could be used to lead small focus teams when the appropriate occasion arises. The key is to construct a toolbox of skills and expertise which can be drawn down in the most effective fashion dependent on local needs. Having the occasional "champions" of specific techniques, in the same way as we created functional champions within the teams, promotes interdependence and greater harmony.

The most effective form of training we found for teams came simply out of opportunity for quiet reflection, facilitated by a particularly empathetic manager or technician. It's true we tried the outward-bound type bonding exercises, which were great fun for all but of limited application back in the plant. A Saturday morning, away from the stresses and strains of the great "iron horse" (the track), often generated lots of common sense and some great ideas. One exercise, which all groups eventually took up, was simply to agree amongst themselves what they wanted from the company and what they thought the company wanted from them. Although unsurprisingly there were many variations, the same common themes reappeared. Figure 23 shows one example, which was signed by all and proudly posted in the area. I'm not entirely sure what an OFU stands for, although I hope it's Occasional Foul-up and not something ruder.

Figure 23: Sample Team Contract

**Contract — Team 3147 (Pre-Dyno) with
Manufacturing Engineer support**

We the undersigned agree that during the "Development of the Empowered Team Process", we will act and behave with the following considerations:

- We will trust in each other, by showing honesty and openness

- To develop belief in one another and in what we are trying to achieve

- We will adopt a flexible attitude

- We will show full support of each other, allowing input from all

- Advice will be offered not dictated

- We will operate in an environment which allows OFUs, and constructive criticism is valued

- We will commit to the team and the development process with enthusiasm

Signed

This sort of exercise to me is the most valuable. We in management may be quick to see the benefit of teams, and indeed of the need to create a more harmonious culture. However, we operate from the perspective of a helicopter pilot. Down in the jungle, the visibility is not that clear and therefore allowing other people from time to time the opportunity to levitate themselves above it all can be enormously beneficial.

Summary

Some form of teamworking is in all probability an essential ingredient of a successful Team Enterprise. And as we've seen, the infrastructure is in turn the key determinant of the successful team. Starting afresh, one must resist the temptation to focus exclusively on creating an effective *micro-unit*. Nor should we exercise excessive patience and set about establishing a healthy infrastructure without some attention to team development. The trick is to move forward on both fronts slowly and patiently, recognising that this is a long process. However the novelty, enthusiasm and energy generated even in these early stages can be highly beneficial on both motivational and financial fronts. So this should be sufficient to satisfy both the altruistic and the purely mercenary!

CHAPTER 11

TEAM ENTERPRISE IN ACTION: EMPLOYEE SYSTEMS

The subject of employee systems is vast and far beyond the scope of this book. Libraries and bookshops are full of step-by-step approaches to the necessary portfolio of employee systems required by any organisation. The fact that a lot of this advice is contradictory is something, sadly, you'll have to work out for yourself. We've enough to do in this book without worrying about that as well!

However, Poskett's Law (Chapter 6) tells us that in order to attain a successful Team Enterprise we must have a range of employee systems, both formal and informal, which achieve at least acceptability in the eyes of the workforce and which approximate good, if not best, practice. We therefore must give some thought to the key principles involved. There's little point in attempting to be prescriptive. Across a range of successful businesses one can find huge differences in style, content and approach. Something that seemingly works exceptionally well in one arena may fail disastrously in another. Effectiveness seems to be a heady cocktail of personality, management style, market stability, workforce pliability and too many other factors to enumerate. The message is, I believe, *think simple and be prepared to experiment*. If it doesn't work, find out why. And if the "why" seems insuperable, ditch the initiative and find something else.

Don't expect current systems to last forever. People can get fed up or complacent. Anomalies may creep in to damage credibility. Circumstances may change, rendering your once-proud edifices ineffective. Be prepared to be flexible and to experiment. If you do see good practice elsewhere, adopt it lock, stock and barrel. Don't change the imported system for the sake of changing. You may enjoy the intellectual satisfaction of restyling, renaming or readjusting but you are probably ignoring a lot of experience and trial and error endured elsewhere. Others have paid expensively by making mistakes. Don't risk your reputation by doing the same.

FORMAL SYSTEMS

Pay

Pay has the highest profile of all formal employee systems. Individual requirements for remuneration packages vary enormously, even in the most stable and balanced of environments. Demands are more often than not mutually exclusive. You either pick one model and stick with it through thick and thin or you accept that each new scheme has only a limited life of, say, five to seven years and you act accordingly. Team Enterprise cannot resolve this dilemma. You can only resort to constant communication and constant reminders of the impossibilities of generating a universal panacea. In Optima, despite numerous request for us to do so, we don't "do pay". We'll advise on the features of a helpful pay system but don't expect us to design one for you. There are plenty of experts about in this field, so let them screw up instead of us!

The reason we don't "do pay" is very simple: *ownership*. Any pay system has to be owned by management. They have to believe in it and be committed to it. Even more importantly, management must own the vitally important *transition* process. It is far too easy to blame a third-party contribution. It is also difficult at times not to experience a tinge of sympathy for those who feel disadvantaged by perceived anomalies in the new scheme because there will always be winners and losers.

Take the annual pay round at Leyland, for example. The lower paid employees — warehouse operatives and junior track workers — always want a flat increase each year. Everybody, they argue, should be paid the same increase in pounds rather than percentages for obvious reasons, to them. Other employees want percentage increases to sustain differentials. You definitely *cannot* please everybody in this situation. Management must weigh up all the variables, make a decision *and stick by it*. If it's your own idea, you're much more likely to convince yourself of the need to resist change. If it's the consultant's idea, you might waiver, with potentially catastrophic consequences. So please don't ask me about designing your pay system, as a categorical refusal might simply offend!

However, there are some key features of pay packages which are more compatible with Team Enterprise than others. Consider each against you own profile before deciding:

Differentials Kill Teamwork

Lots of companies set about restructuring their organisation into teams without thinking this through. They then find that they cannot get the essential levels of flexibility, job rotation and shared responsibility because of perceived differences in pay. I have seen instances where some employees were expected to control the output of others and yet receive only 70 per cent of their colleagues' weekly pay. I can understand the historical reasons for this glaring anomaly and I can understand the difficulties in reaching a generally accepted solution. But I cannot understand why so many managers blindly continue with the expectation that people "will eventually forget about them". They won't: inequality of remuneration is one of the strongest demotivators around. I have also experienced a situation where, as a matter of company policy, salaries were confidential to the individual and to the organisation. A huge problem arose about suspected pay differentials when, in reality, the differences were much smaller than generally believed. However, the damage had been done and even tiny differences were seen to create a disenchantment way beyond their scale.

The key determinant is "felt fair". People will accept differences if they see good reasons for them. These could be experience, consistently good performance or additional responsibilities. But history tells me that you should only generate differences in pay within groups doing the same work if there is an absolute and acceptable case for them. Otherwise you'll be forever coping with resentment and damaged morale.

Piecework Kills Team Enterprise

As advisors to many companies, my colleagues and I here have a big problem. We do not recommend any specific pay system, but we are to a man absolutely convinced that you cannot *ever* have an effective Team Enterprise with a traditional piecework system. The reasoning is fairly obvious. A Team Enterprise demands a holistic view of the world of work from all of our employees. We want them to be concerned about output certainly but also about quality, productivity and customer delight. And then we want them to give their attention to safety, to the environment and to working with colleagues right across the organisation. In short, we want them to look at the world of work in totality and concern themselves with every single variable that impacts on their contribution, intellectual as well as physical. We want a purer form of motivation to support this involvement.

Unfortunately, piecework systems come from different times. They are based on a combined Tayloristic/Theory X view of working life. If people are paid by results, that's exactly what will dominate their daily thinking. They will focus exclusively on getting as many widgets out of the door as possible to maximise their earnings. Once the requisite maximum has been achieved, you can forget everything else. Quality, customer satisfaction, on-time delivery and so on do not figure in their personal vocabularies. Job-and-finish mentalities can often free up huge tranches of spare time but, in their minds, that's theirs. They've earned it, so you can't have it. Managers may tear their hair out with frustration, seeing this huge window of opportunity for addressing all the other ills of working life. But we shouldn't blame the workers. Management created the system, management created the values and management have to accept total responsibility for the situation.

Piecework is therefore incompatible with Team Enterprise. However, in many organisations this particular payment system has been in place for years and has presented the distinct benefit of high productivity. There is a real fear that switching from piecework to, say, measured day work will result in a sharp loss of efficiency. Figure 24 shows the desired profile alongside the ideal and worst-case situations.

Figure 24: Moving from Classical Piecework Systems

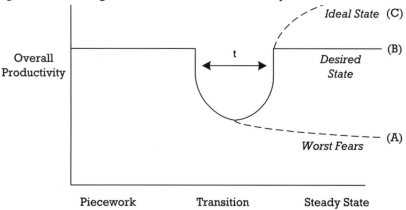

If workforce motivation is solely driven by pay, then simply removing the "threat" of lower earnings may well reduce the incentive. Profile A will ensue with a sharp drop in productivity. Leyland did exactly this in the 1970s: removed a long-established pay system and relied solely on the "felt fair" characteristics of the new scheme, with a consequent drop in productivity of 20 per cent. Profile B assures that "something" is put in place to ensure that employees are sufficiently motivated to continue to produce at their previous level. The issue here is to ensure that the time for transition "t", is kept as short as possible. Ideally, we would like to see an *improvement* in productivity (Profile C), particularly when measured by total operational efficiency, as opposed to direct labour efficiency alone. But again, we want to see "t" at zero or at an absolute minimum.

You have to plan this transition carefully and ensure that the negotiating process includes checks and balances to protect you against either scenario A or an extended transition time. One thing you mustn't do is act on blind faith. Giving away the benefits of the new pay system without an absolute commitment from the workforce could be catastrophic. In my experience, you never get them back. Changing pay systems is fraught with risk and changing from piecework systems to more modern pay practices is the riskiest of all. My advice is simple:

- Take your time

- Look at best practice elsewhere, especially those who have successfully made the transition

- Negotiate carefully, emphasising detail and consequences

- Communicate, communicate and then communicate again to ensure that there is no ambiguity or misunderstanding in either content or intention

- Monitor in fine detail.

However, this is just the theory. The practice, I am relieved to say, is totally down to you. And the best of luck!

Bonus Systems Can Damage Team Enterprise

We mentioned earlier that Leyland suffered an enormous loss in productivity in shifting blindly from traditional piecework systems to a fixed payment system called *measured day work*. In the latter, individual and team performance were measured and reported but few financial penalties existed for underachievement. The new system relied on goodwill and management attention. Such checks and balances proved totally inadequate and the consequences are a matter of history.

However, it was not all bad. Apologists for the revised system can justifiably claim significant improvements in capacity planning, inventory management and general manufacturing controls — but scarcely enough to pay for the costs of transition and lower labour efficiencies.

After a few years of stagnating performance, something had to be done. Unfortunately, once again the organisational decision-makers, no doubt heavily influenced by the oversimplistic views from both sides of the negotiating table, decided that a return to monetary motivation was needed. We went back to the carrot and stick. A plant-by-plant bonus scheme was introduced which paid on a ratio of productive hours generated divided by actual attended hours. It seems simple and in principle it was. But in execution it proved enormously complex and absorbed a huge amount of management time. However, its principal weakness was that it returned the average employee back to the mindset where effort equated a financial payback. Other issues faded into the background as every worker in this huge empire demanded the opportunity to maximise earnings. Inventories grew, management became increasingly distracted from the real issues of working life and morale plummeted. Other important facets of output suffered as well, such as quality, on-time delivery and mobility/flexibility. We even had the nonsense for a few years of employees being paid a quality bonus, almost inherently accepting that bad quality was a fact of life!

Many bonus systems share the same weaknesses as the Leyland productivity scheme. If you must have a bonus, in a Team Enterprise environment it should have five characteristics:

1. The scheme needs to reflect a holistic view of performance and not emphasise one element above any other.

2. The scheme needs to be perceived by the workforce as genuinely reflective of their overall contribution.

3. The scheme needs to be perceived by the workforce to be intrinsically fair and simple.

4. The scheme needs to be easily managed and not draw management into constant tinkering or horse-trading.

5. The scheme needs to be relatively stable and free from dramatic fluctuations, particularly downwards.

I hope that some of you are now thinking that the above is too demanding, that no scheme can ever totally satisfy all five of these desired characteristics. Because that is exactly right. Any bonus scheme, seen as a *motivational* instrument, is going to be imperfect. There are contradictions in these requirements that can never be 100 per cent satisfied. The last characteristic — the need for stability of earnings — is at total odds with the desire to see earnings reflect effort. But in truth, whilst employees might find the idea of an occasional unexpected windfall quite acceptable, the reverse is hardly ever palatable. This is particularly the case after long periods of positive payments. People become dependent on their new standard of living and, negatively affected, can react badly to the change in circumstances.

So our conclusion is quite challenging. Bonus systems are a threat and rarely a boon to Team Enterprise. If you have to have them, ensure that they comply to the five characteristics noted above or be prepared for negative consequences!

Performance-related Pay Doesn't Help Either!

I appreciate that some of my earlier comments on pay systems may be somewhat contentious, as they are not the stuff of perceived wisdom. If I have managed to upset you in the last few pages, forgive me. However, I fear that I am going to do so even more in this next section!

Everywhere I go nowadays, I encounter the gurus of performance-related pay. Whether it be the worlds of education, government, quasi-government or industry, the message seems to be that linking pay to performance is unquestionably always a good thing. Permit me to differ for a while as I try to delete "always" and replace it by "very occasionally".

We have dealt to a large extent with our concerns on direct labour performance pay in the previous three sections. Linking remuneration only to output overfocuses employees' concentration on one single parameter — volume — to the exclusion of everything else. Developing a fair and equitable system of measurement is also, in most instances, extremely difficult and perhaps unsustainable over the medium term. Performance-related pay is, if you accept my argument, usually an ineffective device for motivating direct labour. So why should it be any different for any other group?

To illustrate the point, let us examine the common practice of *merit pay*. Merit pay is usually delivered in the form of a "merit budget" accompanying the annual "cost of living increase". So a general increase of, say, three per cent may be augmented by an additional payment of, say, two per cent, to be distributed individually according to performance over the previous year. Most companies seek not to publish the overall cost of the merit budget, as this will only raise expectations. The whole scheme is shrouded in secrecy, as the majority of managers try to deal with each of their charges on a confidential basis. Unfortunately, this is usually undermined very quickly by the natural curiosity in the department to find out whether you've personally done well, badly or indifferently. Problems can also be anticipated with other groups that don't have access to this additional payment and feel aggrieved by the disparity.

The manager is supposed to apply highly objective criteria in their allocation of the allotted pot. However, there is a problem here. What happens if the same people "overperform" year after year? The inevitable consequence is one of great differentials in an area where people are essentially doing the same job — the only justification being apparently one man's perception of relative performance. "So what?", cry the purists, "That's exactly what we are seeking to achieve. The lower paid and poorer performers will be motivated to mirror the achievements of the high flyers."

That's great in theory but not so effective in practice. For a start, the usual reaction is not determination to emulate but a resentment at the inequity of it all. Only rarely can we defend such criticism by reference to the absolute objectivity of the process. You might find it in, for example, some sales organisations where volume, and hopefully margin, are pushed, but elsewhere subjective assessment often dominates. The hapless manager, faced with deteriorating morale, frequently uses the following year's merit allotment to rebalance packages. "Buggins-turn" dominates the majority of practical instances of merit budgets. Unless you can guarantee absolute confidentiality and absolute objectivity, experience tells us that these schemes rarely contribute any positive strokes to working life. And a motivational scheme that turns out to be demotivational is surely not worth the effort.

Humiliating Conditions

One of the key obstacles to effective empowerment in many of the companies investigated by Optima over the years has been the application of practices which are perceived by some or all of the workforce as "humiliating". Often management are shocked by the revelation that their charges see perhaps long-standing and traditional conditions as iniquitous or worse. They might also become quite defensive, arguing that the benefit considerably outweighs the inconvenience. However, such practices can have a cumulative effect which in totality "distances" the employee from the organisation. To quote a few of the many examples of "humiliating conditions":

Clocking

I have no particular argument in favour of or against clocking, *as long as it's done consistently*. However, when, as in so many companies, the discipline is applied to only one part of the workforce, then you have a recipe for disaffection and resentment. Just put yourself in the shoes of Sam, a longstanding, loyal and conscientious shopfloor worker who has to clock in and clock off. If he has to comply with this practice day-in, day-out whilst even the most junior staff or office employee can seemingly come and go as they please, he automatically feels inferior or, even worse, mistrusted. Sam may not have been late for five, ten or perhaps twenty years and yet he still has to endure these oppressive (in his mind) regulations because he is a shopfloor worker, and apparently shopfloor workers cannot be trusted.

This hurts and the hurt will multiply after years of seeming injustice. So when management goes along and pleads for a greater intellectual and emotional contribution to the world of work, Sam's cynicism and reluctance is totally understandable. There are only two acceptable outcomes; either:

- Everybody clocks; or

- Nobody clocks.

There are greater dangers in the first if the device is seen as purely a matter of behavioural control. But if there are good communicable reasons otherwise, say in reportage, accounting or safety, then the practice should be more acceptable.

Separate Facilities

When I joined Leyland Trucks in the early 1970s, I was simply amazed by the proliferation of canteens around the place. We seemed to have canteens for every organisational level. On our South Works site, for example, we had the huge, cavernous shopfloor canteen. This was characterised by poor lighting, bare boards and basic equipment. The workforce ate with plastic cutlery, as apparently they couldn't be trusted not to pinch the steel knives and forks. Many wandered in carrying their own equipment in their greasy overalls. One wonders how many cases of food poisoning this practice engendered!

As the shopfloor worker queued for his food, carrying his ancient, mangled aluminium tray, he could see through to the next canteen. This was the Shield Room, where even junior staff sat patiently as busy waitresses served them a much higher class of fare, complete with real knives and forks! Further down the building, several other rooms existed, culminating in the Directors' Dining Room where attendance was strictly by invitation only. Even the title of director meant nothing until the new incumbent was summoned by the head of the table!

This hierarchy around one of the most basic human needs — the need to eat — sends out a clear signal of your place in the world of work. For those achieving the dizzy heights of silver service, the perception of status may have been very good for the ego. However, for those forever confined to the dingy ambience of the lowest level, a feeling of inferiority or alienation was almost inevitable.

Canteens are just one area where aspirations of a unified culture can be undermined. Car parks are another equally visible signal of differentiation. Unfortunately, at Leyland Trucks I never quite managed to eliminate this altogether, for all sorts of reasonable but, at the death, totally unconvincing excuses. I worked with a company recently where the issue of prime site reservations on the firm's car parks had been a running sore for years. However, to my astonishment, and incidentally against my advice, they scrapped the reserved places for authority but replaced them with service! Those employees with over 20 years in the business were able to move into the spaces vacated by management. All very laudable in intent, I suppose, but the logic is flawed, simply replacing one form of elitism with another. Long service may be more palatable than hierarchy, but it may not be sustainable in the long term. To avoid unnecessary risk and complication, my advice is simply to eliminate all badges of unnecessary differentiation.

Your challenge in creating a Team Enterprise is to identify all those trappings of privilege which are capable of contributing to, or simply maintaining, the perceived differences between management and the managed. You then have to carefully assess whether removing the privilege will make a real difference. This can be a difficult decision, but fortunately you can have more than one go at getting it right. Don't fall into the trap of assuming all differences are necessarily bad. Few would seriously advocate, for example, harmonising salaries, as such differentials are generally accepted. I made the mistake of assuming that the type of company car used by senior management would be a key driver of dissent in the organisation. After all, I'd heard enough negative remarks made about "fat cats in their company machines" over the years. However, when I adopted a cheap MPV which doubled up as the firm's "van" as my company car after receivership in 1993, I received just as many comments about giving the wrong signal to the outside world about the status of the new company. We need to think through these differentiations and, ideally, see them through the eyes of others in the organisation. Only then can we ultimately distinguish the important from the trivial.

Humiliating Procedures

The good thing about the weaknesses portrayed in the foregoing is that they're easy to spot. People will talk about them and, no doubt, they will feature frequently on the bargaining table, particularly those more obvious differentials in payment systems, holidays and pensions. However, beneath them may lie a raft of equally pernicious practices that continue to reinforce this sense of mistrust and inferiority. Identifying such activities can be extremely difficult, as both sides often take them for granted. However, they equally need to be removed or modified if efforts at creating a unified culture are to be successful.

One of my colleagues talks about an incident in our early days of attempting to introduce self-directed work teams. He was deep in discussion, trying to persuade one such group to engage in more of their own decision-making, when he was abruptly challenged and accused of being insincere. An argument developed about the seriousness of the company's intent, which culminated in an operator saying that as long as we continued with practices like the "pen replacement system", we could never be serious. As he said, "If this new process is as stupid as getting a new pen, it'll never work."

All operators have, as part of their job descriptions, to write comments and information on a range of documents. To do this, unsurprisingly, they need pens. However, if a pen ran out, as it inevitably would, they were obliged to follow this routine:

- The unfortunate operator, now bereft of a writing implement, had to find a foreman or supervisor to authorise a replacement. This was not always easy, as their superior could be in a meeting or occupied elsewhere. Often the operator would have to leave the job to locate somebody endowed with the necessary authority.

- Upon finding the foreman, or equivalent, the operator would present the old pen. A piece of cardboard, specifically used for the purpose, would be brought out of pocket or office, and the pen would be tested to ensure that it genuinely had yielded its last drop of ink.

- Once satisfied that a new pen was now needed, the supervisor would hand a "chit" to the operator, authorising the bond stores to release a new pen.

- The operator would join the queue for the bond stores, hand over his chit and receive, at last, his new writing utensil.

As the operator so powerfully emphasised, the cost of a new pen to Leyland Trucks was probably no more than eight pence. The price of the above farce, measured as lost time plus the opportunity costs involved, was more than likely to be several pounds. The only justification for this ridiculous and irrational state of affairs had to be that the company didn't trust the shop-floor not to walk off with their writing implements, despite the fairly obvious conclusion that to justify the expense, the firm had to be in danger of losing about a hundred pens to every single employee!

In traditional businesses, there are probably scores of processes and procedures that are built on a foundation of suspicion and mistrust. However dressed up, eventually this will be the way they will be perceived by the workforce. Fortunately, as the empowerment process gathers momentum, such situations will come progressively out into the open. The challenge here is to see the process or procedure in true perspective and not to comfortably resort to the rationalisations or justifications of the past. An empowered workforce will only be really effective when they feel valued. Unfortunately, management have a habit of unconsciously sending out signals to the contrary.

Flexible Working Systems

The world of work is changing in an obvious fashion in terms of working patterns. Where once, for example, the retail industry traded on a longstanding system of a five-and-a-half-day week with Wednesday afternoons and Sundays off, life has completely changed. Seven-day opening is now commonplace and further augmented by late night, if not all-night, availability. The customer may be king but competition is a more likely candidate to become emperor. Regardless of whether or not the market really needs this widening access, it's a brave retailer who tries to knock the trend.

Similar developments are seen in other spheres of commerce and business. Competition is demanding greater and greater levels of flexibility as businesses become more and more pressurised. In the truck industry, short-term fluctuations in market demand were always managed through a "build-to-stock" policy. Increases or decreases in customer buying patterns were addressed by simply adjusting the floor stock "float", the number of vehicles between the customer and the market. Factory and supplier schedules could be smoothed to minimise disruption. However, the costs were considerable. Funding an inventory level of perhaps between three to six months' supply of vehicles could be inordinately expensive in interest payments alone without taking into account stock losses, obsolescence, damage, rework, repair and so on.

In collaboration with our partners, DAF Trucks, Leyland developed a build-to-order philosophy, which simply said that no buffer stock would be held between the factory and the customer. Instead, it would rely on super-fast and reliable lead times to get the product to the customer when he wanted it. As well as the obvious and dramatic financial savings, the customer also benefited by getting access to what became known as a "factory-fresh vehicle". This simply reflects the fact that the vehicle the customer buys hasn't been stuck in a compound or a field for six months before being exposed to the danger of a sale. From a marketing point of view, this is an excellent story. From a financial standpoint, it is even better. But for the factory, such a colossal change represents the world of work being stood on its head. The factory is no longer isolated from the market by the huge tranches of stock lying around the country (or countries). Any fluctuation in customer demand is felt immediately by those making the product. And whilst a certain amount of "damping" can be achieved by making small adjustments to lead times, the level of volatility for the plant increases dramatically.

Leyland, like other automotive companies subsequently, tackled this by flexing the working week. We could no longer guarantee a 37-hour week, week in, week out. Something different had to be developed and this something became known as AVDs, Additional Vacation Days. If the demand next week, say, was worth 42 hours, then we worked 42 hours with the incremental five hours going into a "bank", rather than being paid as overtime. Eventually, the programme might fall and the time would be "repaid". Wherever possible, we tried to arrange this payback to match social requirements. Most time off was engineered at Bank Holidays, for example, to give greater quality time for employees with their families.

There are many similar arrangements to this across a host of businesses. As I said earlier, life is changing — but the manner in which such changes are introduced is vital to the preservation of the ethos of a Team Enterprise. There are six key stages:

- **Stage 1: Background Explanation.** The need for such a radical upheaval of employee working patterns should *never* come as a surprise to the workforce. Using the devices described earlier in our chapter on Communication, the workforce should be constantly informed on developments surrounding their industry. We must always remember that *opinions* and *views* are probably more important than *facts* and *statistics*. The conveyance of mere facts will never create trust and reliance. However, consistent and transparently honest interpretation of the way external parameters impinge on your company could go a long way in this direction.

- **Stage 2: Consultation.** Once the specific factors relating to the change in circumstances are known, the workforce should then be consulted. Whilst trades unions and representative bodies are obviously important here, the need of the workforce at large should not be neglected. Managers should be encouraged to communicate and debate the broad issues involved so that a cogent understanding of the situation is achieved by all. Rumours and grapevines can be fuelled by unnecessary secrecy, so ensure that all the drivers for change are communicated in a simple, open manner.

- **Stage 3: Selection of Strategy.** During Stage 2, it is likely that most of the practical ways of addressing the situation would have been revealed and debated. If this is not the case, then time should be taken to do so without prematurely concluding or "leading" to a personally preferred option. Each strategy should be carefully laid out and the merits and disadvantages discussed. Care must be taken to highlight the importance of the business need and the ongoing requirement to do a lot more than simply satisfying customers. The consequences of failing to achieve either of the latter points may need to be explained, if they are not immediately obvious. Management must then declare its preferred option, giving clear reasons as to why the route

selected has been chosen. Wherever possible, such information should be conveyed verbally through cascade and
supported by written briefs, not the other way round.

- **Stage 4: Communicate the Implications.** If the route selected has far-reaching consequences on working patterns
  or perhaps even job retention, some time must be allowed
  to enable the workforce to digest the full implications of the
  new strategy. Management too often underestimates how
  long this process will take. They forget about the inherent
  advantages they have personally had in terms of a greater
  familiarity with both the facts and the nature of the issue.
  Communication must be exercised with patience and tact.

- **Stage 5: Introduction.** There is often a presumption in
  businesses, particularly in those with strong union representation, that a negotiated settlement is both the object and
  the end of the matter. Once the workforce signals its acceptance of the proposed alternative, so the reasoning
  goes, the arguing is over and the employees will simply
  have to get used to it. However, whilst the battle of the negotiating table may be complete, the fight to win over real
  employee commitment goes on. We don't want employees
  to simply and reluctantly resign themselves to the new
  working pattern. We want them to be utterly convinced of
  the inevitability of it all. It may be too ambitious to expect
  everyone to embrace the change enthusiastically but that
  should not stop us trying to do so. The implementation
  should be handled carefully and sensitively. I have seen too
  many examples of managerial triumphalism undermine
  well-intentioned initiatives. Even at Stage 5, it is still "game
  on". We're not there yet.

- **Stage 6: Maturation.** An unpopular working pattern will
  always be unpopular. I'm sure many of the multitude of retail workers who crawl out of bed on a Sunday morning
  yearn for the good old days of a traditional five-and-a-half-
  day week. As one of the shop stewards once memorably

said to me of our Additional Vacation Day scheme, "You can expect me to understand it, you can expect me to accept it but, for God's sake, don't expect me to like it!" In other words, there is an appreciation of the business need and an acceptance of the inevitability of the chosen practice, but in reality a lingering sense of discomfort and even latent resentment is understandable. In such cases, one has to guard against the reasons for the change simply being forgotten as time passes by. The sensible manager will routinely think up excuses for raising the matter on a regular basis and use their ingenuity to dream up new ways of rehearsing the same old arguments. "Repetition, repetition and . . . repetition again", may seem Machiavellian but it's not. It protects against complacency as well as the occasional mischief-maker who may, for their own reasons, wish to use the unpopularity for an unwelcome agenda. In the same way as car makers use their advertising to reinforce the purchasing decision of existing buyers, managers must continue to be vigilant, recognising that distance from the point of implementation may lead to eventual rejection.

A world-class Team Enterprise competing in an aggressive market will inevitably encounter challenges which shape new working patterns and discard old practices. The art of good management here is to ensure that the old simplistic routine of "negotiate and implement" is handled with far more subtlety and sensitivity than hitherto. It sounds sensible and it sounds easy. But in the hurly-burly of business life, it is so often forgotten. This is another example where a little patience and planning can pay huge dividends downstream.

INFORMAL SYSTEMS

Finally, let's examine the potential for informal employee systems to help establish a Team Enterprise. This is an area of some dispute. There are those who say that straying into the world outside work is both wasteful and potentially damaging.

Like most things in life, there is a balance. The informal employee systems in the world of work should be an add-on and never, ever, be seen as a dominant part of the organisation's culture. I've spent too much time in my career fretting about the amount of resources spent on charity work, Christmas celebrations, football competitions, quizzes and their seemingly never-ending ilk. Whilst the sentiment may be Scrooge-like, and I've often been accused of that, anything that deflects attention or resources from the key deliverables of working life is, in my view, dangerous. However, properly constructed and properly managed, these informal systems can have a unifying impact within the organisation, as well as creating a bond between the individual and the company. The art is in striking the right mix.

In times past at Leyland, investment in the social life of the working community was considerable. The wonderful Leyland Motors Social and Athletics Club stood for decades as a monument to the paternalistic interest of the company directors of old. Such large-scale interventions are, sadly, decreasingly appropriate. They appeal less and less as value for money for the company or as suitable venues for the employee. Something else is required.

In the 1990s, we concluded that we in management had little idea what to do. We couldn't even agree amongst ourselves. I, perhaps over-sentimentally, wanted to resurrect the declining ideal of the "club" and introduce a more modern approach. Others wanted to move in diametrically opposite directions. In the end, we made the correct decision and abdicated responsibility. A view was taken that the people who know best what the workforce want are the workforce themselves. We therefore invited a group of employees who seemed to be interested in this sort of thing to decide the best way forward. Terms of reference were established, a budget agreed and, by and large, all decision-making was left to this cross-departmental team.

Called the Links-Lifestyle Committee, over the years this group has established a reputation for innovation and novelty backed up by plenty of enthusiasm. Events include:

- Trips to places of interest, including museums

- Rambles with families and friends

- Shopping trips

- Zoo visits, again for families

- Tenpin bowling nights

- Football/cricket competitions

- Golf

- Aerobics

- Pub quizzes

- T'ai Chi.

The list is endless!

The costs of these events are subsidised by the company and they are generally well attended. I am very much in favour of this approach (and not just because it's cheap!) For a budget of around £20 per head per year, we have a series of events held outside working hours with managers only in attendance as participants. Rank counts for nothing. The benefits include the development of a social interaction with one's closest work colleagues; friendships extended over departmental boundaries; and a greater sense of affiliation with the company. With the committee having full authority from the firm for its expenditure, there are none of the hassles, challenges and criticism so frequently experienced when management were actively involved. It is basically much friendlier and much less formal than an "orthodox" approach.

The company also financially support a Charity Committee on a pound-for-pound basis. For every pound the Charity Committee raises, the company matches it. I'm not sure that there is any real correlation between the activity here and any greater benefit to the organisation. The occasional distraction from the real business of making trucks can also be a bit worrying. But on balance, the feel-good factor, particularly when the cheques are distributed to deserving causes, probably makes it worthwhile.

Other devices for informal employee systems have proved less successful. As previously mentioned, the Dutch idea of giving a present each Christmas to every employee did not go down too well due to the inappropriate selection of the gift itself. In fairness to our continental cousins, in this area you cannot please all of the people even some of the time! The overall effect was one of scepticism and resentment. My advice here is to sup with a long spoon. Similar reactions were encountered with the distribution of mementoes to celebrate specific occasions. One man's treasure is another man's tat! Distributing huge quantities of cream cakes proved another disaster as overnight storage in the allegedly refrigerated lorries turned the cream rancid and grey. Only those with the strongest of stomachs enjoyed that one.

Another area of contention was the 25-year service celebrations. I say "contention", as I disagreed but my thoughts were shared by very few. However, I did always worry about the lavishness of the affair and whether we could keep it up even in times of recession. Fortunately, my fears were never tested but I do believe you should never start these things unless you can maintain them through thick and thin. Cancellation will cause enormous damage to morale as potential recipients feel "robbed" of their natural entitlement. Management credibility will also take a fearful hammering, which will make you think twice in future.

Informal employee systems are there purely and simply to reinforce the collective spirit in achieving the desired unity of purpose. Each proposal should be carefully vetted against this end, taking into account value for money and longer-term sustainability. Get them right and they can be a powerful force in attaining your ideal. Get them wrong and wasting money might be the least of your concerns.

CHAPTER 12

TEAM ENTERPRISE IN ACTION: THE ROLE OF REPRESENTATIVES

In this chapter we will consider the role of the "representative" in the world of Team Enterprise. By "representative", we mean any of those people nominated by management to speak on behalf of their colleagues or those who are elected by the workforce in either unionised or non-unionised situations. Before we begin detailed consideration, let me emphasise that I am not knocking trade unions here. I believe after many years of good, bad and indifferent experiences that, properly constructed, the representative body can be a positive force within any company. Unfortunately, examples of good practice seem to be few and far between, and the cause of the problem lies, as usual, more with management than anywhere else.

Workplace Attitudes

To explain, let us consider a general profile of workplace attitudes, as illustrated by Figure 25. In any organisation, we can divide up employee attitudes into three categories, which we describe at Leyland as the "20:60:20 Rule".

Figure 25: The 20:60:20 Rule

Positive	20%	Highly conscientious, hard working, strongly positive towards the company
Neutral	60%	Good employees, reasonably hard working, generally positive towards the company
Negative	20%	The whinging, whining negative underbelly

The top 20 per cent element are our crème de la crème. These employees are highly conscientious, often going way beyond the usual call of duty. They work hard, usually arriving before everybody else and leave only when the car park is well nigh empty. They are loyal to the company and feel a strong bond between themselves and company ideology.

The next 60 per cent are Joe and Joan Average. Their characteristics are "reasonable" — reasonable attitudes, reasonably hardworking and reasonably positive towards the company. However, they are definitely not unquestioning — not for them the unchallenging obedience of the top group. They can at times be suspicious, cynical and disbelieving — the world of work's equivalent of the floating voter. And there are usually a lot of them.

The bottom 20 per cent are the negative minority, Jack Black's "moany-faced sods". They have a tendency to permanent cynicism and sarcasm. They never believe any company communication nor give credence to any new initiative. They've seen it all before, used to have the T-shirt and know it will never work, whatever "it" is. However, from time to time you may find jokers in this pack, the shopfloor or office comedians who use humour to convey their world-weary cynicism. A dangerous breed indeed.

Now this isn't meant to describe every single situation in traditional establishments. Some places may have different proportions in each category. It could be 14:60:26 or 10:70:20. The actual numbers don't matter for our argument; it is merely the classifications that are useful. The real concern arises when we juxtapose Figure 25 alongside the level of *management attention* each category is given.

Figure 26 attempts to do this. Management's attention tends to get drawn to the lunatic fringe disproportionately here. Obviously, management find the top 20 per cent both useful and attractive. To have working for you self-starters who can be trusted at all times to pursue the right objectives in the right manner without detailed scrutiny is an absolute blessing. The world of work is increasingly complex, stressful and unpredictable. This top 20 per cent can often relieve the oppressed manager of many of the hassles of workaday life for little in the way of attention or time. As long as you ensure that the efforts of this group are routinely recognised and rewarded (not necessarily in financial terms), you can leave them alone to concentrate elsewhere.

Figure 26: The Paradox of Management Attention

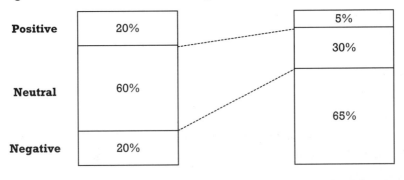

Workplace Attitudes   **Management Attention**

The bulk of our employees (the 60 per cent) may give us relatively few problems. Their complaints are never likely to be vocalised but are more usually internalised, as inner resentment or suspicion. However, they need guidance, they need encouraging and, occasionally, they may need hurrying along or even chiding. So management may have to spend a fair amount of time with them.

The vocal minority, however, swamp the managerial timetable. They are always complaining vociferously, drawing attention to even the most minor discomfort or disruption. They have the loudest voices and constantly demand our presence to argue about trivia. Resolution is rarely achieved with any degree of appreciation. Matters put to bed will only be grudgingly acknowledged with accusations, silent or otherwise, that their concerns shouldn't have been allowed to happen in the first place. These are debates that can never be won, as these negative elements only infrequently defer to logic, and that's only when it suits their argument.

However, the fear most of us carry in management is that the fires stoked up by this lunatic fringe could quickly spread elsewhere. We worry about that middle, neutral element being alarmed by the scaremongering or the griping and therefore feel obliged to spend valuable time dealing with their concerns. The great managerial paradox is that we end up spending a disproportionately large amount of time with the least useful section of the workplace community. It may not be exactly the 5:30:65 ratios shown in Figure 26, but the profile will be similar.

Having fallen into this trap for years in my management career, as evidence by the "Managing by Walking About" anecdote in Chapter 3, I can understand the reluctance to change tack here. We in the upper echelons justify this trait by:

• Persuading ourselves that these people are dangerous in that they are quite capable of influencing others to turn away from the company line; we have to try and quell them;

• Convincing ourselves that, whilst perhaps exaggerated, the arguments articulated by the negative 20 per cent do reflect real concerns in the world of work and hence need to be addressed;

- Being sufficiently arrogant to assume that our personal presence in *ad hoc* shopfloor or office debates is necessary both to win the argument and to convince the protagonists and their onlookers of the validity of the management line; and finally

- Convincing ourselves that the rest of the workforce believes that our disproportionate allocation of time is essential to maintain equilibrium.

I wouldn't wish to excessively criticise those many managers who adopt one or more of the above arguments. Their claim that spending time reasoning with the negative fringe is infinitely preferable to another common management response — avoiding the issue altogether — is irrefutable. I have much admiration for those managers who display such courage and discipline in confronting the problem head-on. It is, I agree, far better than locking ourselves away from the sharp end of the business and spending our time in more predictable and less controversial pursuits. However, despite the good intentions, one must examine the consequences of this "paradox of management attention". These are, in no particular order of priority:

- Spending a disproportionate amount of time with the negative minority satisfies their initial craving for attention. But the more you do it, the more they'll demand. Very quickly, a wasteful spiral of less and less value-added activity is created.

- Spending a disproportionate amount of time dealing with the arguments of the negative minority is likely to persuade you that these arguments have a greater relevance to the *total* organisation than is the case. Your subsequent policy and strategy formulation could end up missing its target by a long way, if you are reacting to the wrong signals.

- Rather than being admired by the rest of the workforce for "taking on" the negative fringe, you are likely to encounter dismay and criticism at being duped by the organisation's lunatic fringe, the barrack-room lawyers and loony-tunes of Chapter 3. Your credibility as an individual as well as a manager will be undermined.

- The lunatic fringe are only dangerous if they are given a platform for their negativity, cynicism and hostility. The most effective platform is that constructed by intensive management attention. The more you pay, the more potentially dangerous they become!

The conclusion I have reached after many years of personally getting it badly wrong is that management needs to maximise their attention to the organisation "good guys", that top 80 per cent who conform to the idea of positive corporate citizenship. Our allocation of management attention needs to shift to 90–95 per cent of our time spent with the positive and neutral community and as little as possible with the others. We need to demonstrate to the majority that we care for them, we understand their concerns and that we are prepared to listen empathetically. We need to lead by example in marginalising those who are inherently at odds with both the company and, perhaps, even the world of work. As we emphasised earlier, the culture of any organisation is largely created by what we as managers pay attention to, what we care about and what we reward. We may not intend to convey that impression when we devote a disproportionate amount of time with that bottom 20 per cent, but we most certainly do so.

Avoiding the Pitfalls

If we accept these arguments, then we must be absolutely certain that the *representative structures* adopted for an organisation don't create similar weaknesses. Unfortunately, this is often precisely the case. The representative body simply provides a fast-track conduit for the bottom 20 per cent, with all the disadvantages that entails. I hear so many managers complain about latent "Ludditism" or disruptive caucuses in their union or representative ranks as if this is a natural consequence of having such structures. It never occurs to them that the root of the problem is the design of the consultation process which they themselves, or their equally important predecessors, threw together. Once you're in this mess, it is one hell of a job to get out of it, so wherever possible I suggest you avoid the dangers at the beginning.

At the risk of being perceived as negative, let us start our consideration of best practice by deciding what representative groups are *not* good at. We can point to at least four areas:

1. Representative channels should not be used for routine communication;

2. Representative channels should not be used to "sell" management policy or persuade employees of the merits of a company line;

3. Representative channels should not be used as a substitute for management practice;

4. Representative channels should not be used to develop policy or strategy in areas of potential contention.

Routine Communication

In our earlier discussion of communication, we established the requirements for good practice. The role of management here was emphasised as being vital in both the design of the communication systems and in their delivery. People want information from those who they consider to be proactive in the decision-making process which affects their future. They do not want communication routed through a perceived third party because:

- The third party doesn't carry the same authority

- The third party doesn't have the same informed outlook, and

- The third party cannot be assumed to be able to convey the necessary nuances and subtleties.

However, even in this new millennium, I still encounter a significant proportion of companies who entrust much of their routine communication to shop stewards or their ilk. This is not just inefficient but a total dereliction of managerial responsibility. Not only are these companies wasting time, they are failing to serve their employees properly and placing representatives in an impossible position.

The average shop steward/representative is not selected or elected primarily on their ability to communicate. They are much more likely to get there by dint of personality or negotiating skills. To expect them to convey the routine day-to-day detail of workaday life, much of which may be of little interest to them, is folly of the highest order. Those who persist in this fashion will see all the necessary nuances and subtleties lost, with perhaps some unwelcome ones added.

Selling the Company

The first prerequisite of an effective shop steward or representative is to have a high level of credibility with their constituency. That will not happen if they are perceived to be management lackeys. To be remotely effective, they must distance themselves from management to a degree and be seen to be taking an impartial line. In times of disagreement, they must show the workforce that they will convey their concerns with commitment and passion. Using your representatives regularly to persuade employees of the merits of a company approach or to sell specific managerial policies is never going to be effective in the long term. We have enough problems with communication through middle managers and front-line supervisors, who do not have the same conflict of interest, without attempting the impossible and the unfair.

Substituting for Management

In many traditional concerns, the shop steward can be seen by default to take over activities which should be the exclusive province of management. Again, the fault lies totally with the latter rather than the former. As well as the routine communication and the marketing of management thinking noted above, we have encountered recruitment, training plans, rostering and more being left to shop stewards. This is pure abdication of the most cynical variety. Shop stewards are not equipped, trained or motivated to undertake those activities in a manner likely to coincide with either the corporate or general workforce interests. However, once conceded, these duties are very difficult to withdraw without inadvertently sending out signals which could create a potential power struggle. Managers should manage and representatives should represent, with each party clearly understanding and respecting the challenges and difficulties of the other's role.

Developing Policy/Strategy

Over the years I have been to several seminars on involvement and participation. To me, these concepts are there to draw the total workforce into a more proactive engagement in working life. For others, however, the terms are used to denote a closer and more harmonious relationship with local trade union or representative bodies. Their objectives are laudable. For decades, the UK in general, and the British Leyland empire in particular, was bedevilled by the absence of a common agenda between management and unions with the consequent loss of a whole section of our industrial society. It is quite likely that the damage caused from over four decades of turmoil is irreversible. We have lost companies, skills and sheer industries which will never be replaced. Any attempt to solve such a fundamental weakness has to be applauded.

However, I do feel that, in their enthusiasm to right the wrongs of the past, many companies go overboard. They build into their management decision-making processes routines for elected representatives to play key roles. Unions find themselves contributing actively to policy and strategy development as well as deployment. That is the theory anyway. In practice, the truth probably lies nearer to posturing, to façades and to game-playing, none of which is either remotely convincing or effective.

Such machinations fail to appreciate the underlying role of representatives. They are there to protect the interests of employees, individually and collectively, in the face of potential abuse or misguided management. Being part of the decision-making furniture can distract substantially from this core responsibility as well as undermining their credibility in the eyes of those they are supposed to represent. It is better, therefore, that with issues of potential conflict or contention, management alone should take responsibility for the consequences of their decision-making. If you have to have "worker-directors" or the equivalent, I strongly suggest that they should be separate to the usual negotiation body. The European model, now increasingly fashionable, is, I suspect, a triumph of style over substance. It may appease those inclined to political correctness but I have seen little evidence of any real value aside from a sense of self-importance conveyed from both sides. By all means play these games if you perceive some worthwhile political or cosmetic benefits, but exercise real caution over issues of potential controversy. Otherwise, the longer-term consequences could be detrimental.

Developing the "Right" Model of Representation

As I said earlier, we have introduced this debate somewhat negatively by focusing on what representatives should *not* be doing. Starting at this end of the argument hopefully emphasises just how wrong so many companies have got it. Team Enterprise demands a unity of purpose tightly controlled from a single agenda. The most important player in this equation is the manager as everything they do, consciously or otherwise, dictates the culture of the organisation. The representative here acts as a safety valve or even perhaps as a *watchdog* to ensure that management's motivation remains well intentioned. Figure 27 attempts to demonstrate these respective roles. The representative body stands alongside the relationship between the management and the workforce. It will have conduits to and from both parties but never so large as to damage the essential dynamic in the bigger picture. Should this happen, we lose the unity of purpose to confused agendas, conflicting priorities and an inconsistent culture.

Figure 27: The Role of Representation

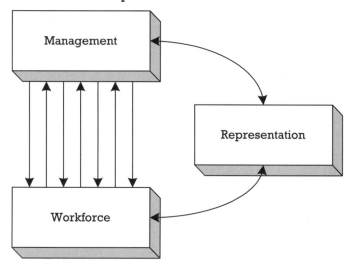

The role of the representative now becomes more difficult. The classical and traditional stance of a shop steward is an easy one to adopt for those sufficiently thick-skinned and oblivious to longer-term issues of competitiveness and survival. To management, you can voice the oft-quoted "I am but a prisoner of democracy" argument in situations where logic fades and a defence for irrationality needs to be found. To the workforce, you can play the crusader, fighting hard to right the evils of mismanagement where, in truth, behind the closed doors of the negotiating forum you might privately concede to the arguments. The whole crazy dance is characterised by irrationality, smokescreens and political manoeuvring — an enjoyable game for the mischievous or egotistical to play but a game nevertheless. Playing the *watchdog* effectively demands a much greater set of skills and one can only admire those who possess them.

In addition to the watchdog we can see five other distinct roles for the representative:

- The *counsellor* or facilitator

- The promoter of *proactive health and safety*

- The sponsor of *workforce training*

- The encourager of *lifelong learning*, and finally

- The *negotiator*.

The ideal representative will act as a *counsellor* or *facilitator* to their constituents where problems of a non-managerial nature crop up. This could include personal difficulties where, in unionised environments, the resources of the union at large can be used. These skills are also put to good effect when difficulties arise between individuals and local management. A good representative who has established their credibility with both sides can be a highly effective mediator in such situations.

Such interventions are expected, particularly from unionised shop stewards. However, to be really effective, a broader agenda is needed so the representative can be seen as an influential and constructive contributor to the world of work. If we examine the basic needs of an employee — once we get beyond pay, terms and conditions and job security — the next area of significant interest is around health, safety and the environment. Trade unions have traditionally played a reactive role in this area, focusing on finding fault and getting management to do something about it. This inevitably leads to criticism and controversy, creating a hostile climate around an area of vital importance to everybody. In recent years, a realisation of the benefits of a more holistic, less adversarial approach called *proactive health and safety* has emerged. This will be covered in detail in the following chapter, but suffice to say here that such a philosophy affords numerous opportunities for the well-intentioned and well-informed representative not just to contribute but also to lead. The success of proactive health and safety seems to be helped enormously by stewards not just promoting the culture but acting as exemplars. This can be a rewarding, informative and immensely satisfying adjunct to the rep's portfolio.

Similar views can be expressed about constructive involvement in *workforce training*. The need for all companies to constantly change is reflected in a parallel requirement for ongoing development of the workforce. In former times, the workforce's involvement may have been oriented around attendance on formal training packages, usually off-the-job. Team Enterprise, with its emphasis on self-directed or autonomous workgroups, necessitates a wider view of training with classical techniques augmented by on-the-job packages, open learning and a host of continuous improvement initiatives. The representative can have a huge influence here, not just through their local understanding of the dynamics and requirements of the workforce, but also through the message they will convey through their constant attention and commitment.

Another increasingly important dimension is the need for much of the responsibility for self-development to be accepted by the individual. We can all quote personal experiences of colleagues and acquaintances whose livelihoods have been fundamentally affected by the march of technological change. Whilst the company may carry much of the onus for helping employees maintain their skill base for existing jobs, the responsibility for future "portability" of talents and expertise lies firmly with the individual. The concept of *lifelong learning* is now well established in governmental and academic circles. "Jobs for life" is disappearing fast as a concept and "skills for life" is not far behind. We have to accept that society will demand a portfolio of occupations in a single working life supported by a constantly developing battery of skills. Representatives, particularly those from unionised backgrounds, need to strongly emphasise this approach if they are genuinely going to look after the long-term interests of their colleagues. Whether "learning representative" will be as commonplace as safety reps or shop stewards in the future remains to be seen, but the unity of purpose within Team Enterprise demands increasing attention here. The involvement of representatives in the encouragement of lifelong learning is a worthwhile and highly effective means of positioning them positively in the organisation.

The role of the representative as a *negotiator* in Team Enterprise needs careful thought. If our ambition is to have the entire workforce using the full array of their talents and expertise to constantly challenge the status quo, then the representative, as a key influencer, cannot be excluded. There is a view that knowledge is power when it comes to negotiations. Accordingly, the "other side" is generally kept in the dark so as not to erode that power. However, such enforced ignorance can lead to misunderstandings, confusion and even confrontation. In Team Enterprise, the reverse philosophy is applied. The representative body is kept fully up-to-date on all matters relating to company strategy, subject only to the limits of commercial confidentiality or sensitivity. At times, information is shared with this group on a "need to know" basis where the representatives commit to holding the matter confidential until disclosure is practical.

In conclusion, most organisations are served best by having some form of representative body, unionised or not. In Team Enterprise, it is vital that such a group *adds* to the effectiveness of the organisation rather than distracts or endangers it. To achieve this, we must ensure that representatives are not lumbered, consciously or otherwise, by those duties that should always be fulfilled by management. However, we must also secure a full, varied and relevant agenda to enable the representatives both to play an important role in the world of work and to be perceived as doing so by their constituents. The selection of would-be candidates is also all-important but management cannot play too large a role here. They can create an air of acceptability by promoting, encouraging and recognising the contributions made at appropriate moments, taking care not to jeopardise the whole proceedings by over-patronising. The ideal representative will share the same "character ethics" as our ideal manager — integrity, honesty, courage and fidelity.

Many organisations may see the above as a long way off, particularly if they still experience the pain of traditionalism. Having lived for years in an atmosphere of hostility, controversy and conflict, such people have my deepest sympathy. However, I remain absolutely convinced that the trigger for change is management behaviour. I once heard a national union official voice privately the thought that "companies get the shop stewards that they deserve". And if anyone should know, he should!

CHAPTER 13

TEAM ENTERPRISE IN ACTION: PROACTIVE HEALTH AND SAFETY

One of the unforeseen pleasures of writing a book like this is the opportunity it affords to reflect. When looking back at the successes and failures encountered at Leyland since the early 1970s, there is a tendency to focus on people, identifying one's heroes and one's villains. The laws of libel probably prevent too much discussion on the latter, but I doubt whether contemplation here would add any value. On the other hand, I have been fascinated by the realisation that my own personal "heroes" emerge from the most unlikely sources. There have of course been some senior members of the great Leyland empire who have been influential on my thinking over the years. I owe a particular debt to the great Les Southworth, who was revered by several generations of aspirant managers. However, looking down the list of people who have inspired me over the past three decades, I have been astonished to see how many have come from the junior ranks. Their names will mean nothing to the reader, nor will they be remembered by too many at Leyland. But the Bill Fairbrothers, the Bill Colcloughs, the Bill Nuttalls and the Ronnie Snows all had a number of things in common. They were incredibly conscientious, hardworking, immensely loyal and always willing to help. Not exactly the

phraseology of Stephen Covey's "Highly Effective People", but
not a million miles away. I doubt whether Leyland is any different to anywhere else in having such a rare breed of individuals
who sit at the very top of the upper 20 per cent noted in the last
chapter. But I wonder whether we all share the same weakness,
admittedly identified in retrospect, of taking such exceptional
people for granted. Perhaps it's because they never complained or sought gratification for their efforts. Their seeming
contentment to simply carry on doing their jobs with a rare excellence may perhaps reflect a purer form of inner satisfaction.
Nevertheless, with the benefit of hindsight, I do wonder
whether we should have cherished these unlauded champions
more and perhaps even stood them on a modest pedestal for
others to emulate.

These thoughts occurred to me as I started to write this
chapter, which reflects upon one of the great successes of Team
Enterprise at Leyland and revolves around another hidden talent, one Alan Lark, health and safety manager *extraordinaire*.
Alan is not a junior in the company, having been in a demanding
senior role for many years, a former RoSPA Safety Professional
of the Year and now nationally known through his pioneering
work with Optima. However, Alan shares all those exceptional
talents noted earlier which distinguish the long-term achievers
from the career grasshoppers, so-called because they rarely
stay in one position long enough to be found out.

Reducing the Casualties

The story of health and safety at Leyland is, to my mind, one of
its great successes. Alan played a key role in first seeing the
opportunity to achieve fundamental change, and then having
the tenacity and ingenuity to carry it through. If we go back to
the early 1990s at Leyland, all was not well in the world of
health and safety. Some successes had been achieved within
the company with Manufacturing Resource Planning (MRPII)
and then Total Quality Management (TQM). The first flushes of
what became known as Team Enterprise also began to bite into

mainstream activity with surprisingly beneficial early results. But the world of health and safety seemed immune to all this, locked in a time warp where old practices, habits and attitudes rigidly resisted the march of progress.

In the assembly plant alone, reportable accidents in 1990 totalled an enormous 65 separate instances, with around 8,000 production hours lost as a consequence. Employer liability claims thundered in (40 related to accidents in that year alone) alongside numerous submissions for occupational diseases like noise-induced hearing loss and vibration white finger. We had, in truth, a "claims culture". It was not unknown for shop stewards to approach an injured party being carted away on a stretcher to remind him of his rights! The American nightmare of "ambulance chasers" was right here on our doorstep!

Such a perceived lack of safety was not down to resources. Huge financial allotments were made annually to cover training, plant renewal and safety equipment. Senior safety professionals were expensively recruited to each plant to ensure that the best of traditional practice could be applied to each individual area of working life. But nothing changed and the adversarial, exploitative mentality simply continued.

Within the automotive industry, Leyland languished around the bottom of the safety league. As a consequence, our safety professionals simply found themselves overrun by constant arguing, fighting, dealing with accident investigations, liaison with the HSE, insurers, solicitors, unions, etc. Hardly the right background for a revolution.

Safety committee meetings were a class apart. These were battle royales! Shop stewards and safety representatives would meet an hour before these monthly conflagrations to develop the tactics of their attack. How many remedial actions had management *failed* to complete since the last meeting? What new weaknesses in the systems and procedure could they *surprise* us with at this session? Where had management demonstrated *ignorance* or *fallibility* this time?

In another room, management planned its response. What excuses could they come up with to silence or moderate the criticism? "Work is ongoing", "estimates are on the way", "lack of progress due to well-known production pressures" were all trotted out with monotonous regularity. But the truth was that management knew they could never win; this was simply a matter of damage limitation. In those circumstances, "postponement", "carried over to the next meeting" or "referred to engineering" were minor victories.

The meeting would commence around a long rectangular table with the sullenly aggressive shop representatives arranged along one side. Opposite the tight-lipped and often white-faced managers would await the onslaught. And once the session was opened, it inevitably came. Shop stewards loved health and safety issues and managers hated them. On other areas of workaday life, management could duck and dive. However, if a metaphoric brick came hurling your way with "H&S" emblazoned on it, you had to catch it. Sitting at one of these meetings was akin to being an Aunt Sally at a coconut shy. Most managers, after years of bitter experience, simply took the punishment quietly and patiently. Losing one's temper was definitely not recommended. As plant director, the senior man on site, I exercised my prerogative to delegate chairmanship to my next-in-line. Being neither a hero nor a masochist, I didn't see why I had to subject myself to this monthly nonsense. But of course I couldn't escape the consequences.

The watershed came at one particular meeting. Amongst the usual mish-mash of trivial complaints such as missing toilet chains and extra pay for phantom dangers, one serious issue emerged. At the front gates of the factory where 2,000–3,000 people poured out each evening, a potential hazard had been spotted. Outside these gates would be parked cars with wives, girlfriends, partners, etc., waiting to pick up employees. One look at the series of cars weaving their way through these exiting masses, particularly in the dark of winter time, was enough to convince even the most hardened manager that danger really existed. Something had to be done about it. After the usual ranting and railing, the chairman agreed to refer the matter to the company architects who would report back in eight weeks. He had bought time and the meeting returned to its normal state of sullen aggression rather than the firecracker of contention.

Two months later, an ashen John Dwyer, the chairman of the safety committee, came to see me. It was the day of the report-back and he expressed deep concern over the architect's response. As he unravelled the numerous drawings and supporting documentation, I began to share his anxiety. In front of us, we gazed at an expensive combination of traffic lights and swinging arms. It was going to cost tens of thousands of pounds. At the time I couldn't guarantee tens. We had a problem.

An hour later, John reached the point in the meeting where the issue came up. He waited until he was asked if the architects had replied and then he threw the plans on the table in a gesture of absolute disgust. For the next few minutes he ranted on about the incompetence of these so-called professionals, their inability to see any situation simply. Everything had to be complicated, everything had to be expensive. It was totally ridiculous, he stated, and added that "people in this room could do a far better job". The other side were at a loss. It wasn't done for managers to slight their own. So when John picked out three of them and offered them a couple of weeks to come up with a better alternative, they were totally non-plussed. A few murmurs were heard but the general demeanour was one of confusion. John returned to me and reported that he had "bought" two weeks and could I please get on to the architects to come up quickly with a more realistic solution.

However, a few days later John was asked to report to the gatehouse where the three nominated safety representatives stood there proudly and smugly. One of them carried the solution to the problem, a £37 length of plastic chain which could be attached to two existing stanchions to separate the cars from the crowds. It worked perfectly and negated any need for the vast sophistication of the architect's traffic lights and swinging arms. John immediately called a special meeting of the health and safety committee and challenged the assembly to come up with some key learning points from the experience. There were three, in retrospect simple and common-sense, but at the time far-reaching:

- Safety problems were everybody's problems, not just management's;

- No-one should bring a problem to the meeting without at least some tentative proposals for resolution;

- No-one should be "actioned" by the minutes of the safety meeting unless they had actually attended the session.

The last point was vital. It meant that both problems and solutions were "owned" by the meeting as a whole and not some distant bureaucracy. It created teamwork and a sense of realism. From that day on, a platform was established where Alan and John were progressively able to take the mutual aggression and conflict out of the formal forum and replace it with co-operation and mutual objectivity. The results, as can be seen from Figure 28, were truly astonishing.

Figure 28: Reportable Accidents — Safety Performance

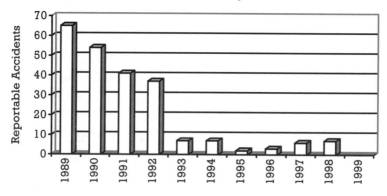

Reportable accidents fell by 90 per cent (90 per cent!) from 65 in 1989 to single figures in 1993. Employer liability insurance costs *fell* by 50 per cent in 1994 when most other companies experienced sharp increases. Attitudes to safety in the general population improved markedly. Accidents and even near-misses were logged and investigated meticulously as learning points for future action. The world turned on its head. All the futility and gross inefficiency of the former adversarial climate disappeared, to be replaced by a healthier and more fulfilling unity of purpose.

To understand what had happened, we need to go back to the old world and examine the dynamics of the situation. Alan uses McGregor's Theory X and Theory Y management styles to understand the process. He believes that in the late 1980s many of our managers, at all levels, were inclined towards a Theory X view of working life. They believed that employees intrinsically disliked work and would avoid it if at all possible. The only way to get people to work effectively, went the argument, was to exercise a high degree of control and direction. Punishment was threatened if orders were not carried out. Not surprisingly, Theory X managers generate an "anti-Theory X" response. The workforce simply reacts and attempts to subvert the dictates of the autocrats. Elsewhere in the organisation after the advent of Team Enterprise, such polarisation had been eroded. But the special circumstances of the health and safety forum allowed this clear schism to continue.

However, we should be careful not to take a one-sided view of this situation and merely blame the shop representatives for their Ludditism and blatant mischief-making. Management was also culpable, perhaps much more so. One can argue that the safety reps were simply reacting to events. Managers, driven by the incessant pressures of production, quality and cost, often gave tacit approval or turned a "blind eye" towards corner-cutting or unsafe practices to keep the lines going. Health and safety was often seen as a chore or even a distraction from proper business. As a result, managers simply regarded safety as a peripheral burden that they were obliged to carry whilst the reps saw management alone as being responsible for safety and for taking the actions necessary to correct unsafe conditions. Consequently, unsafe "acts" were rarely mentioned, all the emphasis resting on unsafe "conditions".

With the initial success of Team Enterprise, the safety professionals in the plant saw a golden opportunity to "hitch a ride". A new system for managing health and safety based on the key objectives of this new philosophy was developed. *Proactive health and safety* was intended as a vehicle to take the company towards zero accidents, the ultimate goal. Using all the principles of the larger initiative, a bespoke package was introduced to utilise the interest and involvement of the *entire* workforce rather than just the committed few. By-products of this new safety culture were targeted as:

- Reductions in employers' liability costs

- Elimination of damage to property, plant and equipment

- Increased operating efficiencies through risk assessments

- Improved employee relations

- Best business practice

- Fulfilment of humanitarian obligations

And, equally importantly, to establish credibility in the eyes of senior management:

- A contribution to reducing overall business operating costs.

Building a Safety Culture

The first step taken by the safety team under Alan was, quite logically, to tackle management attitudes. In his words, he had to get all the Theory X managers to convert to Theory Y. He had to persuade them that, under the right conditions, employees do not inherently dislike work but in fact would relish the opportunity to contribute to a safer working environment. Even more radically, people will manage themselves quite capably and safely if they have objectives that are at once realistic and

challenging. Providing managers could learn to delegate effectively, not only would the vast majority of the workforce take
this responsibility for their own safety, they would more than
likely look to ways of *improving* it. This approach was identical
to that taken elsewhere in the plant on more general matters
but, for whatever reason, health and safety had seemed permanently locked into the old traditional schism.

Alan spotted a window of opportunity with the establishment
of the first shopfloor teams, the forerunners of the autonomous
work groups noted in Chapter 10. He immediately set about
integrating health and safety responsibilities into those elements delegated to the team. Local management welcomed the
approach with open arms, as they needed to demonstrate a few
quick "victories" to authenticate the approach. Everybody
agreed that the general arena of safety was an ideal vehicle to
generate early progress. Alan then initiated a significant education and training programme. He maintained that a company's safety culture was fundamentally determined by the way
people treated each other. In particular, he pointed to the degree to which managers and employees worked together
against a set of underlying safety values, beliefs and behaviours. The key to achieving this proactive approach to health
and safety management lay in creating a mutual trust across the
company. This might be argued as relevant to all areas of corporate activity, but health and safety has an immediacy and a
relevance that cannot be challenged. People may not get particularly enthusiastic about efficiency, productivity or even
quality. But to talk about ways and means of promoting a
healthier and safer environment, against a background of a
generally perceived unsatisfactory situation, is usually quite an
attention grabber. Assuming, of course, that we manage to dis-
pel the belief that safety is simply a political football to be
fought aggressively between management and representatives.

Once persuaded, local management played a vital role in
ensuring that health and safety featured as strongly in the world
of work as production volume, productivity and quality. This

had to be communicated and reinforced *daily* in word and deed. They had to demonstrate that they understood that "people are the company's most valuable asset and management do really care about people's health, safety and welfare". It was easy to say the words but much more difficult to convince the workforce to believe it.

The first step down this road of conviction was to establish a clear "no-blame culture". Employees were encouraged to report all near-misses, minor personal injuries or unsafe acts. Genuine mistakes did not result in individuals being blamed or disciplined, as had happened so often in the past to demonstrate management's "seriousness about safety". Instead we learned to "celebrate the error" by using the experience to draw lessons for future avoidance of perhaps greater catastrophe. If you go down this path, you have to ensure as near 100 per cent conformance as possible. An occasional reversion to type where the traditional rollicking or punishment follows can arrest the progress of the entire initiative. There is occasionally a fine line between genuine error and incompetence. Over-zealous policing can leave the workforce both confused and suspicious. Those who usually think in black and white may disagree here, but we would recommend that guidelines are put in place to ensure that the perceptions of the workforce are always taken into account. Care should be taken to make sure that proper communication and involvement is carried out thoroughly, particularly where the issues stray near the borderline.

There is a need, particularly at the outset, to send out signals reinforcing the significance of the change. One device used by Alan was a poster campaign, which baldly said:

> **If It's Unsafe, Don't Do It!**
> **Someone Expects You Home Today**

This message would have been quite inconceivable prior to 1990 in the days of reactive safety, as management would have anticipated regular downing of tools or stopping of tracks at the merest pretext. But the workforce didn't. They knew they were being taken on trust and no-one wanted to damage this demonstration of faith. The prize — a better way of working — was too great. Even the lunatic fringe, who in times past would have certainly led the charge into mischief-making, feared the consequences of a new peer pressure. It worked.

One illustration of this in practice was the story of the forklift truck driver reporting to the safety manager that he had just driven his forks into a 25-litre drum of oil in the factory yard. Shamefacedly, he confessed that he had been driving too fast when he saw the drum. Despite turning the truck with brakes hard on, he failed to stop and punctured the container. Fortunately he had the sense to contain the spill himself. Despite there being no witnesses, the driver still reported it. After a discussion with the safety manager, they both agreed that the best course of action was a refresher training course.

Prior to 1990 there would have been two other alternative outcomes. Firstly, if there had been no witnesses, he would have fled from the scene as quickly as possible. Containing the spill wouldn't have crossed his mind! Alternatively, had he been spotted, he would have been up before management for a formal disciplinary meeting and no doubt warned on record as to his future behaviour. Many managers may maintain that this is still the right action, as the accident could have had serious ramifications and the causal factor was unquestionably either a lack of concentration or worse. However, you have to gauge whether, in the longer term, the application of the disciplinary process would have greater overall adverse consequences than leniency. Nobody can really advise you in advance; each situation needs to be examined on its own merits. Previous practice needs to be taken into account, as consistency is also all-important. But you need to remember that the rulebook is not always the best way of securing a healthy culture!

Spreading the Gospel

Such has been the success of proactive health and safety at Leyland that in 1993, when Optima was formed, it seemed natural to incorporate the approach into its new portfolio. A dedicated and separate health and safety team, headed by the soon-to-be famous Mr Lark, was created to provide customised consultation services to other organisations. Hundreds of companies and thousands of visitors have flocked to their training courses with a remarkably high satisfaction level. Many have gone on to achieve similar success with their own companies: organisations like Albion Automotive in Preston who have just recorded their sixth RoSPA Gold Award since Optima became involved. The encouraging sign here is that Albion is a 100-year-old company which has achieved a 90 per cent reduction in lost-time accidents. Who says you can't teach an old dog new tricks?

Conclusion

Health and safety is, in most organisations, a fertile ground for sowing the seeds of involvement and participation. Proactive health and safety is now a proven approach to ensuring speedy acceptance and early gains. The temptation, again, to re-invent the wheel may seem irresistible, but my advice is simple — don't!

CHAPTER 14

TEAM ENTERPRISE IN ACTION: MANAGING STRESS — THE MINDSTORE PROGRAMME

Leave Your Prejudices at the Door . . .

Readers of a conservative disposition are strongly urged to skip this chapter. The rest of the book is hardly controversial. You may disagree with some of the techniques advocated but in general most managers leafing through it will recognise the issues involved and hopefully empathise with the approach. Those of a more traditional or autocratic nature are hardly likely to entertain either Optima or this tome anyway! However, here we are about to go somewhat off the wall and take an excursion into areas where conventional practice rarely ventures. None of the following owes anything at all to either Leyland or Optima, save for introducing the process. Although we'll accept culpability for anything that went wrong, any credit for the staggering success that ensued lies firmly and squarely in one man's court — Jack Black. We will hear more about him later.

But first, the beginning. In the early 1990s, we at Leyland Trucks had divided emotions about our progress along the road to Team Enterprise. Financially, the results were way beyond expectations. Our overhead structures were in balance, our organisation was working much more effectively and attitudes generally had improved significantly. Change Initiation had impacted on the latter and much of the old adversarial climate had slowly abated. But a feeling abounded that we really hadn't got to where we wanted to be on employee morale and attitude. Memories linger a long time in companies as troubled as ours and this baggage of history seemed to be continually holding us back. Our desire for a totally proactive workforce seemed an awfully long way away, despite steady progress in the right direction.

We began to fret about this issue and impatiently sought an answer. Many of us had hoped that Change Initiation would have helped more but there were obviously deeper forces at work. We needed something more potent to shift this organisational mindset.

The problem was articulated in what I refer to as *Oliver's Theory of Workplace Motivation*, called that simply because no-one else would own up to it! I have never shown this model to any industrial psychologist for fear of ridicule but since its only use is to illustrate a point, just humour me. Our vision in the early 1990s is shown as in Figure 29.

Figure 29: Oliver's Theory of Workplace Motivation

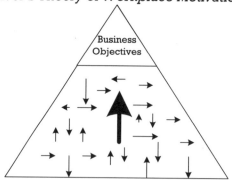

If one imagines the area within the triangle as the totality of every individual's motivation in the world of work, what we are seeking is to have all employees focused on achieving those business objectives at the top of the pyramid. Our ambition is to have everybody working together to their utmost towards this one end, an end which hopefully will be mutually beneficial.

This is represented by the large black arrow. Unfortunately, at an individual level in companies which have yet to reach this utopian state, things are never that straightforward. Again, using the 20:60:20 guideline, some people will naturally be comfortable with this ideal, the majority will be less convinced but nevertheless gravitate towards the same end, and the bottom 20 per cent will have no affinity at all for company objectives and perhaps even work against them.

Our task as senior managers is to use all the resources at our disposal within the world of work to realign the entire organisation in the right direction. You will have read earlier of the devices we used to facilitate this. I am still very proud of the work we did on communication, recognition and organisation restructuring, all of which proved enormously beneficial. Nevertheless, none of these techniques seemed to posses the power to dislodge this negative legacy of history. And as long as this fatalism and guilt lingered, we could never really make the progress so necessary for survival in our fiercely competitive market.

It eventually occurred to us that this model was perhaps oversimplistic. At an individual level, an employee may not feel motivated at all to give of their best towards company objectives due to factors outside the control of the company. They could have health problems, family problems, relationship problems or any number of problems totally outside the world of work. The model was therefore far more complex (Figure 30):

Figure 30: Oliver's (Modified) Theory of Workplace Motivation

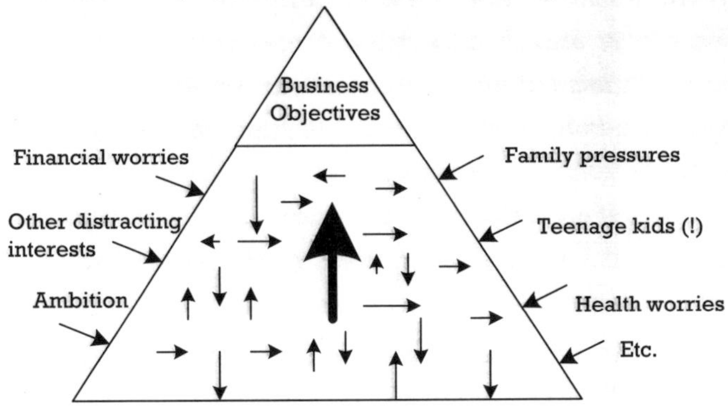

If this new analysis was valid, our challenge was even more ar-
duous than we first thought, and a bit depressing. We couldn't
possibly contemplate intruding into people's lives for the sake
of business performance improvement. Such a thought was both
intolerable and impractical. However, if external influences
were so powerful, we couldn't afford to ignore them either.
Failing to achieve competitiveness wasn't going to suit anybody.
We didn't want to have this discussion in the dole queue!

Mindstore

We therefore looked for a common denominator that could aid
our colleagues in both the working environment and in the
world outside the factory gates; something that wouldn't seem
intrusive and would be readily recognised as useful by all
members of the company. Despite discouraging mutterings
from some quarters about meddling into areas beyond our
proficiency, we persisted. The credit for the eventual solution is
lost in the sands of time but I think it might have been our
manufacturing manager, John Dwyer, who found the answer —
stress management.

His suggestion met an enthusiastic response. Stress was very
fashionable at the time! Workplace stress had started to figure
prominently in the daily broadsheets. And the stresses and
strains of domestic life in the materialistic 1990s were known to
all, even to us truckworkers up north! If we could find a suitable
stress management programme aimed mainly at life outside
work, went the argument, the company might in turn benefit by
having healthier and more settled employees in the workplace.
This seemed a logical approach and, in the total absence of any
other good ideas to address our dilemma, we set about finding
a stress management programme.

This wasn't easy. After all, the ideal model would be something that could be used on a mass scale, something light and
interesting but at the same time useful and enjoyable. Most of
the alternatives that appeared initially seemed learned and
long-winded. Not at all suitable for our purposes.

Around this time I had an important speaking engagement. I had been asked by an organisation called SI Associates to deliver an address at a highly prestigious International Strategic Management Conference in the Gleneagles Hotel in Scotland. There I heard a fellow give an absolutely electric presentation. Its content was hardly academic, being more emotional and motivational than anything else. But he seemed to possess lots of ideas which were pertinent to our situation. His name was Jack Black and he was undoubtedly the star of the show.

In a chat afterwards, I learned from Jack that he worked in the area of personal development, part of which dealt with stress management. He told me of his programmes and later sent me details. It seemed logical therefore to investigate this further, so when I returned to work, I chatted the matter through with Stewart Pierce, the personnel director. We decided to send three candidates to his next two-day programme in Edinburgh: Brian, our quality manager, a natural enthusiast; John, the manufacturing manager, a natural cynic; and Charlie from industrial relations, who had an uncanny understanding of workforce motivation. Their brief was simple — find out whether Mindstore, the name of Jack's programme, was any good and, as a saving grace, study his brilliant presentational technique for possible use in Optima!

From the nature of the people selected to go, you may correctly deduce that Stewart and I expected a mixed reaction to the visit. We wanted a balanced view and the likely varying responses of the different individuals who attended would give us exactly that. Or so we thought. However, the totally unexpected outcome was all three returning completely smitten and using a language totally unfamiliar to the rest of us mere mortals. They were incredibly enthusiastic and positive about pursuing their own personal change programmes. Whatever Jack had done over the two days, it certainly had profoundly influenced my colleagues.

Naturally, Stewart and I had to go as well, alongside other key players including the senior shop steward on site, works convenor Dave Alty. Without exception, we all returned excited about the possibilities of using Mindstore to accelerate our vision of greater organisational empathy. There was something here that we could use, but the question was: How?

Let me now digress for a while and talk about the Mindstore product offering. Jack's portfolio is extensive but our primary benefits came from four areas:

Negativity

Jack explains in a highly entertaining way how negativity can be so devastating both personally and organisationally. He teaches how to avoid the unconscious damage of negative language by adopting a more positive phraseology. In a very amusing section, he reveals simple techniques to protect oneself from other people's negativity using devices such as Ballesteros's belljar, which one commissions to the theme tune from *Thunderbirds*. It sounds crackers, but it works and is a lot of fun.

Success

He talks about the four characteristics of successful living:

- Putting *oomph* into your life, gaining energy to handle stress;

- Developing a positive attitude;

- Breaking out of limiting beliefs and comfort zones; and

- Using both the right- and left-hand sides of the brain to best effect, especially in improving our awareness of the possibility of increasing our creative and imaginative faculties.

Interestingly, although the above are defined as *individual* characteristics, at Leyland we felt that there was a lot of mileage in pursuing them as *organisational* traits. The message is simple but it's communicated so powerfully that both personal and collective mindsets are instantly challenged, to great effect.

Using Relaxation Techniques to Conquer Stress

This was our original objective and Jack's approach meets it in full. By adopting a unique Mindstore version of classic meditative techniques, any of our employees who participated in the programme could now manage better those fractious moments in both private and working life. Jack also ensured that each attendee had a clear view of exactly what was going on here so that a life discipline could be developed, if desired or required.

Using Relaxation Techniques to Set Goals

Like many companies we had been used to setting goals for years and had attempted to involve our employees in a cascade where they in turn could establish their own targets. Jack's approach not only refreshed this process, it also in turn made those involved in the system more ambitious, more challenging and simply more interested. An unexpected benefit!

There is of course much more to the Mindstore programme than I've just mentioned, but these are the key relevances to Leyland Trucks. The system, marketed as the Ultimate Mental Fitness programme, covers most areas of personal development and is introduced in his book *Mindstore for Personal Development* as follows:

> It teaches you to have a positive attitude towards life, to manage your stress levels, to take control of your life, to enhance your creativity, to realise your full potential and to become the person you have always wanted to be.

And on that basis it was little wonder that this subject matter became so popular with his attendees from Leyland. Jack also strays into other areas, which you can take or leave without detracting from the key elements I noted earlier. However, even these alone constitute an approach that is far removed from conventional techniques to shopfloor training! Imagine the reaction to the following description of what it's all about from somebody returning from a Jack Black event. It would go something like this:

> "... and he told me that, if I ever felt stressed or over-anxious, I should retreat to my Alpha closet, which for me only the toilet would suit, and there I would close my eyes and go through his House on the Right Bank routine. By doing this, see, I can take my brain activity, which normally operates at Beta level, down from my usual wide-awake state into Alpha Theta. It's these brainwaves, you see, which emerge when you fall into light sleep or daydreaming, that allow you to use your right brain more. And if you do that, you can more easily become more imaginative, more creative ..."

It's little wonder that the approach caused such a stir!

So having seen the Mindstore product and having been persuaded that this could be of use to us in resolving Oliver's (modified) Theory of Workplace Motivation dilemma, the question was: How could we do this on a mass scale?

There were three key problems: logistics, costs and motivation. Ideally we would like to have stopped the company for two days and sent all 700 employees off to sit at Jack's feet. Unfortunately, whilst from time to time in our cyclical business such opportunities do arise, they were hardly likely to coincide with Jack's availability. In addition, such a scheme would have been very expensive, as we would be paying labour costs as well as Mindstore's not insignificant fees. There had to be another way, and in conversations with Jack we found it.

Jack was keen that, to maximise the impact and to further emphasise that this was a *personal* development tool not targeted directly at the world of work, partners should be permitted to come along too. So each employee was entitled to bring along their wife, husband, partner or close offspring. He took the view that this would both personalise the course and provide a source of mutual support for each individual attendee if they elected to follow the techniques downstream.

Consequently, we hired the largest lecture theatre we could find in the area for a weekend, at the University of Central Lancashire, and set about encouraging and cajoling a large tranche of the Leyland workforce to give up some of their precious time, unpaid. Eventually around 300 in total from Leyland (around 200 employees plus 100 "friends") attended the event supported by others who came through the usual Mindstore entry.

The following Monday morning, I waited anxiously to see the response. The weekend had gone well, fantastically well in fact. However, there is always a difference between being on a course and having slept on it. Within the company there had been a fair degree of opposition to the idea, incidentally only from those who hadn't been on the course. So these were anxious times.

I need not have worried. The reaction was way beyond anything we'd even dreamed about. People were excited, enthusiastic and eager to put into practice the techniques and lessons acquired over the weekend. Initially, even little Mindstore meetings sprung up over lunchtimes where people could swap experiences. And those who hadn't attended the programme began to express an interest. A second session was eventually held to cater for those who couldn't or wouldn't attend the first one, this time augmented by local companies including the training and enterprise council, the local borough council and a housing association. In total, around 40–45 per cent of all full-time employees from Leyland completed the course, giving us a comfortable critical mass.

The benefits of Mindstore at Leyland have been generally accepted — even by the hardened cynics — as exceptional. A new, more positive language emerged replacing the defeatist "been there, got the T-shirt" mentality. It became acceptable to be creative, to be innovative and, most important of all, to be optimistic. The reaction of the partners who came along was even more enthusiastic. Shoals of letters appeared thanking the company for including them on such a worthwhile endeavour.

This manifestation of goodwill from outside the operation was in marked contrast to earlier times when all we were known for was redundancy, rationalisation and restructuring.

We have never tried to quantify the financial impact of Mindstore. I do not think that it's even possible. How do you value goodwill, renewed energy, improved teamworking or simply a friendlier working environment? One of Jack's bigger customers, a worldwide name in electronics, rang us to ask us to financially justify the programme. They were somewhat disappointed when we said we couldn't do it quantifiably but were more than willing to do it qualitatively. There is no doubt in my mind or in the minds of any of the key players around at the time that we recovered our investment many times over. We'll never know what proportion of the imaginative projects, ideas and suggestions since then owe their roots to the Mindstore training. But we can take a guess and say it's considerable.

Since that second session, Jack has been a regular visitor to the north-west, attracting large crowds each time. Lots of his attendees have been inspired to take the Mindstore programme after visiting the factory or talking to its employees. The numbers in this category must now be in the thousands with the vast majority enjoying a similar reaction to the one we experienced. These regular sessions have allowed us to maintain the numbers trained in the techniques. In all honesty I doubt that there are many participants who maintain the disciplines with the regularity that Jack advocates. But the lasting legacy is the continuation of a positive ethos, a willingness to challenge established practice and a collective ambition to achieve what was previously held to be unachievable. Off the wall or not, the only test is whether it works or not. And to repeat Jack, it only works!

Chapter 15

How to Get Started

If you've taken the trouble to plough through this book page by page (and if you have, very well done!), you may now be tempted to give Team Enterprise a go. The initial questions to be asked are, firstly, "How do I start?" and, secondly, "How do I avoid screwing up?" In this chapter we certainly put you right on the first and perhaps give a few pointers on the second. However, if the comment earlier about "celebrating failure" was correct, a few of your own mistakes along the road may well be useful in making you a little more sympathetic to others!

Reminding ourselves of the "preferred process" described very early in the book (see Figure 1 in the Introduction), you can see that experience points towards a controlled and patient stage-by-stage process. The following makes the assumption that you are one of the key influencers in the organisation with the capability and authority of initiating such a far-reaching change. If you're not, I suggest you rehearse your "hand washing speech". This presupposes that your only contact with your boss is as you pass a few seconds at the wash basin after answering the call of nature! Your task is, in a sentence, to awaken interest in this brave new world by the selection of an irresistible fact or two. You could try:

> "Have you heard how *Leyland Trucks saved £10 million a year* by simply changing the culture of the organisation?"

or, if you're really brave,

> "Did you know that *Runshaw College became No. 1 college* in the UK by simply changing 'its management culture'?"

If you wish, you could alter the items in italics to any other example you feel is more likely to catch the eye than those above. This could be particularly useful if any of the specific examples noted elsewhere in the book are keen competitors of yours!

First Steps

To get started, your first task is to convince and familiarise yourself further about the world of empowered systems. There is always a distinct advantage for the organisational champion to know a little more than their colleagues about any new initiative and the case for Team Enterprise is probably even stronger. Everybody, you will find, will have a view about workplace motivation. Many will not wish to adopt best practice seen elsewhere without tinkering or customising, which usually results in the total neutering of the discipline. Accordingly, you must be sufficiently well versed in the subject, first to spot the dangers and then to fight them off. Reading this book will hopefully have assisted here and at the end of the chapter we will recommend a short additional reading list which will strengthen your resolve as well as expanding your knowledge.

There are, however, two other vital steps that you as initiator/leader must take before setting forth on the formal path. First, you should get out and about, visiting best practice organisations from a range of industries and businesses so that the nuances and subtleties of change can be understood. Fortunately, nowadays most companies are more than willing to open their doors and extol the virtues of participation and involvement. Like Leyland, they feel it to be good external public relations as well as reinforcing the message internally that this is a serious and permanent way of life. Organisations like Inside UK or your local Business Link/Learning and Skills Council could also help here. However, you must also immerse yourself in your own culture. Change initiation will help here downstream, but you have to be prepared for any bottlenecks that emerge in the earlier stages. Fortunately, all you have to do here is to talk and to listen, preferably in a ratio of about one to ten! Speak to people individually and in small groups to engender an organisational debate on a matter which might represent a radical departure from the usual small-talk in your business. The novelty, if nothing else, will normally get everybody chattering. I also find an introductory statement like "Tell me what you think is preventing this company becoming genuinely world class" is sufficient to open the floodgates. Carefully facilitated, such dialogue will not only inform but also provide you with a ton of ammunition to use against the inevitable cynics and doubters.

Persuading Management

In Chapter 5 we examined *why* it was important to first "convince and educate the senior management team" and then do exactly the same with middle management. Here we will explore *how*.

Persuading senior management to actually undertake Team Enterprise can be a problem. Despite the almost irresistible financial arguments for participation systems, managers can always be relied on to think of numerous excuses why they shouldn't proceed! I don't want to give such cop-outs any more airing than they deserve, but it is worthwhile examining the underlying reasons for their surprising lack of enthusiasm, recognising that what they say may not reflect their real motive:

- They didn't invent or introduce the idea

- They feel personally threatened by the process

- They feel challenged by the consequences of change

- They feel personally exposed by the debate

- They feel they cannot personally adapt to a participative style

- They feel that this is yet another airy-fairy, HR flavour of the month which will soon pass over

- They worry about the complexity and the size of the task

- They have too many other competing initiatives.

All these situations will be familiar to those who work in the change industry. When I started on the "stump" in 1993, fuelled by an altruistic vision to spread the word to everyone about the power of Team Enterprise, I fully expected a conversion rate of over 90 per cent. After all, where else can you find a means of radically transforming your business bottom line at virtually no expense! My presentations, and those of my colleagues, seem to go down fine with participants. As well as registering over 95 per cent satisfaction levels, the latter always appeared ready to discuss enthusiastically the details of the approach. But then they would go away, sleep on it and seemingly lose interest. At our Introduction to Team Enterprise Days, we have had quite senior people come back two or even three times and still ultimately do nothing about it! Even the ones who decide to go down this path often take several years before taking the plunge. We're always far too polite to enquire why these people come back after such a long time to seek more information. I suspect that we're simply too grateful for the chance of a potential convert!

Despite the obvious potential of the subject and, dare I say it, the excellence of the message, the actual conversion rate seems to be no higher than two to five per cent. That may be something of an understatement, as perhaps many go away and do their own thing, but measured by those who come back to us for further advice, the percentage is very low. And before someone throws in a concern about costs, let me emphasise that these first steps are provided free of charge, so finance has nothing to do with it!

Anecdotally, the key reason why senior managers shy away from what appears to those who have been down this road as blindingly obvious seems to be a proliferation of other initiatives. Whether already underway or simply in contemplation doesn't appear to make any difference. The harassed and overburdened executive finds it impossible to take on yet another major programme. I can sympathise with their plight to a degree but find it difficult to understand what can be more important than developing the most important resource in any organisation — people. I would not argue with the validity of the claims of competing initiatives in actually achieving significant benefits. However, most of the fashionable structural initiatives, whilst very potent if done correctly, do seem to be characterised by a relatively high failure rate. Experience tells us that a great proportion of these failures are due to an unhelpful organisational culture. Where the workforce at large is prepared to embrace such change, success rates multiply. Figure 31 illustrates the benefit that Team Enterprise brings in creating this foundation for a healthy and supportive ethos.

Figure 31: The Benefits of a Sound Cultural Foundation

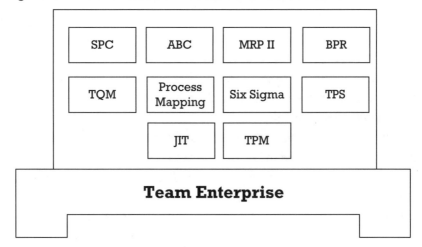

Once in place, the acceptance of initiatives like TQM and MRPII, to name but two, is much higher and therefore the predictors of success much more positive. So whilst I appreciate that nearly all executives and managers have severe constraints with their activity levels, not only will Team Enterprise improve organisation effectiveness, it will also help them optimise their own time management.

Sadly, however, I suspect that many executives will find both the complexity and the lack of prescription of Team Enterprise too great a challenge to contemplate. The structural initiatives noted in Figure 31 all have carefully and rigorously defined processes and procedures. There is little ambiguity and even less uncertainty in going down such paths. The executive never has to leave his personal comfort zone and, in most instances, can delegate all the donkey-work to others.

Team Enterprise is unlike any other approach in that it demands experimentation, direct personal involvement by senior management and constant monitoring. Inevitably, there will be mistakes and cock-ups which may, God forbid, actually land at the door of the senior executive! Add in the threat of a potentially adverse subordinate appraisal through change initiation and you now begin to understand why only the brave or desperate choose this path! However, the counter argument is that, if the various phases of competition are ultimately going to drive *all* companies down the Team Enterprise road, why wait until you're desperate? You could be too weak or too far gone to get on board by that time.

Your task in persuading your senior management to adopt a full-blown Team Enterprise programme could therefore be difficult. If you do fail, then despair not. There are many of the basic elements described earlier which can be introduced slowly and progressively. Communication, recognition and the concept of multifunctional project teams are hardly the stuff of controversy and bear little in the way of risk. Your overall rate of progress may be slow compared to a full-blown initiative, but you will be moving in the right direction.

Middle managers share many of the same common concerns as senior management. However, once the latter have adopted the initiative, there is really no place for middle managers to go. Their attitudinal conversion will depend on a combination of belief in senior management's seriousness of intent, of the actual example set by the latter and by the efficacy of the education/training programme. Experience tells us that if these three are done demonstrably well, a high percentage of this group will fall in line and a significant proportion will become real enthusiasts and drivers of change. So allow these people time to debate the issues as they see them, to visit best practice elsewhere and to actively participate in the development of the concept. The last point is not just advisable, it is probably mandatory, as middle management is so influential within the organisation at large.

A Word of Warning!

At some point at the start of this process, you need to reflect for a while on the nature of Team Enterprise and its relevance to your business. As was said right at the beginning of the book, Team Enterprise is a philosophy. It may be a powerful philosophy, but it remains just a philosophy. As Figure 32 shows, having an ethos such as that generated by Team Enterprise can both engender a truly supportive infrastructure and help improve the performance of the fundamentals of the business enormously. However, if there are major structural weaknesses in these fundamentals which necessitate urgent and comprehensive attention, perhaps a diversion into the world of culture change isn't the biggest priority. You simply have to ask yourself if the key constraint towards addressing this fundamental weakness is either attitudinal or cultural. If the answer's yes, fine. If not, put Team Enterprise on the back burner (perhaps at simmer!) and look elsewhere.

Figure 32: The Importance of Fundamentals

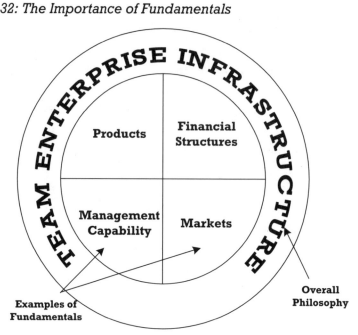

Two examples may illustrate the point. In one organisation, we discovered through our initial training work that their overhead structures were far too heavy for the new circumstances facing the company and constituted a financial burden which was simply unaffordable. There was little option but to put the culture change programme into cold storage, whilst local management and ourselves aggressively reviewed cost structures in a fairly traditional fashion.

The consequent remedial plan was of such sizeable proportions that it could not be tackled in any way other than a painful redundancy. Time, as the lawyers say, was of the essence as no short-term means of improving added value sufficiently to absorb the excess labour could be found. Team Enterprise was then used to remotivate the survivors behind a clear joint objective of ensuring that the workforce would not be exposed to that situation again.

Another example came on a visit to a company that desperately wanted to embark on a culture change programme. However, as we walked around the shopfloor, we were staggered to see such an obvious lack of control. Material covered the floors up to ceiling level, often completely obscuring the assembly lines. Operators worked in cramped conditions despite seemingly having one of the highest floor areas per man I'd ever encountered. Semi-finished products lay everywhere and a quick wipe of the dust with a finger reinforced impressions about its average age. We immediately raised our concern that the attitudinal problems in the factory might have a lot to do with this chaotic workflow. If that was the case, then logistics rather than culture would have to be the first port of call. Twenty minutes looking at their Manufacturing Resource Planning (MRP) processes confirmed that. This was a factory crying out for a *kanban* pull system rather than an MRP push.

There are many other business fundamentals which demand a greater urgency than culture or attitudes. Examples may include:

- Products that don't work

- Products with inherent margin deficiencies

- Inadequate market access

- Financial structures, particularly excessive borrowings

- A lack of management capability, etc.

Whilst I don't want to furnish any more timid senior managers with excuses not to go forward, a breathing space after the "convincing and education" phase is well worthwhile. By then you should be able to appreciate the limitations of Team Enterprise as well as its phenomenal potential. If your constraints to future advancement prioritise attitude and culture, go for it. If they don't, then you could be spending valuable time working on the wrong priority.

The Change Committees

Assuming you decide that Team Enterprise is the way forward, your next step is *change initiation*. The merits and processes involved in this are described in some detail in Chapter 6 and therefore need little elaboration here. You will have been through Stage 6, Feedback, and will undoubtedly be quite shaken at the realisation that the real world of work doesn't quite fit your earlier cosy view of it. You may even have had some criticism that affects you personally. However, once the inevitable bruises to the ego have had time to heal, the potential for using the information to organisation betterment should now be enthralling you. The big danger here, I always feel, is for managers to get overexcited and start to move at a pace faster than the rest can sustain. To repeat something said several times before, be patient and take your time.

If your operation is of any size, then your Action Planning architecture is likely to be as was shown in Figure 10 in Chapter 6, repeated below, for ease of reference, as Figure 33.

Figure 33: Action Planning Architecture

MFFG = Multi-Function Focus Group

The Senior Management Steering Group is ideally the driving force behind the whole initiative with the leaders of each function fully committed to the goals of your Team Enterprise. If sadly this isn't the case, the Steering Group plays an equally important role in keeping the lukewarm on-board. The Senior Executive should regularly use measurement data to ensure that the execution of the initiative is evenly balanced. Where a functional head is not as enthusiastic as one might desire, as inevitably will happen, subsidiary committees should be used to champion the cause in the defaulter's area. Spotting a natural enthusiast and seeding them in the Culture Change Committee could pay more than sufficient dividends to justify the effort!

The real work will take place in these subsidiary committees. Their workload is likely to be fairly onerous, hence the need to subdivide into three specialist areas. There will be a pronounced difference in timescale. Culture change will cover activities that will impinge in the short as well as the longer terms. Change requiring the intervention of employee development and corporate strategy will probably necessitate a more extended time horizon, so don't drive for quick fixes here. The dangers of conflicting priorities in human resources issues are well known and hence time must be allowed to ensure you're not simply jumping into a bigger hole!

The boundaries between the three groups can at times be blurred, but this can easily be addressed by the overall Steering Group specifically allocating duties as they see fit according to appropriateness and, occasionally, load. Areas may include:

- Culture change:
    - Communication and recognition systems
    - Management style
    - Interdepartmental relationships (silos)
    - Informal continuous improvement activity (e.g. ideas generation)
- Employee development:
    - Pay and conditions
    - Training analysis and execution
    - Career progression
    - Formal continuous improvement activity (e.g. Kaizen)

- Corporate strategy

  - ◆ Equipment (yield, up-time, replacement strategy)

  - ◆ Logistics systems

  - ◆ Marketing and product strategy including customer focus

  - ◆ Manufacturing strategy.

Each committee must therefore be equipped with a range of skills to handle the various tasks set before it. Both Culture Change and Employee Development must have a high level of line/operational management representation. Whilst central or corporate nominees can perform a valuable task in administration, facilitation and generally driving the philosophy forward, at the death the whole thing will fail without clear ownership and commitment from the "sharp end". If line management is actively engaged in the derivation and monitoring of policy, they are far more likely to see it through to completion. If they believe that they're simply dancing to another's tune, the end result will be lip service. And Team Enterprise cannot survive in an atmosphere of gestures and tokenism. The committees must therefore have teeth, brains and belief.

The Role of the Facilitator

The multifunctional focus groups which define the necessary actions need not be such a great cause for concern, as you can readily retrace your steps if things don't go to plan. However, we wouldn't want that to happen too often, as credibility may be damaged. On one memorable occasion, despite the best efforts of local management to populate a group focused on communication with a range of balanced talents, it was discovered that one member had developed a very personal agenda. He was so influential that he intimidated the rest of the group into agreeing with his highly distorted view of the world. Fortunately, the facilitator spotted the danger quickly and moved in to restore equilibrium. The end result was highly satisfactory and the delay marginal. The errant member, ironically a high profile member of middle management, was carefully excluded from such activity thereafter.

This little example illustrates the important role that facilitators bring to this process. Within Optima, we always strive to promote local facilitation. A pool of employees trained in getting the best out of people in small group situations can be a real boon to any organisation. These multifunctional groups do not need permanent assistance but certainly, at the start of any new group, the use of a skilled facilitator is to be encouraged. This is important, as we are not just seeking outcomes here. The process, and the way it is perceived, is equally vital as the teams must be portrayed to their peers in a manner that demonstrates that this was an exercise in democracy where every member played their part and had their say. A skilled facilitator will encourage both teamwork and a systematic approach to ensure that both these ends are met. The teams may only have a lifespan of four or five meetings before being disbanded but experience tells us that team members will seek other opportunities to get involved and contribute again to the problem-solving process. The techniques and disciplines established by the facilitator will therefore progressively multiply until they become organisational norms. The early spadework is therefore very much worthwhile.

Teamwork in Practice

To illustrate how these teams may work in practice, let's examine a typical situation:

- **Step 1:** Change Initiation Stage 6 identifies that *communication* generally is a weakness in the organisation.

- **Step 2:** The Senior Management Steering Group discusses the implications of this feedback and then delegates the issue to the Culture Change Committee.

- **Step 3:** The Culture Change Committee asks a multifunctional focus group firstly to reflect upon the criticisms of

communication coming out of the feedback and then to recommend some initial remedial steps. The MFFG is formed
from a cross-section of employees across the organisation
including a representative of personnel, a line manager, a
staff supervisor plus three other nominees from the
workforce and office areas.

- **Step 4:** Using the services of a skilled facilitator, the group
  determine:

  a. Whether they agree with the criticisms expressed on
      Communication in the feedback;

  b. If so, what they believe to be the key features of the
      weakness in organisational communication; and

  c. How they believe they should go about resolving them.

  The last point may involve visiting a perceived best practice
  installation, getting an experienced practitioner to talk to
  them or purely researching the subject through books,
  magazines, journals, etc. All members will be encouraged
  to discuss the matter with their peers in informal settings so
  that others can contribute as well. The weekly/fortnightly/
  monthly written brief (see Chapter 7) can also be used to
  communicate more widely the objectives and the status of the
  committee's work.

- **Step 5:** Once Step 4 has been exhausted and firm conclusions reached, a report is sent to the Culture Change Committee. This may be in a written form, a presentation, or
  both. The committee reviews the conclusions in a broad
  context and decides on action.

- **Step 6:** The MFFG meets, are thanked for their efforts (and
  recognised formally if warranted) and are either disbanded
  or are given further work.

- **Step 7:** The Culture Change Committee implements and monitors, after once again detailed communication through written briefs and cascades.

By adopting this routine, the company gains from:

1. Exploring the local knowledge of a broad cross-section of employees;

2. Gaining acceptance through a process which may be seen as democratic; and

3. Gaining ownership of the eventual strategy.

All those points are highly valuable in constructing the Team Enterprise. Some might argue that the final outcomes are in essence no different to those that could be reached directly either by management or by the Culture Change Committee in a quarter of the time. In many, but not all, instances, we may agree. But as implementation is often far more difficult that the identification of the preferred solution, the overall timescale from complaint to resolution is likely to be much shorter if it is done in the recommended way. In addition, the chances of achieving a permanent change in mindset are much stronger with the preferred route. So once again, be patient, take your time and do it correctly!

Swinging the Pendulum

The routines established in your Action Planning Architecture, it should be strongly emphasised, are *permanent* features in your new management process. There will always be areas of culture, employee development and strategy that need refining and exploring. In addition, there will always be new challenges and changes to which the organisation needs to respond. Senior management can break these down into manageable chunks and let the workforce at large contribute to a satisfactory outcome. Your objective must be to create a sustainable framework which permanently addresses the issue of ongoing development. The model shown in Figure 33 may be as good as any.

In conclusion, what we are trying to achieve in this book is expressed by the three triangles in Figure 34. The left-hand triangle (a) is supposed to represent the sum total of all the talents and expertise of our average employee. Years of Tayloristic and Theory X-type approaches, from the dawn of the industrial revolution in fact, have led us to believe that the world of work needs only a very small proportion of these skills as shown by the shaded portion in (b). In order to achieve predictability, repeatability and control, we have in the past deliberately designed jobs to access very little of the average employee's capability. Too much individual discretion or judgement would, according to the theory, lead to variation, variability and even anarchy. So in essence the real message to the workforce was "leave your brains at the gatehouse and do as you are told". Nowadays, organisational needs have changed. The competitive market and the new nature of the world of work has placed more decision-making at the elbow of those at the bottom of the classical organisational pyramid. The Taylorist may simply say "So what?! Simply redesign the jobs around the new requirement!" — but we disagree. Team Enterprise recognises that we are not just enlarging responsibilities, we are looking for new levels of flexibility, responsiveness and individual judgement. The game has changed.

Figure 34: Unlocking the Potential

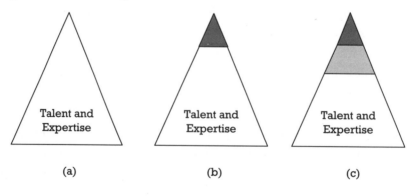

(a)   (b)   (c)

Successful companies will move towards (c) where the proportion of individuals' talents and expertise used in the world of work will increase sharply. Your task within Team Enterprise is to unlock this potential whilst at the time maintaining or even increasing control and predictability. The pendulum of Figure 35 has been used at Leyland to illustrate the desired effect.

Figure 35: Average Employee Mindset

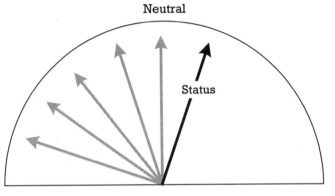

In most companies the "average employee mindset" is to the left — "Reactive". People come to work for the money. They work to job descriptions. Demarcations between individuals and departments are legion. "Getting away with it" is fair game. There is no natural affinity between the company and the employee.

Team Enterprise works on the principle that, in the twenty-first century, such companies will soon be out of business. The aggressive competitiveness of all markets will undoubtedly expose these dinosaurs as being too slow, too predictable and too inflexible to survive. What is needed is a totally proactive workforce where the status quo is challenged routinely by everybody.

The success of Leyland is reflected in Figure 35. Ten years of blood, sweat and tears have probably only managed to move the pendulum just to the right side of neutrality. It still occasionally moves around. Some days may be better than others. A period of prolonged overtime working, complex new product introduction or perhaps even something as trivial as a summer heat wave (in Preston?) can cause the pendulum to move backwards a little. But the movement is never substantial nor irreversible. The philosophy is robust enough to ensure that violent, damaging fluctuations would never be allowed to take hold. The only real threat is a long, attritional erosion by a complete change in management attitude. However, given the long memories at Leyland of life before Team Enterprise, this has only the remotest chance of happening.

Nevertheless, no one at Leyland would claim that the journey is complete. The potential of moving from just north of neutrality to total proactivity is unquestionably one of enormous benefit. A former colleague once said that we didn't want "1,000 employees at Leyland, we need 1,000 mini-entrepreneurs". I shudder to think what would happen if that became a reality, but his general sentiment is appreciated. Perhaps our challenge is to "release the entrepreneur in all of us" within the context of a controlled and customer-focused environment characterised by teamwork and a clearly understood unity of purpose. Putting it that way doesn't seem difficult, nor should it be. The seemingly endless lists of "do's and don'ts", prohibitions and recommended actions may seem daunting to the uninitiated. However, if it was that problematic, how come Leyland Trucks did it? And if Leyland can do it, anybody can!

The very best of luck!

CASE STUDIES IN TEAM ENTERPRISE

Selecting candidates to feature as case studies in this book was no easy task. Should we feature big companies to demonstrate the power of Team Enterprise in tackling huge, complex edifices? Or should we major on those clients where the most startling returns have been registered? After long discussion, we decided on neither approach. Instead we picked five differing operations to demonstrate the universality of the approach. There is no claim that these are the best examples of Team Enterprise in action. Far from it: some are still in the stage of active development. Instead, each in its way illustrates both the sheer complexity of changing mindsets and the wonderful benefits in at least starting down the path.

CASE STUDY 1: RUNSHAW COLLEGE

Of all the organisations I have encountered working in the fields of empowerment and involvement, Runshaw College is my particular favourite. As a case study, the college is a fascinating subject, as it is a long way away from the usual commercial examples of empowerment quoted in business literature. Nothing could be farther from the world of truck-making than teaching 16–19 year-olds. And yet the principles apply equally effectively, demonstrating the universality of Team Enterprise.

Background

Runshaw started life in 1974 as a small (350-strong) sixth-form college serving the communities of Chorley and South Ribble. By 1983, the numbers had grown but quality hadn't. Despite a 150 per cent increase in student numbers, achievement and retention were, frankly, poor. The local County Council decided to do something about it and went for "tertiary" status by merging the college with the boroughs' two small adult education services, the education unit of a prison and a small engineering college. Shortly afterwards in 1984, the most significant move of all was made with the appointment of Bernard O'Connell as Principal.

Bernard set about improving the quality, range and balance of the curriculum as his first priority. Things began to improve, particularly in the high profile areas of achievement, retention and recruitment. Progressively, all the relevant performance criteria seemed to be moving in the right direction — except for one. Staff morale remained stubbornly low. One incident summed up the situation. In a farewell speech to his assembled colleagues at the end of summer term in 1990, a departing lecturer said, "This is a great place for students, but an awful place for staff!" And to Bernard's horror, he obtained a prolonged round of applause, despite the Principal's presence.

Bernard knew this had to be tackled as a priority, but the question was: how? In desperation, he read every management book he could lay his hands on before finally deciding that Total Quality Management (TQM) fitted the bill. By the middle of 1991, Runshaw had adopted TQM as its management philosophy and consultants engaged to help it on its way.

Unfortunately, things didn't go at all according to aspirations. The emergent weaknesses and mistakes will be familiar to many who have followed a similar path. But that was of little consolation to Runshaw. Like every other college in the public sector, Runshaw had in mid-1992 become "incorporated". This effective "privatisation" of the further education network was intended to free colleges from the bureaucracies of local authority control and maximise the benefits of self-management. Sadly for Runshaw, the iniquitous structure of financing in this brave new world left the college at the bottom of the funding barrel, being the tenth-worst out of nearly 500 in the entire country. Add in the burdens of an inherited deficit and an urgent need to review much of its building stock, and one can easily see why the Principal had enough problems on his plate without an ineffective and time-consuming central management ideology.

Adopting Team Enterprise

To quote Bernard, it was then that "an unlikely white knight came to the rescue in the shape of Leyland Trucks". In late 1993, as covered elsewhere in the book, Leyland Trucks was sponsored by the government through the TEC Challenge to disseminate its unusual people practices. Runshaw became one of the six organisations which successfully applied for a "buddying" — or mentoring — programme. They were attracted to Leyland because these practices had utilised TQM, so it seemed sensible to get Leyland to review Runshaw's version.

Accordingly, some of the senior members of the Leyland management team, including myself, sat in on the college's quality meetings. As we listened and observed, a horrible sense of déjà-vu hit us. The college appeared to be making exactly the same mistakes as we had so many times before in the 1970s and 1980s. Their underlying weakness was undoubtedly one of culture. After all, even the way they defined the problem's key observable symptom, poor staff morale, was all about people and people management. But the device they'd selected for addressing the issue, TQM, was being applied in an impersonal and objective fashion focusing on systems and structures. And their distraction and diversion into process definition was, if anything, worsening matters. Despite therefore all the attractions that a successful quality initiative could offer, it seemed to us that a totally different emphasis was required. Runshaw needed to change its culture. It needed a step change in communications, recognition and involvement. It needed a radical change in management style. And it needed a culture of listening to the workforce.

The process employed downstream mirrors the recommended path described earlier in the book. Reg Hardy was commissioned to undertake the survey, the first time he had ventured outside the familiarity of the business community. Over a period of 15 months he carried out detailed employee surveys, using structured interviews, questionnaires, workshops and reports.

A number of key issues emerged which were probably familiar and commonplace across the education sector. However, this time the recognition was accompanied by a strong sense of "ownership" of what they perceived as "our problems". Managers moved from what Bernard describes as unrecognised incompetence to recognised incompetence: "The data was stark and it was impossible to deny it or avoid responsibility for responding to it."

This response was all-embracing. The senior management team was completely restructured, adding a Vice-Principal for Human Resources and Communications plus four heads of faculty to support the overstretched line management functions. New ground rules were established covering management behaviour and style alongside routine measurement and monitoring to ensure compliance. Communication systems were ruthlessly overhauled and new systems for intensive staff participation introduced, particularly through Academic Board Structures and a new Suggestion Scheme. Recognition became an important concept with systems engineered to support it. A radical "delegation" strategy was developed, allowing teams to take most of their own resource decisions. An Activity Based Costing system was also incorporated to further aid the teams in formulating their own solutions.

And that was just the start! Runshaw differs from most other organisations in two respects. Firstly, there seems to be an almost restless energy to move further and further in this direction. Each year, the entire organisation aggressively reviews its progress and starts again with a new theme or focus. Secondly, they take enormous care in detailing and documenting good practice. To an industrialist from the private sector, this looks at first sight to be massively overprescriptive. But it has proved over the years to offer a clarity and coherence rarely seen elsewhere. In particular, Runshaw seems to excel at:

1. *Strategic Planning*: Runshaw's model incorporates a competitive strategy analysis alongside core process, support process and thematic strategies in a fairly conventional fashion. However they've cleverly adopted an annual "theme" to illustrate the difference between last year's plan and the new one. As long as the new theme relates to real, pressing business issues, this regular renewal can be extraordinarily stimulating, rather than causing the type of confusion often encountered elsewhere. The end result is complete ownership of the outcomes through the active involvement of everybody in the college in setting the agenda for the following year.

2. *Involvement and Participation*: Runshaw has succeeded in effectively "institutionalising" involvement and participation. Whereas elsewhere, an effort is made to consult and to involve, at Runshaw, it's simply the way they do business. Their approach is built around six "stop-the-track" days each year when staff attend a full-day conference. Each is themed around specific aspects of college life — for example, student support, assessment or teaching and learning.

3. *Leadership*: Runshaw have defined very carefully their own approach to leadership, which is extensive, rigorous and auditable. In this comprehensive analysis, which is cascaded to every employee, all middle and senior managers are viewed as leaders. All other staff, and indeed *students*, are expected to share the values and exhibit the behaviour inherent in what they describe as an "ethical partnership".

The Benefits

To name but a few:

1. In the period immediately post-Change Initiation, the further education sector was riven by disputes, overtime bans, work-to-rules and generally abysmal labour relations as the government pushed radical new contracts. These contracts were designed to eliminate both restrictive practices and demarcation, and to improve productivity by over 30 per cent in a very short timescale. In the midst of all this disruption, relationships at Runshaw remained cordial, supportive and co-operative.

2. A-Level pass rates, originally at around 67 per cent in 1984, rose to 95.7 per cent in 1997 and 97.3 per cent in 1999. At the same time, grades improved dramatically — so much so that the average point score rose from 16.4 in 1993 to over 23 in 1998, placing Runshaw as the *No. 1 further education college* in England for A-Level results. It has retained that position for four years up to the point of writing.

3. Vocational results also rose considerably. Advanced vocation pass rates rose to 95 per cent with distinctions rising to 23 per cent and merits to 37 per cent by 1999.

4. A rigorous inspection by the FEFC (Further Education Funding Council) in 1996 gave the college rarely attained Grade 1s on *all* cross-college management criteria. It commented:

   ". . . in a relatively short time, staff perceptions have been more positive and favourable. Morale is now generally high, staff feel the senior management is open, flexible and accessible."

   This transition took less than two years.

5. In 1995, the college was awarded Investors in People. The following year, it won the North West Quality Award administered by the British Quality Foundation in a category which covered every public sector institution in the North

West of England. In 1997, it was "Highly Commended" and described as a "role model organisation" at the highly prestigious national UK Quality Awards. In 2000, it won a Millennium Award at the regional event in Manchester.

That should be sufficient to convince anybody that the application of Team Enterprise to an educational establishment can generate quite outstanding results. Runshaw has become an exemplar to public and private sector alike in using "the pursuit of excellence" as a stimulating and rewarding unity of purpose which galvanises both management and the managed. It really is Team Enterprise in action.

CASE STUDY 2: MOORES FURNITURE GROUP

The second case study is a world away from education and concerns a leading kitchen and bathroom manufacturer in Wetherby, West Yorkshire. With in excess of 1,000 employees, Moores Furniture Group is a major player in an aggressive and highly competitive industry. We were approached by Peter Wilson, the Manufacturing Director, who wanted to use the principles of Team Enterprise as a means of improving performance solely in the manufacturing area. Ideally we would have liked to undertake a full company transformation, as only rarely do production areas work in isolation from the rest of the organisation. However, for all sorts of understandable reasons, that wasn't possible.

Background

Moores Furniture Group was formed in 1947 by an entrepreneur who owned the company until 1987, when there was a management buyout. During that time, it developed a very hierarchical and autocratic style of management in which internal promotions were rare, especially in Manufacturing. Moores produces kitchen, bathroom and bedroom furniture for both the public and private sector house-building industry and more latterly the DIY market. By far and away market leaders, its financial performance had always been exceptional for the furniture industry and in 1996 it became part of the giant MASCO Corporation of America.

The years 1997 and 1998 became critical for the company. Although still market leaders and financially very sound, it was becoming increasingly obvious that it was beginning to "creak at the seams".

The company was seeking new markets for its goods and customers were demanding more and more product to satisfy the need for differentiation among builders and from "last year's models". Methods of operation that had stood the company in good stead for many years were increasingly inappropriate to meet the demands of this changing marketplace.

For example, the capacity of the machine shop which made the panels for the furniture was virtually saturated. Overtime was almost a permanent feature, with some major machine processes not producing panels due to set-ups, breakdowns, etc., for approximately 85 per cent of the time. It appeared that the only solution was heavy capital investment in machinery. However, due to the physical constraints of the factory, there wasn't the space for either major machinery or an extension to the buildings.

In assembly, people weren't coping with the proliferation of products (by now the theoretical number of kitchen units ran into many millions): mistakes were being made, products not completed on time, items went "missing"; quality (in its widest sense) was suffering.

Moores Furniture Group measured its delivery performance by a simple index. If one item on an advice note was not delivered "right first time", the whole advice note was classed as a failure. As a result of the above, the delivery performance started to deteriorate; from averaging between 96 and 98 per cent, it fell to 94–96 per cent.

Although the management team were aware of the situation it is almost certain that this had not communicated itself to the shop floor.

The employee working on a machine or assembly bench remained distant from the customer, oblivious that he/she was the company and that the interests of the individual and Moores Furniture Group were inextricably linked. This manifested itself not only in a lack of involvement in any improvement measures but also in such areas as health and safety. There was a lack of commitment, responsible/mature attitude and approach. Many people would "hang up their brains at the gates on the way in and collect them on the way out".

For some time certain members of the senior management team recognised that team working had been introduced in other industries with remarkable results. However, it had always been felt that, for various reasons, it would not be appropriate or necessary to their own situation.

Adopting Team Enterprise

Initial attempts to move in this direction by restructuring the manufacturing organisation to match the complexities of the new world had some success, particularly in indirect headcount and in health and safety. However, problems occurred elsewhere, as Peter indicates:

> "We knew the direction in which we were going but hadn't taken the workforce with us. In short we had underestimated the resistance to change and the amount of input required to get people to understand the need for it. . . . Having gone to several consultants, all with impressive credentials, Richard (the Works Manager) visited Optima and urged me to do likewise. The reasons were obvious. John Oliver and his team weren't theorists, they'd done it! We could use the lessons they had learnt from successfully implementing team working in Leyland Trucks to drive us towards our vision."

The process employed was again the preferred route outlined in the book, using the Optima Change Initiation process. Peter's comments here are quite typical:

"The first thing they advised us to do, and indeed conducted for us, was the Change Initiation survey of all of
our employees — their independence ensuring that we
would receive honest answers from a high proportion
of people working within manufacturing at Moores. All
of the warnings John gave us about how painful this
process would be could NOT prepare the management
team for the shock and hurt inflicted by the results of
the survey. It was then that the importance of having a
team 100 per cent committed to the change process
was highlighted. Those 'going along for the ride',
paying lip service to the vision of team working would
have crumbled and fallen by the wayside."

To accelerate the process, Peter sent scores of employees on
factory tours around Leyland to show them what a real teamworking environment was like. We used the opportunity also to
do some training in basic Team Enterprise principles, which
were incredibly stimulating experiences. To see a bunch of
people arrive as cynics and leave as enthusiastic converts was
an absolute joy. Moores followed the prescribed route and
formed steering committees and sub-committees. Multifunctional focus groups were formed to examine hitherto controversial areas. The vexatious No Smoking Policy, an issue of
longstanding contention, was soon sorted out amicably. Another problem area, clocking, was also resolved. Communication, recognition and even the state of the toilets became
subjected to the same routine, with favourable outcomes. To
quote Peter again:

"The forming of the groups themselves sent out a definite signal that things were changing. They were made
up of volunteers from all departments — not hand-
selected individuals who could be seen as 'cronies'.
They were given a framework to work in but were
completely free to decide upon the proposals that
would be put forward to the steering committee for final approval before becoming policy. So, although the
management still retained the right to manage, employees had a real say in the decision-making process,

their views were taken seriously and were seen to be so."

Looking back at the first year since the attitude survey, the number of improvements that have been made has been staggering. A whole variety of improvement initiatives have been launched with good effect, including:

1. A complete restructuring of local management with the introduction of team leaders to replace traditional supervision and the creation of "business unit technicians" to support and coach.

2. Ideas generation capture.

3. Improved communication techniques including regular "Meet the Boss" sessions with the manufacturing director.

4. Improvements in cell layout and support infrastructure.

5. Quality improvements.

The Benefits

1. Introduction cycle on a new product cut from six to nine months to six weeks!

2. A new manufacturing cell introduced, saving 2,400 linear metres of storage space.

3. Direct labour productivity improvement of 20 per cent.

4. "Right first time" delivery performance has risen to 98–99 per cent.

5. Stockholding reduced by £500,000.

6. Changeover times reduced by 70 per cent.

7. Labour turnover and absenteeism slashed.

All in all, the financial benefits of a programme costing around £70,000 probably equate to in excess of £2,000,000 per annum. And that's just manufacturing doing it by themselves! Just imagine the rewards when the rest of the organisation comes on board. But we'll leave the final word with Peter:

> "The one thing that has surprised us all is the commitment required and the time needed to manage change in a company. The resistance to change and the "dependency" of the workforce on management and "others" should never be underestimated. However, it was (and is) vital that we found the time. Time and again, subsequent events showed how important it had been for us to hold our nerve; the benefits prove that it is worth it, but there is an awful lot to do!"

CASE STUDY 3: HANSENGLASS

Lots of visitors to Optima courses leave feeling very impressed by what Team Enterprise has to offer but still harbour the feeling that "it's really only for big companies". Nothing could be further from the truth; SMEs can benefit as powerfully and as quickly as their bigger cousins. To illustrate the point, have a look at the case of HansenGlass, a glass processing company in Liverpool employing 88 people.

Background

HansenGlass cuts, shapes, polishes, drills, paints, toughens and laminates glass, and manufactures insulating glass units (IGUs). Its predecessors had rather a chequered history, twice going into receivership in the early 1990s. After the second business failure in 1992, HansenGroup purchased the assets from the receiver with a single aim of supplying glass to other companies within the Group, both in the UK and in Europe.

Their purchase was a classical brownfield company sharing many of the old bugbears of Leyland Trucks. They inherited many negative attributes arising from a long troubled history. Traditional hardened attitudes, "us and them" practices and a strong unionised environment with a high reliance on overtime were just some of the inherent weaknesses. Each machine centre operated like a separate fiefdom, producing as much as it could but oblivious to adjacent centres, often just yards away. The pay structure underpinned this method of working. Product damage to the glass, breakages and scratching were all high.

The new directors of the business, led by Stewart Barnes, had heard all about lean production and world class manufacturing. But, understandably, they did not possess the knowledge or experience of introducing and establishing such practices against such a background. In these situations, you only get one crack at the whip; they could not afford to make a mistake. After nine months of networking, reading and canvassing, they finally decided on Optima. To quote: "After two meetings with Optima, we were clear on what to do and how to do it. We decided to make the 'lean leap'."

Adopting Team Enterprise

Stewart elected to follow the classical Team Enterprise steps in the first stages before adopting a more bespoke approach downstream. This approach is vital to ensure an appropriate, speedy and best value Action Planning phase. Accordingly, the first three stages were, as ever:

1. Convince and educate the senior management team.

2. Convince and educate the middle management group and other key influencers.

3. Change Initiation.

Stewart's action planning phase initially prioritised Investors in People certification. He reasoned that this was a vital step in convincing the workforce that the company really had a different agenda. A four-day intensive teamworking and leadership course, run by Optima's Dave Graham, reinforced this message.

Once the above had settled down, 12 volunteers, representing all parts of the business, were trained in classical *Kaizen* techniques. These individuals were then used to lead teams of various sizes in on-the-job investigation of process improvement. Coupled with a simultaneous communication to all employees on *Gemba Kaizen*, a programme of structured and continuous improvement was progressively rolled out.

To quote Stewart:

> "We wanted a motivated, skilled and involved workforce with a payment system relevant to targets, improvements and productivity gains. We needed to take the blame out of the system and recognise good work, ideas and positive thinking by changing our language, finding new ways of saying things as well as doing them. To win involvement from everyone, the pain of change was supported by a promise of training for all."

This transitional process was difficult for HansenGlass because, like many other longstanding, traditional organisations, ingrained beliefs and attitudes had developed, hardened and been reinforced over decades. But this makes the company's transformation even more remarkable. Now two-way communication is routine and structured (daily, weekly, monthly, always), decisions are made at the lowest possible level and the organisation is slick, flat and non-bureaucratic. There is a programme of supporting continuous improvement through mentoring and training so that people know what they have to do. But best of all, there is now a very strong customer focus both on internal as well as external customers.

The Benefits

Stewart again:

> "We were cautioned that, after leaping into Team Enterprise, the benefits would be staggering. No matter how much we were warned, the outcomes were WAY BEYOND our most optimistic forecast or wish!"

To quote a few:

1. On-time delivery rose from 80 per cent to 98 per cent

2. Wastage was cut by 67 per cent

3. Customer complaints were down 73 per cent

4. Inventory was down 50 per cent

5. Sales were increased by 130 per cent

6. Profitability was double the target.

In summary, for a £30,000 investment, they have realised annual permanent savings of £500,000. Quite significant, I'm sure you'll agree, on a £6 million turnover! However, Stewart's final comment on the benefits speaks volumes for the robustness of the Team Enterprise approach:

> "What is more difficult to measure but is so obvious to anyone visiting us or buying our architectural glass products is that everyone is much *happier* at work. All the improvements we have implemented have made us one of the foremost, independent European companies specialising in thick glass and toughened IGUs. HansenGlass plan to grow a further 55 per cent in turnover in the next three years without increasing factory size. Another example of getting *more* from *less*."

Summary

The HansenGlass experience is fairly typical of those who have had the courage and the foresight to adopt Team Enterprise principles. Senior management at the company must be commended not just for adopting the philosophy — that's the easy bit — but for seeing it through. Experience tells us repeatedly that the key determinant of a successful empowered culture is the ability and willingness of the key decision makers to live, breathe and act these new disciplines. Mistakes will inevitably be made; the nature and the extent of the change makes this almost inescapable. However, the consistent and focused exercise of, in particular, new levels of communication, recognition and leadership will lead to such challenges being seen as mutual learning experiences rather than matters of regret.

HansenGlass is characterised by this healthy acceptance of the well-intentioned error and by a constant restlessness with the status quo. Many organisations fall down when pursuing teams or teamworking through the phenomenon of "initiative overload". However, this case study clearly proves that, providing the organisation can see the need for change and understands the multifaceted nature of the philosophy, companies can take on far greater dislocation than is usually considered both manageable and tolerable. And apparently enjoy it!

HansenGlass have proved yet again that Team Enterprise can not only considerably impact on bottom-line deliverables, it can be fun as well.

CASE STUDY 4: BRADLEY DOUBLELOCK

Background

Bradley Doublelock is a producer of components for the light trailer industry and is situated in Bingley, West Yorkshire. Currently employing 85 staff, the company has endured a period of sustained economic turmoil in which turnover has remained static in real terms. Its experience with Team Enterprise is very different to that of HansenGlass but nevertheless is equally relevant in demonstrating the power of the philosophy in even the most vexed circumstances.

The business was founded over 50 years ago by two brothers who recognised the need for a better quality trailer coupling and developed a cast range to compete with the pressed steel products in use at the time. The Bradley range became synonymous with quality and its UK market share grew to 80 per cent by the early 1980s. During the 1980s the company influenced market prices with automatic increases in line with inflation, indicative of a strong market position.

However, this comfortable situation came to an abrupt end with a build-up of pressure in the market to match European prices irrespective of quality. Coupled with the emergence of low-cost competition, the company began to feel the heat. Unfortunately at this crucial time, new product developments failed to capture replacement business.

Adopting Team Enterprise

In 1992, Bradley Doublelock set about correcting this new weakness by subscribing to a government-sponsored World Class Manufacturing programme. This enabled them to access good quality consultants at a fraction of normal costs. As a result, the company acquired a powerful tool to improve processes in an objective and focused fashion. Using classical business process re-engineering techniques, the company began the slow climb to competitiveness. However, translating the theoretic into effective and practical change proved difficult and so visits to Leyland were organised to investigate the benefits of a greater focus on organisational culture. In 1995, Bradley Doublelock adopted the principles of Team Enterprise to work hand-in-hand with the lean engineering concepts adopted earlier.

Changes included:

1. Hierarchy stripped out of the organisation structure with four levels of management replaced by one.

2. Workforce flexibility emphasised with a strong focus on the external customer.

3. Communication systems introduced to ensure openness and feedback.

4. Build-to-order replaced build-to-stock on a daily basis.

5. Rationalisation of the supply chain.

The Benefits

1. Sales per employee increased by 30 per cent.

2. Stock turnover ratio increased by 30 per cent.

3. Overhead staff to direct labour ratio was reduced by 65 per cent.

4. Productivity of manufacturing rose by 20 per cent.

The financial savings stemming from the above, according to local management "saved the business from closure" and the process itself "has created a service level to customers which has provided growth and a much more stable business". However, much remains to be done and the management are refreshingly honest about their mistakes and the areas of weakness which still need to be addressed. Like so many other companies in a similar situation, they have encountered those obstacles that incentive-based pay systems place on achieving the new levels of flexibility and responsiveness needed in this increasingly competitive world. Pay anomalies within the new cells are not perceived to be fair and hence create resentment. They also feel that they have underestimated the demand of the workforce for improved communication. Whilst the process has been transformed, feedback indicates that not enough has been achieved and that, perhaps, a broader approach is required.

However, one of their most interesting experiences with the process engineering techniques beloved of the "lean" engineers is in the formation of what they term "natural groups". Here, whilst the theory firmly pointed them in the direction of a new process-based structure, in practice the latter failed entirely due to "personality differences". In particular, the difficulties of mixing extrovert sales staff with pessimistic production people proved to be unworkable! This really reinforces the need to take stock of organisational culture before superimposing process or structural change. I am not for one second saying the latter is wrong but, in so many instances, a little attention to the softer side of working life can pay dividends in the longer term.

The management at Bradley Doublelock have proved that traditional attitudes and practices can be changed quickly to good effect. They may well have some way to go but their openness, honesty and ambition will get them there.

CASE STUDY 5: W. & J. LEIGH & CO.

One of the great joys of the consultancy business, when compared with the occasional monotony of pumping out trucks day after day, is the variety of companies one encounters. They're all different, even if the problems are largely the same. Some are exciting, some are challenging and some are . . . plain nice. Now 'nice' may not represent a great compliment in these days of aggressive competition and hyperactive management, but it is such a rarity that dealing with concerns of this nature is nothing less than a huge pleasure.

W. & J. Leigh & Co. (or "Leigh's Paints") is a beacon in terms of niceness. The whole place seems to encapsulate civilised values. People are friendly, the atmosphere is convivial and the ambience a combination of helpfulness and mutual respect. Perhaps it's the history of the organisation, being some 140 years young. Or more likely it's the fact that throughout that time the company has been in private ownership under the careful stewardship and paternalism of the Leigh family, including the fourth generation and current chairman, Brian Leigh-Bramwell. I particularly like their definition of management style: "A strong emphasis on teamwork, enthusiasm, honesty and good humour at work."

Background

Founded in 1860 by William and Joshua Leigh (the W. & J. in the company name), it started as a building and property development company. Paint remained a sideline until the end of the First World War. It was left to Herbert Leigh as the second generation of the family to really focus on paintmaking; it was Herbert in particular who developed the idea of "ready-to-use" paint for ships, culminating in the launch of the famous Leigh's marine white in 1924. Previously, paint had been made on board by the bosun and his mates.

Since those early days, Leigh's Paints has grown through natural evolution and acquisition to become a market leader in the UK, specialising in the manufacture of heavy duty and industrial coatings. A large part of the business these days is based on the treatment of steel surfaces, such as on commercial and defence shipping, oil rigs and refineries, tanks and pipe-lines, bridges, steel buildings, sports stadiums, power stations and production line applications, from JCBs to electric motors, cranes, valves and compressors.

Employing 316 people, the company is a small player in global terms but punches much above its weight. It continues to secure major projects against strong foreign competition, such as the coating for Hong Kong's new Chek Lap Kok Airport, and the Tsing Ma and Kap Shui Mun Suspension Bridges that join it with Hong Kong Island.

Adopting Team Enterprise

My first real encounter with the company came with an invita-tion to address their management conference in 1998. Brian and his works director had attended one of the Optima "Introduc-tion to Team Enterprise" Days somewhat earlier and this had been followed up by further visits from other senior personnel. In a nutshell, the company had entered a fairly flat period. Prof-its were down with less than sparkling performance parame-ters. A fresh start was needed to enthuse and invigorate the organisation, and Team Enterprise seemed to fit the bill admi-rably.

Interestingly, the company had already gone some way down the teamworking road. Back in 1997, they had adopted a "market-led" approach to give better penetration into their marketplace. In short, this entailed studying the marketplace, identifying those areas representing profitable opportunities and then hitting them hard with multidisciplined, market-focused teams. By definition, this also meant taking tough calls to get out of mature or saturated markets that were no longer viable. However, it also necessitated the total organisation ex-hibiting world class characteristics of flexibility and respon-siveness.

Initially, the company followed the classic introductory steps that are essential to get the initiative off to a controlled start — once again:

1. Convince and educate the senior management team.

2. Convince and educate the middle management team.

3. Change Initiation with the total workforce.

However, as the process wound its way through these careful initial stages, two issues came to the fore with repeated emphasis. The first was most unusual and proved a fascinating intellectual challenge. A couple of year earlier, Leigh's had abandoned the role of a single chief executive/managing director and instead substituted a "managing triumvirate" comprising the directors of sales and marketing, technical and finance departments. The idea was that this novel arrangement would promote interdepartmental harmony and avoid functional sub-optimisation at the expense of the overall interest.

The second issue was an increasing awareness that perhaps the paternalistic over-concern of recent years, where job security was taken as read, had resulted in a significant degree of overmanning throughout the business. In short, the company carried too much overhead and too much resource for its trading situation. But first, back to the managing triumvirate ...

Whilst the idea of sharing authority seemed workable in theory, in practice it simply didn't function. In their efforts to ensure that a harmonious and conducive atmosphere existed between themselves, each of the three directors became excessively cordial. There was none of the creative tension or positive conflict so essential in keeping organisations constantly challenging the status quo. Decision-making slowed and the company progressively lost its edge. Each director privately understood what was happening but felt that articulating their concerns would have been disloyal or offensive to their colleagues. So they continued working exceptionally hard at trying to make their chosen model work, despite the odds. Allowed to

debate the matter in a forum where fellow feelings were set
aside for a while, a unanimous conclusion quickly emerged that
a more orthodox approach was needed. It had been a brave experiment but, in retrospect, a dangerous one.

Solving the first problem was straightforward and delivered
amicably with solid consensus. The second unfortunately didn't
have the opportunity of a painless resolution. A zero budget review had to be undertaken, using existing and prospective
business profiles as its starting points. For an organisation unused to the traumas of restructuring and rationalisation so familiar elsewhere, this was an extremely difficult period. No
manager ever finds such a process less than difficult, but for
Leigh's it was inordinately stressful. However, with the culture
change programme put in temporary cold storage, the necessary actions were taken, albeit with a heavy heart.

Once through the redundancy programme, Team Enterprise
was tackled in earnest. The new managing director, Dick Frost,
ably supported by his colleagues, immediately stamped his
authority and enthusiasm on the process. Communication systems were considerably enhanced with a combination of a
monthly brief, the "Hawk and Trumpet" (named after the company logo), "Meet the Team" sessions and cascaded team
briefs. Recognition systems were enthusiastically embraced
and a "working environment committee" assembled to address
some of the humiliating systems and conditions discussed earlier in the book. Self-directed work teams were introduced in
the manufacturing area, supported by a massive training support. Every area, from sales at the sharp end to the backroom
boffins in the research department, became engaged in this
step change in attitude, approach and effort.

All this sounds relatively straightforward in retrospect. However, a few comments from Dick may shed a more realistic light
on events:

> "The first part of the process was an employee survey.
> None of us realised what was coming in the results,
> which blew apart the view we had that we were basi-

cally a paternalistic and caring company. The survey showed that the employee perceptions were of a company that failed to communicate or listen, and where in many cases both middle and senior management were felt to be overbearing and even tyrannical. I will never forget the demoralising effects of the results, and the shock of wondering how on earth we were going to transform the situation and improve things.

The first thing we learnt is that, when John Oliver said in his initial speech to the company that 70 per cent of the task was about people, he lied! It's at least 90 per cent. The second and most difficult challenge was for our management itself to undergo a major change in its style, and show a massive commitment to the process to encourage the employees to actually buy in.

The third thing we didn't understand was that, even with the support of John and his team, the process is a long and tortuous one, with progress lurching on a "three steps forward and two steps back" basis with monotonous regularity, and to everyone's frustration. You must be prepared to admit when you get it wrong, and hold your hand up to all the employees, while telling them we are still going to keep trying even though they don't like it."

The Benefits

The improvement in profitability by an estimated £1.5 million per annum (Leigh's doesn't publish its results) was a huge boom to a company turning over "in excess of £20 million a year". Major advances in product quality helped enormously in achieving Dick's personal obsession for a more customer-focused organisation. Employee morale improved significantly, despite the painful interlude after the zero budget.

To quote Dick again,

"The combination of the market-led team approach alongside Team Enterprise has led to the company continuing to make profits even when the heavy duty and industrial paint markets have been in deep recession. Sixteen new products are being brought forward for launch in 2001, and according to British Coating Federation Statistics, the company achieved the largest improvement in employee productivity in the UK paint industry during the year 2000. This was a tremendous result, and the company had moved significantly up the league table.

Without a doubt, even though many of our old "doubting Thomases" and cynics don't like to admit it, many major beneficial changes have taken place in the last two years. We are still learning to remind everyone what these are, as anyone tackling the process will soon find people are great at refusing to acknowledge when changes have actually happened. They need to be told time and again, and even then don't believe it!

A key goal and primary company objective is to keep Leigh's independent and family-owned. The Optima survey showed a surprising loyalty from employees to the company, with an amazing 85 per cent response rate. Most employees wrote extra pages to the survey questions, which Optima felt showed they wanted the company to succeed. The financial turnaround means that if the company continues to satisfy the shareholders, it will remain independent. Without the changes, there is little doubt the company would be running with significant losses."

And, I'm delighted to say, the company has retained its characteristic "niceness", It's still a joy to visit with all the gentlemanly courtesies now augmented by a new enthusiasm, zeal and restlessness with the status quo.

INDEX